Rural Development in India: Scope for Industrial Development

Rural Development in India: Scope for Industrial Development

Editors

Y. Gangi Reddy
Shankar Chatterjee

SERIALS PUBLICATIONS
NEW DELHI (INDIA)

First Published - 2010

ISBN: 978-81-8387-321-5

Published by

SERIALS PUBLICATIONS
4830/24, Prahlad Street, Ansari Road
Darya Ganj, New Delhi-110002 (India)
Phone : 23245225 Fax : 91-11-23272135
E-mail: serials@satyam.net.in

CONTENTS

AN OVERVIEW ABOUT THE CHAPTERS

India witnessed a fundamental change in its economic policies during the last decade. The economy came under Structural Adjustment Program and opted for liberalization, privatization and globalization as per the dictates of the World Bank. Several studies suggest that the new economic policy regime did have an impact on primary, secondary and tertiary sectors of production during the last decade. Impacts are, however, both positive and negative. India being pre-dominantly rural with enormous surplus of labor, rural industries has not lost its relevance in the context of global competitiveness since they continue to be significant sources of employment generation in the rural areas. It is true that they are perennially handicapped with the problems of shortage of capital, obsolete technology, lack of market etc. But, these are the problems that are essentially structural and can be addressed through appropriate interventions. Opinions differ between scholars about the impact of the implementation of the new policy regime on rural industries. Some argue that new regime is hardening the existing problems rural industries are encountering for several decades and pushing them to the brink of destruction. However, others argue that they are now embedded with new opportunities and, therefore, they have more potential for development. Both streams of argument throw several issues, which may be mutually exclusive, but assumes great importance in the context of new development initiative that already passed through a decade after the economy was globalize. Analysis of strengths and weaknesses of these industries, threats they are facing and opportunities that are lying ahead of them could perhaps help us in understanding the likely impact and strategies that could be adopted.

The biggest strength of this sector, needless to mention, is higher employment elasticity with respect to capital investment. In a capital scarce country like India, which is yet to succeed in attracting capital from abroad as aspired, employment potential of this sector with low capital base lends credible support to the above argument. The second most important strength is that, it fetches large export earnings to the nation mainly due to its orientation towards eco-friendly production. This sector, therefore, deserves to be considered even from the point of view of environment as an important contributor to development. The worldwide concern for environment seems to have created space for VSI sector to flourish since the latter nurtures its production ethos giving due regards to the ecological imperatives. Besides, there are other inherent strengths of rural industries that cannot be wished away even in the context of increasing market competitiveness. These are found in respect of (1) expanding value addition (2) decentralized nature of production (3) type and range of product (4) poverty alleviation and (5) improvement in quality of life, etc.

The weaknesses are inherent and many. They are also well documented by the researchers. They include (1) lack of credit support (2) lack of appropriate skill development (3) Raw material constraints (4) Market imperfection (5) absence of improved technology (6) adequate infrastructure, etc.

Government of India initiated several programmes to promote this sector at different levels time to time. Several institutions have been created to facilitate their promotion. Despite these efforts for last several decades or so, process of rural industrialization continued to be peripheral to the mainstream industrialization process.

A major fall out of globalization seems to be deceleration in employment generation in rural areas. One of the distinguishing features of employment situation in the country is that a large number of workers are either self-employed or casual labourers. The increasing trends of employing labour force on casual basis among educated workforce accompanied by declining growth of rural employment and declining employment share of the organized sector are certainly disturbing for the economy. It is, therefore, necessary for the government to work out appropriate measures for the growth of rural industries that could supplement the process of employment generation on a sustainable manner.

Liberalized Import Policy of the government has its own ramification for the growth of employment in the VSI sector. Dumping of small industry goods by countries like China, import of footwear from several countries, which are under consideration and several other imported goods are reducing the space of the VSI sector in the market. This can be accomplished by means of following better management techniques based on professionalism and adoption of improved technology wherever it is required. This will definitely bring down cost of production that finally leads to enhance competitiveness of the VSI sector.

One should not overlook the implications of WTO Agreements on the prospect of rural industries. The issue is how the process of rural industrialisation can be reversed for its betterment by means of confirming the stipulated standards of WTO related to total quality management. Rural industries sector is yet to absorb technological advancements that are taking place across the globe. The effects of these advancements that have reduced the distance between the production and consumption are yet to be utilised by the VSI sector.

Liberalized EXIM policy facilitated the growth of export not only of handicrafts but also several agro-based products, which are environment friendly. Several rural industry products are considered natural and eco-friendly. It is possible to develop entrepreneurship among the persons of non-entrepreneurial background through proper training, orientation and motivation. RUDSETI model of rural entrepreneurship development has proved successful in motivating and confidence building of youth and women thereby acquiring a productive identity and generating employment for quality products and services in the rural areas. Consortium of export units is being encouraged to assume greater responsibilities to participate in the international exhibitions and gatherings. They facilitate tie-ups to increase with importers in other countries. This may speed up the process. The emerging thrust for natural resources based products such as vermin-compost; neem extract, organic and bio-fertilizer offer promising opportunities. Increasing demand for natural products in the global market is now opening up better opportunities for Indian manufacturers for scaling up exports.

The winds of change seem to have opened up new vistas for large number of VSI units, which are flexible and adaptable to changes. Low volume specialized markets and diversification to different product lines with appropriate manufacturing processes could be advantageous to VSI sector in the present context. It may gain through establishing both backward and forward linkages with large enterprises or export houses.

India being pre-dominantly rural with enormous surplus of labor, rural industries has not lost its relevance in the context of global competitiveness since they continue to be significant sources of employment generation in the rural areas. It is true that they are perennially handicapped with the problems of shortage of capital, obsolete technology, lack of market etc. But, these are the problems that are essentially structural and can be addressed through appropriate interventions. Opinions differ between scholars about the impact of the implementation of the new policy regime on rural industries. Some argue that new regime is hardening the existing problems rural industries are encountering for several decades and pushing them to the brink of destruction. However, others argue that they are now embedded with new opportunities and, therefore, they have more potential for development. Both streams of argument throw several issues, which may be mutually exclusive, but assumes great importance in the context of new development initiative that already passed through a decade after the economy was globalize. The following is an overview of different aspects of rural industries sector in the context of changing economic scenario in India.

Economic Reforms and Rural Industry: India in the 1990s by V.B. Athreya in his paper has explained impact of economic reforms on rural industry. The first part deals with the macroeconomic outcomes of the decade of reforms, focusing on growth, equity, employment and poverty. The second part deals with rural industry in the context of India's overall strategy of development as it has evolved since independence. In the third and brief final section, he has offered some concluding remarks.

Rural Industries and the International Market: Some Issues by P.M. Mathew narrates as how the globalization has made the functional role of rural industry extremely difficult against the background of the emerging role of the nation state in economic activities, which is getting progressively eroded. The conflict is basically between, the social objective of providing employment opportunities to millions of people through rural industries, and the economic aspects of catering to market opportunities and challenges. The paper analyses as how the structure of India's exports is biased towards rural industry products while discussing constraints and opportunities with the help of two case studies, handlooms and handicrafts. He also discusses as how both direct and indirect agreements under WTO relating to Textiles, is likely to affect both handlooms and handicrafts. Intellectual property rights under the new TRIPS Agreements are likely to steal away the opportunities with regard to rural products.

B. Yerram Raju in his paper on Marketing holds the future for Rural Industrialization has drawn the attention on decreasing employment trends during the recent past. He has highlighted a few emerging areas for employment generation in non-farm sector. They include (a) rural enterprises, (b) agro-processing, (c) contract farming, information technology and (d) marketing. In order to make rural industries sustainable, the paper concludes that it is desirable to strengthen the Rural Connectivity, Agricultural Market Yards, Commodity Futures, Retail Consumer Points, Quality Standards, Packaging and

Labeling, Information Technology and Information and Communication Technologies.

Anne T. Kuriakose's paper examines the handloom policy scenario and its implications on the ground as well as political explanations for the relative stasis in strategies for the sector. The paper examines the recent application of cluster development programme and textile parks in the state of Andhra Pradesh with specific reference to theories of upgrading and the learning region. The paper suggests that the segregation of social welfare objectives from growth enhancement, consideration of region specific strategic interventions at nodal points of handloom belts, exploring the possibilities of non-state actors and allies including MACS network and long term integration of textile and garment industry could alone respond to the growing challenges faced by textile producers including handloom industry.

A paper on Entrepreneurship development through cooperatives: an experience of women dairy project in Rajasthan by V. M. Rao exposes the emergence new breed of women entrepreneurs from rural India. He further highlights that women can do wonders provided congenial and enabling environment is made available through institutional innovations like Women Dairy Cooperative Societies in Rajasthan.

R. Vidyasagar in his paper on rural industry that thrive on nimble fingers: a case of match industry in Tamil Nadu, has dealt with the growth and development of Hand Made Match Industry in Sivakasi region. While narrating the current profile of handmade match industry including the factors that lead to geographical concentration, he has concluded that demand side factors play a primary role for persistence of child labor, supply side factors also provide a fertile ground for the demand for cheap labor to grow and the industry to expand and get agglomerated.

K. Giriyappa & others in their paper on Artisanal Footwear Industry: Impact of Technology Transfer and Globalisation highlight the need for large scale institutional interventions to give intensive training to strengthen the skills of footwear artisans so as to develop clusters keeping in view of emerging free trade scenario under WTO. He has also suggested that the planned approach to strengthen the skills of artisans through careful implementation of various programmes.

K. Srinivasulu & E.V. Prakash Rao in their critical look at the National Textile Policy (2000) have drawn the attention towards all the committees and reports that dealt with the future and prospects of textile industry in India. Analysis of these committees and reports brings out a striking point of their conspicuous silence on the local markets. The paper highlights strength of the handlooms has been the regional specificity and specialty of their products determined by the historically inherited community skills, techniques and designs and tuned to the local traditions, cultural practices and community needs.

A paper on Handlooms–A model of Sustainable Rural Industry by Dasthakar Andhra presents a glossary of characteristics of handloom industry. Extension of credit facility to primary producers, raw material access on reasonable terms, development of innovative market mechanisms and technical and other kinds of research to support the demands of handloom industry are some the strategies that are suggested based on their own practical experiment on handloom industry.

Sudheesh Kaippachery has assessed the performance of rural small-scale enterprises in Andoor under Industrial Development Plot in the context of economic reforms. While identifying the challenges of liberalization and globalization on rural small-scale units of Andoor IDP he has prescribed a few strategies to make these units sustainable. They include (a) sound business practices, (b) development of financial markets with the help of financial institutions, (c) improvement in the quality of products, (d) trade fairs in rural markets, (e) modifications of electricity policies to suit the needs of rural small scale units, (f) R & D facilities to reduce the cost of production and improve the quality of products and (g) diversification and expansion.

The Promotion of Rural Industry: The Flip Fops of External Impetus by Y Gangi Reddy discusses as how to develop rural industries. The author has felt that resources are sine-qua-non to develop rural industry. In this regard, author suggests some measures in strengthening the resource endowment. Some of these are resource friendly harnessing of the naturally available resources, pressing in service group dynamics and collective action of the local people in the regeneration and sustainable management of natural resources, identification of prospective areas of natural resources etc.

V. Mohan Reddy in his paper on rural industries–The agony of Andhra Pradesh presented a meaningful strategy at the export led growth of agriculture and rural industry holds the promise of catapulting the growth of economy and generating mass employment.

Development of a Rural Industry Based on the Cultivation and Processing of Cassia senna by K. P. Sastry, B. R. Rajeswara Rao, C. P. Singh and Kamla Singh have analyzed how Cassia senna can help to develop rural industry. The authors have explained how by cultivating senna not only farmers but country can be benefited as export potential is very high. They have concluded that about 6000-7000 tones of senna leaves and pods are produced and about 85% of the production is exported. The export earnings range from Rs. 17 to Rs. 19 crore.

Impact of New Economic Policy on Coir Industries of Orissa: A Case Study of Puri District by Dr. Bijaya Kumar Sahu has highlighted scope of developing coir industries in Orissa. He has extended some suggestions for developing this sector, inter alia, of which includes supply of adequate fund for modernization, regular training for up-gradation of technology, uninterrupted supply of raw materials and improvement in infrastructure facilities etc.

M.V. Rama Prasad's paper on W.T.O.And Its Implications on Rural And S.S.I has thrown light about implication of WTO on rural & SSI. He concludes that to enable the rural and SSI entrepreneurs in facing the emerging challenges, there is a need for creating awareness about the implications of WTO and educating entrepreneurs suitably.

The paper on Sustainability of Micro-enterprises in the context of declining Common Natural Resources by V. Annamalai & Y. Gangi Reddy has discussed sustainability aspects of micro enterprises based on common natural resources.

N. V. Madhuri's paper on Rural Industrialisation: Problems and Strategies for Promotion in the Post-Liberalised Era discusses about the changes in economic policies in India under the context of Liberalisation, Privatisation and Globalisation which has tremendous impact on primary, secondary and tertiary sectors of production. The new economic policies may boost new opportunities and expand the markets on one hand, but on the other hand it may also intensify the existing crises in the rural industrial sector. This paper analyses the problems being faced by the rural industries in the post liberalisation era and strategies to deal with these problems.

Rural Industries and New Economic Policies–Human Resource Development Interventions for Sustainable Rural Industrialisation by P.SivaRam has thrown light on how human resource plays an important role for promotion of rural industries. Author feels that the development of partnerships between Government, NGOs, community and institutional building is needed to be addressed properly for the community based HRD.

Shankar Chatterjee's paper on Rural Development Programmes & Poverty In India: A Study With Respect To Gandhiji's Thought has explained major rural development programmes going on in the country. The Swarnajayanti Gram Swarojgar Yojana (SGSY) is a programme for rural poor where poor persons are given loan and subsidy for taking up economic activities. Thus many tiny industries are coming up rural India, which Gandhiji once advocated.

The paper on A Unique Bank Run by Rural Women Self-help Groups (SHGs)of Andhra Pradesh by Shankar Chatterjee & NV Madhuri have explained how women self-help groups run a bank. In Andhra Pradesh, self-help groups have been doing well at village and Mandal level. They are not-only involved in individual activity but also involved in activities like running a bank, which is unique one. Such banks are registered under Mutual Aided Cooperative Society Act, 1995. The case here gives an idea how the bank has been functioning.

The authors are thankful to the Director General and Deputy Director General of NIRD, Hyderabad for their continous encouragement in academic works.

The authors are thankful to all the resource persons for their contributions. The authors also express their gratitude to all the persons, who have directly and indirectly encouraged in bringing out the volume. Last but not the least, authors express their gratitude to Serials Publications, New Delhi for publication of the volume.

Authors

LIST OF CONTRIBUTORS

V. B. Athreya, Professor, Bharatidasan University, Trichi, Tamil Nadu.

P. M. Mathew, The author is Director, Institute of Small Enterprises and Development (ISED), Cochin. He can be contacted at *ised@md2.vsnl.net.in or insmall@eth.net.*

B. Yerram Raju, Managing Director, Sandilya Consultants Pvt. Ltd., Tarnaka, Hyderabad.

Anne T. Kuriakose, Development Studies Program, Land Tenure Centre, University of Wisconsin-Madison, 1357 University Avenue, Madison, WI 53715 USA, *E-mail: atkuriakose@wisc.edu.*

V. M. Rao, Professor and Head, Department of Research and Publications, Vaikunth Mehta National Institute of Cooperative Management, University Road, Pune.

Giriyappa Kollannavar, D. Chandramouli and B. Krishnama Naidu, Scientists, Central Leather Research Institute, Adyar, Chennai.

K. Srinivasulu, Professor & Head, Political Sciences Department, Nizam College, Osmania Unversity, Hyderabad.

E.V. Prakash Rao, Assistant Professor, NIRD, Hyderabad

R. Vidya Sagar, *E-mail: rahulvidya2002@yahoo.co.in*

Dastkar Andhra, *E-mail: dastkar1@satyam.net.in*

Sudheesh Kaippachery, Assistant Professor, Department of Economics, University of Kerala, Kariavattom (PO), Thiruvananthapuram, Kerala.

V. Mohan Reddy, Roses; 7-24/5B, JSN Colony, Street No. 8, Habsiguda; Hyderabad. *Email:mohanreddy@eth.net.*

K. P. Sastry, B. R. Rajeswara Rao, C. P. Singh and Kamla Singh, Central Institute of Medicinal and Aromatic Plants, Field Station, Boduppal, Hyderabad.

Bijaya Kumar Sahu, Director, Centre for Socio-Economic and Market Research, Bhubaneswar, Orissa.

M. V. Rama Prasad, Assistant Professor, College of Management Studies, Gitam, Visakhapatnam.

V. Annamalai, Y. Gangi Reddy, Assistant Professor and Associate Professors, NIRD, Hyderabad.

N.V. Madhuri, Asst. Professor (NIRD), Rajendranagar, Hyderabad.

P. SivaRam, Associate Professor, Centre for HRD, National Institute of Rural Development (NIRD), Rajendra Nagar, Hyderabad.

Shankar Chatterjee, Senior Assistant Professor, NIRD, Rajendranagar, Hyderabad, *E-mail: shankar_nird@yahoo.com.*

1

ECONOMIC REFORMS AND RURAL INDUSTRY: INDIA IN THE 1990s

V. B. Athreya

I have worked mostly in the areas of agrarian change, gender, education and development, and must therefore confess to some degree of trepidation at having to deliver the keynote address to this august audience. However, it is not fools alone who rush in where angels fear to tread. Academics do the same. It is an occupational hazard. This presentation is divided into three parts. The first part deals with the macroeconomic outcomes of the decade of reforms, focusing on growth, equity, employment and poverty. The second part deals with rural industry in the context of India's overall strategy of development as it has evolved since independence. In the third and brief final section, I offer some concluding remarks.

SECTION I: GROWTH, EMPLOYMENT AND RURAL POVERTY IN THE REFORM PERIOD

The period of nearly 11 years since the acceleration of the process of economic liberalization in June 1991 has seen an orchestrated attempt by successive governments, international agencies such as the World Bank and the International Monetary Fund (IMF), official economists, and almost the entire electronic and print media, to portray the policies of liberalization, privatization and globalization (LPG) as both inevitable and desirable. Such a portrayal is entirely inaccurate and unwarranted.

As Chandrasekhar and Jayati Ghosh (2002) point out, the neo-liberal reforms "...made curtailment of the fiscal deficit the fundamental task of fiscal policy. It accelerated trade liberalization, which involved doing away with quantitative restrictions on imports and reducing customs tariffs, with attendant revenue implications. It dismantled controls on free operation of large industrial capital, domestic and foreign. It provided a host of direct and indirect concessions to industry, reducing the tax base of the government further. It provided a host of concessions to foreign investors in the hope that they would use India as a base for world market production."

The neo-liberal reformers had argued that economic growth in India was being stifled by the intrusive role of the state as both regulator and participant; that large fiscal deficits crowded out private investment and undermined investor confidence. They argued that the excessive protection provided to Indian industry by the imposition of import restrictions and tariffs prevented the development of an efficient, competitive economy which would enable India to benefit from integration with the world capitalist economy. Their claim, then, was that liberalization would enhance the growth rate. As growth occurred across the board, and the economy became more competitive through domestic deregulation and external opening-up, exports would surge and employment would expand rapidly. As a result, poverty would decline sharply as would unemployment. But what has been the record of the 12 years of reform policies?

In terms of the indicators of growth, employment and poverty, the performance during the reform decade of the 1990s has been no better, and in some respects distinctly worse than in the decade of the 1980s. They also highlight the fact that evens a decade after the reforms; the country faces the paradoxical situation of increased incidence of hunger and food insecurity among a sizeable proportion of our population. This is so even as the government is saddled with huge stocks of unsold food grains despite a rate of growth of food grains production that was lower than the rate of growth in population during the 1990s.

The average annual rate of growth of the country's gross domestic product (GDP) at constant prices was no higher in the 1990s than in the 1980s. According to the Reserve Bank of India, the average rate of growth of the 'growth cycle' over the 1990s amounted to only 4.4 per cent. In the material-producing primary and secondary sectors, the growth performance was even worse. Thus the primary sector, which grew at the rate of 5.72 per cent a year between 1985-86 and 1989-90, grew only at the rate of 3.77 per cent between 1991-92 and 1994-95. A miserable growth rate of 1.95 per cent was recorded between 1995-96 and 1999-2000. Similarly, over the corresponding periods, the secondary sector grew at the rates of 8.66 per cent, 8.04 per cent and 4.99 per cent respectively, reflecting a sharp decline in the rate of growth of industry since the mid-1990s. Even the much-hyped services or tertiary sector showed a decline in the average annual growth rate from around 8.7 per cent in the 1980s to 6.9 per cent in the 1990s. The stagnation or decline in growth rates is not surprising since the key determinant of the overall growth rate of an economy - the ratio of investment to gross domestic product - increased only marginally from around 21.7 per cent in the 1980s to 24.5 per cent in the 1990s. In fact, after touching a peak of 26.8 per cent in 1995-96, this ratio declined, and has been stagnating at around 23 per cent.

The issue of growth rates apart, a decade of reforms has led to a crisis in agriculture. The reduction of public investment in rural areas and cuts in subsidies on farm inputs has led to higher input costs. At the same time, removal of quantitative restrictions on imports has led to a free fall in prices of farm produce in a number of instances. As for industry, except for the short-lived boom of the period 1993-95 and the spurt in demand arising from the implementation of the Fifth Pay Commission Award in 1999-2000, the overall tendency, sharply evident by the end of the decade, was towards deceleration and a distinctly lower rate of industrial growth. Even the apparently more successful case of growth, the service sector, reflects at a deeper level, a more mixed picture. There is a dualism, with a proliferation of low-wage, low-productivity service jobs leading the growth in this sector, rather than 'modern', high-productivity sectors, except for possibly the information technology sector, Even the IT sector has been characterized by sharp fluctuations of fortune. Turning to employment, data from the National Sample Surveys

and Census 2001 show that, while rural and urban employment grew at annual rates of 2.03 per cent and 3.39 per cent respectively between 1987-88 and 1993-94, the rates were much lower between 1993-94 and 1999-2000 at 0.66 per cent and 2.27 per cent respectively. The rural employment growth rate of 0.66 per cent between 1993-94 and 1999-2000, as Chandrasekhar and Jayati Ghosh point out, "... was not only less than one-third of the rate of the previous period 1987-88 to 1993-94, it was also less than half the rate of growth of the labour force in the same period. In fact, it turns out that this was the lowest rate of growth of rural employment in post-Independence history." Over the 1990s, the 'weekly status' unemployment rate was around 7 per cent for men and 10 per cent for women - exceptionally high for a country with little or no protection for working people by way of social security or unemployment compensation. Reduction in public investment, removal of quantitative restrictions on imports, squeeze on rural credit, sharply reduced expenditures on rural development and employment schemes, and the overall deflationary macroeconomic policies deriving from the obsession with the reduction of the fiscal deficit - all these contributed to the sharp decline in the growth rate of employment. Only a small part of the decline can be attributed to increased number of years of formal education for both males and females of the relatively better-off sections of the population.

WHAT has been the impact of the reforms on poverty? While poverty is a multi-dimensional phenomenon, data limitations make it difficult to evaluate the extent of poverty and the changes thereof in a comprehensive manner. Data are, however, available on income-poverty. The most commonly used official indicator of the extent of poverty is the "head count ratio," which tells us the proportion of households below a specified poverty line. The norm used to define the poverty line is the value of food expenditure necessary to ensure the intake of a specified amount of calories a day for a person. The details of how this is worked out need not detain us, since our focus is more on the changes in the extent of poverty, however defined, rather than the level per se. Data on poverty for the latest year available, namely 1999-2000, are not easily comparable with those for earlier years on account of definitional changes. An examination the data on the head count ratio of poverty between 1993-94 and the first half of 1998, as well as the data over a longer period shows that, contrary to the expectations of the reformers that there would be a decline in the incidence of poverty because of higher growth and the rapid expansion of employment owing to reforms, there has in fact been no significant decline in rural poverty as measured by the headcount ratio.

In respect of the overall poverty ratio, the reform period is characterized by the disappearance of the trend of decline in poverty that was observed between the mid-1970s and the early-1990s. This should really occasion no surprise, given the decline in rural development expenditure in proportional terms, the cutback in public investment in agriculture during the period of reforms not adequately compensated by private investment, and the overall macro deflationary policies for most of this period. Additionally, opening up of the economy to imports, gradual abandonment of the public distribution system, accompanied by the successive sharp increases in issue prices of food grains through the PDS, and the move towards targeting of PDS in a context of highly imperfect information would also have contributed to the persistence of large scale poverty despite GDP growth.

The last point about food insecurity and high food prices deserves elaboration. The 1990s have been characterized by a sad paradox, which testifies to the utter irrationality of the LPG policy regime. This is a combination of the denial of access to food grain at affordable prices for a sizeable proportion of our population - amounting perhaps to about 350 million people - on the one hand, and the accumulation of unsold food stocks with the government - to the tune of 62 million tones by the end of 2001 - on the other. The accumulation of a high level of food stocks with the government occurred during a decade in which the per capita food grain availability to the public declined from an average of 510 gm a day in 1991 to 458 gm in 2000. This was despite a much lower growth rate of population in the 1990s than in the earlier decades. An even more glaring manifestation of the irrationality of LPG policies has been the refusal of the government to use the available stock of food grains to carry out a massive food-for-work programme, which would help build badly needed productive rural assets, stimulate industrial growth through its demand effects, and bring down the carrying costs for the Food Corporation of India. Such a refusal arises from an obsession with the fiscal deficit, the reduction of which is touted by the World Bank and the IMF as the panacea for all our economic ills, a proposition that is uncritically accepted and repeated as a mantra by our policymakers.

If the neo-liberal reforms do not offer a solution to our paramount tasks of achieving a higher rate of economic growth in a manner that would expand employment, lower poverty rapidly, and democratize the growth process by ensuring a wider participation and a more just sharing of its benefits, is there any other way out? Contrary to the oft-heard chorus of TINA (There is no alternative), there are alternatives. It is not possible to do justice here to the elaboration of a comprehensive alternative, but the broad philosophy can be stated briefly. One must begin by giving up the obsession with the fiscal deficit, and accept the need for a proactive role for the state in terms of negotiating the challenges posed by the process of contemporary globalization. An appropiate policy regime would be one which includes appropriate restrictions on import of commodities and capital, a serious effort to mobilize resources through direct taxation of large capital, domestic and foreign, the rural landed gentry and the richer sections of the peasantry; thoroughgoing land reforms, a coordinated export thrust in which the state plays a key role in partnership with industry, and a more egalitarian asset distribution. One must also emphasize the importance of democratic decentralization, and the need to grant greater powers to elected local bodies and advocate the greater participation of ordinary working people in economic decision-making.

SECTION II: RURAL INDUSTRY IN THE REFORM PERIOD

Rural industry has been an important concern of policy in India, at least at the level of rhetoric. There have been several distinct strands of argument and ideology concerning rural industry and its place in the Indian economy [Ashwani Saith (2001)]. The Gandhian argument for rural industry has rested on several assumed virtues of traditional rural society, economy and people. The Nehru-Mahalanobis vision-which incidentally was not very different in this regard from that of the "Bombay Plan" proposed by the captains of Indian big business at the time of India's independence and its embarking on development- emphasized the need to provide mass employment, even while the economy sought to develop through large scale investment in capital goods, which were by nature capital-intensive. It saw rural industry as an important source of employment. Additionally, such rural industrial growth was to cater to the mass consumption good needs of the urban population at low levels of capital intensity, thus releasing scarce capital for investment in the capital goods sector. The rural industries were to be made viable and enabled to compete effectively with urban industry, both through subsidies and other means, and by reservation of specific products and services exclusively for the operation of rural industry. Unlike in the classical model of capitalist development where small industry including rural industry would be swept away by competition and the advantages of economies of scale possessed by the large capitalist firms, in the Nehru-Mahalanobis model, state support would enable rural and small industry to sustain itself and also make a valuable contribution to the country's development strategy by providing rural employment, minimizing migration to urban areas and promoting regionally balanced growth. It would also be non-import intensive and enable utilization of scattered rural resources. There were other strands of argument for promotion of rural industry as a policy that did not derive from any specific model but were eclectic in character. These would emphasize, in addition to the ones mentioned earlier, such notions as the presumed "eco-friendly" nature of rural industry. There are also some in the current context who see rural industry as an instrument in the struggle against hegemonic globalization. I shall not enter into a debate on the merits or otherwise of the various arguments and rationales for promoting rural industry as a matter of policy, but merely observe that whatever the policy rhetoric may have been at various times since independence, rural industrialization in India has suffered fairly persistent relative decline throughout the period since independence. It is of course common knowledge that it suffered grievous blows under the colonial dispensation.

The period of reform has been characterized by deregulation, an important aspect of which has been de-reservation. This has negatively impacted on both modern small-scale industry and on village industry. Other policy moves such as opening up of the economy to imports through removal of quantitative restrictions and steep reduction in import duties, as well as the stress on exports without any selectivity have also affected these sectors, removing to a substantial extent the protection they enjoyed earlier. The rural credit squeeze, and the financial sector reforms which have made credit both expensive and difficult to access for those without adequate collateral, especially as compared to the halcyon IRDP days of the 1980s, would have also had a negative impact on the small and village industries. More than the specific sectoral policies, the overall obsession with the fiscal deficit, and the refusal despite ritual exhortation in the *Economic Survey*, year after year, to widen and deepen the tax base, have meant that there has been little impulse for rural growth from government policy. As a result, there has been widespread rural distress, dramatically and tragically illustrated by suicides as well as starvation deaths of both farmers and rural artisans. The plight of the handloom weavers of Andhra Pradesh in the early 1990s and again towards the end of the decade- documented, for instance, in the pages of *Frontline* by Frontline team (1992) and Asha Krishnakumar(2001)- and of Tamil Nadu more recently are cases in point. During a recent revisit to villages I had first surveyed in Tiruchirapalli in 1979-80, I found that the rural non farm occupation of artificial gem cutting, an extremely important source of livelihood in the villages with mainly rain-fed agriculture, had become almost extinct, with a shift to mechanized gem cutting, and a collapse of prices. The power-looms which flourished in the 1970s and especially in the 1980s have been badly hit by the indiscriminate export of yarn and resulting unviable yarn prices as well as by the disasters which repeatedly befell the cotton crop as a consequence, at least in part, of the reform policies. The changes in the global trade and investment environment, with the intrusive WTO regime and the continued protectionist stances of the developed countries, as well as the global deflationary regime imposed by dominant global finance capital, have also been inimical to rural industry.

In terms of the value of output, small scale industry, mostly urban, grew from rupees 7200 crore to 73,125 crore between 1973-74 and 1988-89, and village industry from 122 to 1443 crore over the same period. Subsequently, between 1988=89 and 1996-97, the increase was more modest for village industry from 1443 crore in 1988-89 to 3890 crore in 1996-97. The output of handicrafts grew from 1065 crore in 1973-74 to 8250 crore by1988-89, and to 29,600 crore in 1996-97. Progress on the employment front was rather dismal, especially during the 1990s. Employment in village and small industries taken as a whole grew from 1.5 crore in 1973-74 to 4.26 crore by 1990-91, but grew much more slowly thereafter to reach 5.83 crore in 1996-97. On the export front, the picture is quite mixed, with modern SSI increasing its exports nearly fourfold from9100 crore in 1990-91 to 39,249 crore in 1996-97, but handicrafts declining from 8100 crore to 5628 crore over the same period.

Taken together, the progress of rural industry during the reform period is far from spectacular, notwithstanding the promises made in the small industry policy statement of 1991, and in subsequent policy declarations. The tenth plan document's figures bring out the dismal performance in respect of rural employment during the 1990s, as captured by the NSS, but content itself with pious statements of intention to correct the situation. Worse, instead of recognizing the deleterious impact of reforms on agriculture, it makes the astonishing statement that reforms have largely bypassed agriculture! Its "solution" to the problem of rural unemployment is more vigorous application of reforms, including contract farming and reverse land reforms to corporatize farming and removing all hindrances in the way of leasing of land by corporate. It makes some ritual references to khadi and village industries and to the creation of a new Ministry of Agro and rural industry, separate form the ministry for small industry, but provides little by way of substance as far as a strategy for promotion of rural industry, and through it, rural employment, is concerned.

SECTION III: SOME CONCLUDING REMARKS

It should be clear from the foregoing that the reform period has not been "rural-industry friendly". This should not occasion any surprise, except for those of neo-liberal faith. The reforms are being carried out under conditions of global dominance of finance capital whose main aim is to secure free entry and exit of financial flows across national borders, and unhindered market access to the third world, including the so-called emerging economies. Pleasing finance capital- "retaining the confidence of the foreign investors", in the language of successive finance ministers of India through the 1990s-means reducing the proactive role of the State in development and ensuring the socio-political and economic conditions needed for the unfettered operation of large foreign and domestic capital. These objectives inevitably imply the pursuit of deflationary macroeconomic policies and an obsession with the fiscal deficit to the point where we can have large stocks of food grains rotting in FCI warehouses while millions go hungry, rather than using the food stocks to create real assets through a massive, decentralized food-for-work programme. It would be next to impossible for rural industry as a whole to flourish in such a policy regime, although there may be individual success stories. For rural industry to grow, and to provide meaningful employment, we need to discard the reform policies, and opt for a more proactive role for the State in mobilizing resources for development. Such a State should not be a centralized one, but one exhibiting maximum devolution of finances, functions and powers, and thus potentially more accountable to people at the grassroots. While the State should aggressively pursue exports, it must base the growth strategy on the home market in order to be sustainable. Such a base can only be provided by thoroughgoing land reforms, interpreted not narrowly as pertaining to land alone, but as encompassing all productive assets, including in particular, access to irrigation and credit.

REFERENCES

Asha Krishnakumar in *Frontline*, April 2001.

Chandrasekhar,C. P. and Jayati Ghosh (2002), *The Market that Failed*, Leftword, New Delhi.

Frontline Team, K. Nagaraj, Asha Krishnakumar and N. Rajaram (1991), Cover Story in *Frontline*, December.

Government of India, *Tenth Five Year Plan*, GOI, 2002.

Government of India, *Indian Planning: A Statistical Experience* GOI, 2001.

Government of India, 'SSI Policy Statement', GOI, 1991.

Saith, Ashwani (2001), 'From Village Artisans to Industrial Clusters: Agendas and Policy Gaps in Indian Rural Industrialization', *Journal of Agrarian Change*, Vol. 1, No. 1, January.

2

RURAL INDUSTRIES AND THE INTERNATIONAL MARKET: SOME ISSUES

P. M. Mathew

INTRODUCTION

In the literature on industrial geography, industries have been distinguished according to their locational pattern. A distinction between 'rural' and 'urban' industries has largely been made in a context of the historical experience of economic development and industrialization in developing countries. Developing countries are largely characterized as having a relatively small 'modern sector' of economic activities and a significantly large, and often decentralised, economic activities which are located in the hinterland. The modern activities are often equated with urban centres, and the traditional ones as largely rural-concentrated. Rural areas specialize more or less exclusively in agriculture, while industries are located mostly in the urban areas (Papola, 1982). Such a theoretical paradigm of dualism also pre-supposes, unlimited supplies of labour in the rural hinterland and concentration of capital in the urban centres, such that, as the process of economic development gains momentum, labour migrates from rural to the urban centres. This paradigm, largely explained in development literature as '*economic dualism*', has significant policy implications.

While the process of migration offers some employment opportunities to the "surplus labour" in the rural areas, the urban centres face a significant problem of overpopulation and consequent short supply of basic amenities. The conventional Lewis Model (Lewis, 1954), and critiques of the same which put forward a 'pauperization thesis' (see Bromley and Gerry, 1979), have prompted the search for alternative models of rural development. The 'Redistribution with Growth Model' put forward by Chenery *et. al* (1974), still continues to be the theoretical base of rural industrialisation strategies in developing countries.

RURAL INDUSTRIES POLICY IN INDIA

The political and social rationale of rural industry policy in India far exceeds its economic rationale. The 'Quit-India' movement which was inaugurated in 1942 provided the basic political rationale, while the Gandhian philosophy of *gram swaraj* provided the social rationale of rural industry in a labour abundant and capital scarce India. In the planning era, a strong economic rationale was developed through the Mahalanobis model, in which a "wage goods" role was assigned to rural industries and non-farm activities. The so-called "crisis of planning" in the mid 1960s, and the rediscovery of the so-called 'informal sector' in the 1970s, prompted academicians and policy makers to re-examine rural industries in a new perspective. *Sustainability* became a crucial area of debate. Marketing was considered as a *problem,* rather than as an opportunity. This 'problem' was sought to be addressed through enhanced public policy solutions, such as *Bhandars* and common marketing centres organized by the government, marketing federations, initiated by the co-operatives etc.

The fact that the products of the rural industries do not attract an appropriate market, indicates a basic contradiction in India's rural industrialisation policy. Development of industries in the rural areas has been crucial to the exercise of industrial policy formulation in the country, though the emphasis has shifted from time to time. The policy in this area is more attuned, to the interests of specific institutional structures already existing, rather than a clear-cut policy framework looking for appropriate institutional structures. It was this approach which got reflected in the setting up of a variety of institutions, exclusive as well as general, which consider rural industrialisation as a potential area of activity. Starting from the Cottage Industries Board, which was set up in 1948,and subsequently, the All India Handloom Board and the All India Handicrafts Board, new institutional structures appeared in the form of a separate Ministry for Agro & Rural Industries and development banks like SIDBI and NABARD. While Rural Industrialisation Programme (RIP) was operational in the 1970s, we have nowa National Programme of Rural Industrialization in which the Ministry of ARI and the development banks participate. While the concept of 'growth centres' was evolved in the late-1950s, the place has now been taken by the programme on industrial clusters being implemented by several Ministries such as Rural Development,Textiles and SSI. Irrespective of the policy instruments, programmes and institutional structures, the official focus on rural industry has been primarily viewed as a programme for the preservation and revitalisation of traditional industries, and not as a programme for rural industrialisation (Papola, 1982). As a result, rural industries have not played an effective role in providing a reasonable level of incomes to those engaged in them, or in integrating the rural areas into the overall process of industrialisation in the country. The problem of rural industrialisation, was never considered as an aspect of the spatial diversification of industries, addressing to the wider questions of locational flexibility of industries, economies of scale and agglomeration, infrastructure and incentives and concessions. On the other hand, rural industrialisation was viewed in terms of a limited concept of promoting village industries. Under such a limited approach, a vicious circle of static technology, competition from substitutes and low income elasticity of demand, are natural (Papola, 1982). These issues gain as added complexity under globalisation where markets are characterised by extreme competition and volatility.

INDUSTRIAL SPACE UNDER GLOBALISATION

The process of globalisation seeks to protect global interests. The assumption behind the term 'global interests' is that, in an attempt to pursue such interests, maximum justice is done to each nation state according to its capabilities, contribution and need. However, the term 'global interest' need to be interpreted in terms of its political economy. To the political economist, it means the interest of capital which is globally operating. Therefore, the benefit of a country to gain from trade, under globalisation, depends upon the extent to which the country is 'globalised'.

The extent of globalisation of a country is defined according to two major criteria:

1. turnover across countries; and 2. operational coverage of countries. Based on such criteria, the OECD (1997) has made a fourfold categorisation of businesses: (1) truly global; (2) largely global; (3) partly global; and (4) least global. For example, the extent to which India is globalised, depends upon the extent of the turnover made by India's enterprises across the world, as well as the number of countries so covered.

Under globalisation, the *nation state* is just a managerial instrument. While, in the pre-globalisation era, the nation state could protect the interests of its citizens, under globalisation, the multilateral agreements (e.g., WTO) compell the nation state to follow only those policies which are not detrimental to 'global interests' as defined by such multilateral forum. As a signatory to several of these global agreements, the governments are bound to initiate legislation which may not often be to the best interests of the majority of their citizens. The governments cannot extend support measures (such as subsidies) as before in a regional setting, nor can they effectively spell out and practice rural development as a priority subject.

The concept of rural industry itself, is therefore an anachronism, especially in the present context of globalisation. However, in a functional sense, what has hitherto been described as 'rural industry' will continue to perform its role in a new context. It is this functional role that one should highlight in any discussion on the role of rural industries in the international market.

THE MEANING OF INDUSTRIAL GLOBALISATION

Industrial globalisation is defined as "an evolving pattern of cross-border enterprise activities" (OECD, 1997). It implies a complete paradigm change from an increasingly local individual-oriented economic activity, to more collaborative activities meant for a wider market. The local dimension of production changes to collaborations. Strategic alliances take the place of single-firm activity. Outsourcing becomes the rule of the day, in place of the conventional concept of the single firm, which produces a product for the self-identified market. Local market gives way to world market. Flexible production systems take the place of the conventional rigid production systems. The limited economic interest of a firm gives way to an enhanced thrust on growth. Hence, the conventional concept of a small or micro firm, which is co-terminus with the concept of a rural space, becomes increasingly redundant, though the functional relevance of smallness remains still important.

FUNCTIONAL RELEVANCE OF RURAL INDUSTRIES

Though, in theory, the relevance of rural industry has been decimated, its functional relevance continues. The functional relevance of rural industries needs to be discussed in terms of their present role in the economy. Hence, we may be able to redefine rural industries based on what they actually do. The broad features of a rural industrial enterprise are the following:

(1) located in a rural setting with obvious limited market and linkages,

(2) labour abundant and capital-scarce

(3) focus on local skills and relatively low technology

Based on these criteria, India's rural industries cover its significant informal sector. The term informal sector covers both the micro base of entrepreneurship which spontaneously emerge, as also, a micro sector which has been deliberately created as an appendage of large capital. Viewed from this angle an array of economic activities, falling under the ruberic, 'rural crafts', such as handlooms, handicrafts etc. can form the compass of rural industries.

While we propose to examine the case of a few of these crafts in the latter part of this paper, it is important to examine the basic features of rural crafts, in order to make sense out of a discussion on its international market.

The craft based products are also commodities exchanged in the market. They perform two roles: (1) exchange value; and (2) use value. Exchange value of a craft product arises out of: (a) design and appearance; and (b) ethnic origin. For example, *bathik* produced in Indonesia may be inferior to Indian handlooms. But they attract a premium in the Indian market because of its particular ethnic origin. Both India and Indonesia turn out bamboo handicrafts. However, such handicrafts produced in China attract a much greater premium in the European market. The advantage of China lies in the peculiar design and look of their products. Handicrafts are meant not exclusively for its exchange value; the use value is also important. Therefore, a craft product with greater use value as well as exchange value attracts a premium in the international market, though all handicrafts have at least a limited market share, based exclusively on their ethnic origin. This is true of handlooms as well. The growth of the cotton textile industry at the international level has been phenomenal during the past half a century. However, handlooms from various countries have a place in the international market, though in different degrees, for reasons mentioned above.

INDIA'S EXPORT TREND AND EMERGING TRADE ISSUES

A discussion on the international market for rural industry products cannot remain meaningful, without discussing the new trade regime under WTO. The setting up of the WTO in 1995 institutionalised a rule-based multilateral trading system, and has thereby intensified the extent of global competition. WTO regulates multilateral trade and enforces its member countries to remove import quotas, to reduce tariffs, and to progressively bring down import restrictions. Trade distorting subsidies to exports, as well as to domestic goods, ceases to exist under a full-fledged WTO-led trade regime. The overall implication of the new trade regime is that every single individual enterprise in India, small or large, rural or urban, whether exporting or serving the domestic market, has to face intense competition. While exporting enterprises directly face the challenge in the international market, those confining to the domestic market, face the challenge indirectly, through cheaper substitutes, product obsolescence etc. All enterprises are forced to work as subjects or links of global supply chains, directly or indirectly. Therefore, no criteria can be suggested for rural industries to behave as market players. Probably, the only thumb rule is one of quality, and meeting the international standards, which many smaller enterprises cannot adhere to. However, no enterprise can stick on to its own standard and continue in the market, any longer.

Despite the typical features of low-productivity and low technology of rural industries in India, these industries have a prominent role in India's exports. Until 1970, the small -scale sector did not play any worthwhile role in India's exports. In 1971-72 its share in total exports was 9.6 per cent. During the next 20 years, however, its share increased and became 31.5 per cent in 1991-92. The present share of 35 per cent of total national exports has to be viewed in the light of the fact that while Indian small -scale sector accounts for about 40 per cent of industrial production, its share is 35 per cent in total exports. If we also add up the exports emerging from traditional industries like handicrafts, handlooms, coir, sericulture, etc., the share goes up further to about 50 per cent.

Though there were apprehensions on the potential export scene in the context of the WTO stipulations, the export position of the SSI sector has generally behaved to be more or less constant. But the latest figures brought out by the Directorate General of Commercial Intelligence and Statistics (DGCI & S) hints at the need for a careful examination of the emerging trend and to chalk out appropriate policies (see Table 1).

Table1
Profile of Exports in India: 1999-2000 & 2000-01 (in $ millions)

Exports	*1999-2000*	*2000-01*	*% Growth*
Tea	333.24	289.39	-14.70
Coffee	231.25	157.39	-31.94
Pulses	79.08	90.41	14.32
Tobacco	182.63	127.76	-30.04
Spices	316.62	246.89	-22.02
Nuts & Seeds	578.67	432.20	-25.31
Groundnut	66.33	38.60	-41.80
Oil Meals	191.17	284.59	48.87
Sugar & Molasses	5.71	63.30	1008.95
Processed Foods	271.08	332.48	22.65
Fresh fruits & Vegetables	104.19	127.96	22.81
Meat & Preparations	140.07	206.02	47.08
Spirit & Beverages	12.73	25.29	98.61
Marine Products	906.88	1085.15	19.66
Ores & Minerals	622.28	836.32	34.40
Machinery	1557.73	1879.45	20.65
Iron & Steel	590.61	804.09	36.14
Non-ferrous Metals	21.61	87.93	306.85
Electronic Goods	517.56	734.88	41.99
Project Goods	37.59	5.22	-86.10
Readymade Garments	3395.21	4075.78	20.05
Made-ups	2337.98	2504.23	7.11
Natural Silk Textiles	179.58	231.72.449.68	29.04
Carpets	494.68	11.76	9.10
Cotton Raw incl. Waste	15.24	1310.57	-22.85
Petroleum Products	30.04	920.90	4263.10
Unclassified items	350.23		162.94

Source: Economic Division, Ministry of Industry and Commerce, Government of India.

Disaggregated foreign trade data compiled by the DGCI & S, and collated by the Economic Division of the Department of Commerce, reveal that plantations with a weight of 1.39 per cent recorded a dismal -21.69 per cent growth at $446.78 million during April-December, 2000 against $570.49 million in the comparable months of 1999. Agriculture and allied products exports (weight 8.40 per cent) showed a negative 4.18 per cent growth at $2578.10 million, against $2679.75 million in the comparable months of 1999. Gems and jewellery (weight 16.75 per cent) which was hitherto a star performer in the country's export basket has put on a relatively weak show notching up a modest growth of 5.04 per cent at $5372.39 million, against $5114.48 million.

Export Composition: Enhancing the relative export capability requires some urgent imperatives: Firstly, it is necessary to closely monitor the export composition of India's SSI sector, in terms of products and services, Secondly, it is also necessary to identify, who the exporters are, and how they perform. For example, as per available data, more than 90% of the garment exports from the country are accounted by the SSI sector. But the number of SSI exporters in the garment sector is negligible. It is therefore, necessary to distinguish between exporters and exports. There is a significant data gap in this area, which does not permit evolution of any meaningful policies.

A characteristic feature of the SSI sector in India is that, there is a product concentration with regard to exports: 70-80 per cent of the total exports are accounted by items like, Readymade Garments, Leather Products, Basic Chemicals, Marine and Processed Foods and some Engineering items. While production has substantially grown, efforts towards diversification and quality up gradation remain backward. For example, in the case of Fruits and Vegetables, the processing facilities exist only for around 1 per cent of the output. In the case of Leather, where the country accounts for around 25 per cent of the raw materials, our export share remains very low. Another crucial area relates to the extensive dependence on the traditional exports. While this sub-sector has been considered a milch cow attempts towards quality improvement and design development remain badly neglected. Besides, there has also been a progressive decline in the share of manufacturing exports. During the period of 1992-93 and 1997-98, the share of manufacturing item in the SSI exports declined from 54.44 per cent to 52.84 per cent. The most striking decline is in the case of leather and leather goods, where the share fell from 80 per cent to 58 per cent during this period.

Case Studies

Since database on the export performance of rural industries is not adequate for a comprehensive understanding of the emerging situation, case studies on two representative industries are likely to provide considerable insights into the emerging issues. These are: (1) handlooms, and (2) handicrafts. The selection is deliberate, because these are two major sub-sectors of Indian industry which contribute significantly to output and employment.

The Handloom Sector

The handloom sector in India is very important from the point of view of its size and employment potential. It provides direct and indirect employment to more than 30 lakh weavers and is the largest economic activity second only to agriculture. The backward linkages of the sebsector with agriculture are also significant. It uses agricultural products as raw materials, and therefore, provides a ready market for agricultural goods. Therefore, in an economy where majority of people have agriculture as their mainstay, the significance of handloom is well understood. The inherent resilience and strength of this sector is its high flexibility and adaptability to varying market demand. It contributes nearly 23 per cent of the total cloth produced, in the country. The traditional significance of this sector along with its inseparable links with our ancient cultural heritage further expounds its vitality. Public policy initiatives in the handloom sector include, starting Weaver Service Centers, establishing Indian Institute of Handloom Technology, incorporating National Handlooms Development Corporation, which seek to ensure the regular supply of raw material to the handloom sector. The Parliament also passed the Handloom Act in 1985 with the aim to shield handloom weavers against power loom and textile mill operators by reserving certain textile items for exclusive production by handlooms. The moot question arises here as to the how far the benefits of most of these schemes, programmes and projects percolate down to the handloom weavers who are really in need of such programmes. This sector faces several new challenges, above all, to remain competitive with imports not only in terms of price, but also in product quality and consistency. Since the weavers and artisans do not get proper institutional support, their skills largely remain untapped. Weak financial base of weavers, non availability of adequate and timely credit facilities, technology and traditional production techniques, inadequate integration with modern economy, lack of marketing facilities, design development, training, infrastructure, information about the new international trade regime and developments, slow adaptation to consumer preferences, lack of opportunities for skill up gradation of weavers etc., are crucial problems. Even where this institutional support exists, it suffers because of faulty, inadequate and delayed implementation. An important element of the liberalization process has been the policy of de-reservation. Satyam Committee had recommended the abolition of Handloom Reservation Act and removal of the Hank Yarn obligation. However, the new Textile Policy (2000) has not accepted these recommendations. Whether continuing the reservation policy for the handloom sector would help the handloom sector to grow or not, needs to be seen. Thus, the need is to evolve pragmatic policies for the handloom sector in order to sustain the exquisiteness and novelty of this sector. Economic liberalisation is a reality, and therefore, the need is to tune our handloom sector as per the new challenges and opportunities.

*Trade Implications: Sev*eral Agreements under the WTO affect the Handloom sector. Textiles in particular are of crucial importance to developing countries because of their high export potential. Therefore, all those Agreements that have a direct or an indirect impact on the textiles sector of developing countries are relevant for handlooms as well.

For textiles and clothing, the Agreements in the WTO, could be divided into two parts:

(a) the Agreement that exclusively deals with textiles and clothing (ATC); and

(b) those Agreements, which are not exclusively on textiles and clothing, but nevertheless, are important for the textiles and clothing sector.

The ATCs seeks to ensure the integration of the Textiles and the Clothing sector into the multilateral trading regime by adopting an institutionalised approach. The ultimate aim of this Agreement is to liberalise the textiles and the clothing sector.

Before the Uruguay Round (UR), for textile products, discriminatory Quantitative Restrictions (QR) could be applied under a cover provided by the Multi Fibre Agreement (MFA). These quota restrictions were fixed on the basis of some unilateral or bilateral arrangement. Both these aspects of the MFA i.e. fixing discriminatory quotas and adopting a unilateral or bilateral approach were inconsistent with the basic philosophy of GATT. The ATC, has provided for a structured phase out plan of products under the MFA. This 10 year phase-out plan requires all the contracting parties to phase out their QRs on imports of textile products by 1st of January 2005. This would facilitate the integration of the textile sector with normal GATT rules.

The Agreement also provides a specific transitional safeguard mechanism to protect members from increased imports of textile products that have not been integrated into GATT. Such a provision could be invoked when a member country is able to demonstrate that increased imports are causing damage to its domestic industry. Thus the ATC has a direct bearing on the textile sector because it encompasses issues like market access opportunities, liberalizing the textile sector by allowing imports into the markets of developing countries, allowing countries to invoke the safeguard clause against increased imports. Therefore it would not be wrong to say that the most important international trade law governing the trade in textiles is the ATC.

There are some indirect Agreements under the WTO that unlike the ATC do not deal exclusively with textiles and clothing, but nevertheless, have important consequence on textiles and clothing. They are: (a) Agreement on Anti-Dumping (ADA); and (b) Agreement on Subsidies and Countervailing Measures (ASCM). As per ADA, whenever a country is able to prove that dumping has taken place, and there is a causal link between dumping and material injury to the domestic industry, that country could slap anti-dumping duties on the dumping country. This Agreement, in theoretical terms, should favour developing countries, as developed countries are more likely to indulge in the practice of dumping. But the reality has been just the opposite of what was anticipated. The developed countries have initiated imposing anti-dumping duties against developing countries, and in most cases, these duties have been arbitrarily imposed after exploiting the existing loopholes in the loosely drafted ADA.

These anti-dumping measures, in a number of cases, have been slapped against the textile products of developing countries. The *cotton–type bed linen case* and *unbleached fabric cotton case* against India, are instances of abuse of anti-dumping provisions against the products of developing countries. This also demonstrates how these Agreements could possibly affect even the textiles sector. Gradual opening up of the textiles sector by virtue of removal of QRs is bound to witness more and more non-tariff barriers in the form of anti-dumping duties.

ASCM provides for the imposition of countervailing duties when a particular country provides subsidies to its domestic industry and these subsidies injure the industry of the country where such exports are destined. In the imposition of countervailing duties, like in anti-dumping, the need to prove the causal link between the subsidies being provided and the injury caused, is of paramount importance.

This Agreement also provides for a trade remedial measure. But practice has shown that even this Agreement has been abused for protectionist purposes especially by developing countries. Countervailing duties have often been levied arbitrarily without there being sufficient proof of subsidies being provided to the domestic industry. The misuse of this particular Agreement just like the ADA is bound to increase in the light of disappearing QRs in the textiles sector.

World trade in textiles is regulated by bilateral agreements between exporting and importing nations under the overall framework of the Multi Fibre Arrangement (MFA). In 1974, under the first MFA, cottage-industry handloom fabrics and handmade products of handloom fabrics, as well as traditional folklore handicraft textile products, were exempted from such restrictions, provided that they were properly certified. Problems have since arisen because of an unforeseen increase in imports of handloom products, and also the issue of unsatisfactory certification by the Indian authorities (so that power-loom cloth was often passed off as handloom, owing partly to difficulty in identification, but also to indifference on the part of the inspection authorities).

Thus, in India's two biggest markets, the EEC and the USA, the 1983-86 Textile Agreements placed quotas on a variety of handloomed garments - the former on 10 of India's most successful exports (including women's blouses, skirts, dresses, shirts, trousers), and later on the entire range of garments.

Transport costs can be determined more accurately than any other factor of price and compared with freight rates of competing countries of all the major exporters to USA. India's freight value ratio is the highest, partly because its unit value is also the lowest. The low unit value is a result of the low to medium quality of most handloom products. As transport costs are one of the main factors that influences price and therefore demand for export, government needs to intervene to equalize transport costs comparable with other competing countries.

Under globalization, what happens in one part of the globe has a definite impact on the people and their lives elsewhere. Indian markets are now open for handloom imports from other countries, and the local manufacturers are free to sell their products in the overseas markets. This might bring a monumental transformation in the way handlooms are manufactured, purchased and perceived. With the gradual phasing-out of the QRs, developing countries are bound to gain in terms of market access. On the other hand, imports into the markets of developing countries are likely to rise. Hence, the total impact on the entire textiles sector, including handlooms, would be immense. In India's context the exports of Indian cotton handloom products (fabrics plus made-ups) witnessed a continuous rise from Rs. 1491 crore in 1995-96 to Rs. 2008 crore in 1998-99. However, during the year 1999-2000, exports, constituted by fabrics and made-ups, decreased to Rs. 1892 crore, showing a fall of 5.8%. The export composition has also witnessed a distinct shift from fabrics to made-ups in recent years. For the years 2001-02 and 2002-03 the export of cotton yarn, fabrics and made ups, registered a negative rate of 12.42 per cent. Hand-made carpets also registered a negative growth rate of 17.37 per cent. However, the imports of cotton yarn and fabrics, registered an increase of 56.36 per cent during this period. Cotton handloom products and made-ups are outside quota restrictions in all the countries except USA. The quota restrictions on power loom and on mill made products facilitated handloom exports to these countries, as handloom exports could meet the excess demand of fabrics and made-ups. But, with the phasing out of the MFA, the competition for the handloom exports is bound to increase from countries like Pakistan, China and other South-East Asian countries.

Handicrafts Sector

The handicrafts sector in India provides direct employment to 58.41 lakh persons, mostly in rural areas, and produces Rs. 16457.37 crores worth of items, out of which, about 44% (Rs. 9205.63) crores are exported. The range of handicraft products that are manufactured in India is very wide. The most well known handicrafts in India include metalwork, pottery, woodwork, chikan or embroidery, hand-printed textiles, carpets and zari. These products are not only popular in India but also in the international market. The need is to nurture these products and their markets with the help of a consistent and comprehensive policy.

The rich and varied traditional history of India gets reflected in its handicrafts products. As every state in India has a different traditional history, the handicraft products vary in their design and tenor from state to state. This adds to the variety of handicrafts products that are manufactured in India. These products are exclusive in their characteristics and nature and cannot be replicated anywhere else in the world.

International Trade: The impact of international trade on the handicrafts sector is profound and therefore the importance of having an appropriate strategy for the proper growth of handicrafts cannot be overemphasized. The new international trade regime presents threats and opportunities for the handicrafts sector. The imports of handicrafts in the year 1998 -1999 to 1999–2000 increased by 361.06% and from 1999–2000 to 2000–2001 it increased by 141.56%. The imports have witnessed a phenomenal increase from countries like China, Hong Kong, Japan, Malaysia, and Nepal. While India's exports of handicrafts has been growing, this growth is too meager *vis -a-vis* the imports. The handicrafts exports during the year 1999–2000 to 2000–2001 increased by 5.53% and during 1998–1999 to 1999–2000 it increased by 9.13%. The details about export data on carpet and other handicrafts products from the year 1997–1998 to 2000–2001 reveals that there has been growth in the exports of almost all the handicrafts products. But this growth has been scanty, and a huge untapped potential still exists.

The other significant threat cum opportunity to the handicrafts sector is from the intellectual property rights (IPR) regime. The IPR regime at the multilateral trading level, embodied in the Trade Related Aspects of Intellectual Property Rights Agreement (TRIPS), extends to all sorts of IPR protection. The threat is in the form of expanding propensities of developed countries to get intellectual property rights in their name even of those products that are of paramount importance for developing countries and originally belong to developing countries. At the same time, the TRIPS Agreement could also be used to safeguard the creativity, ingenuity, traditional knowledge and the geographical significance of developing countries by timely action and by ingeniously using the provisions of the TRIPS Agreement.

Agreement on Textiles and Clothing (ATC) could have a tremendous impact on sectors like Chikan or embroidery and carpets. This Agreement seeks to ensure the integration of the Textiles and the Clothing sector into the multilateral trading regime by adopting an institutionalized approach. The ultimate aim of this Agreement is to liberalise the textiles and the clothing sector. There are some Agreements under the WTO that unlike the ATC do not deal exclusively with textiles and clothing but nevertheless have a very important consequence on textiles and clothing. The ADA rules mentioned in the case of handlooms are also applicable in the case of handicrafts, as the functional commonalties of both handlooms and handicrafts are as indicated above.

The Exim Policy of 2002 -07 in order to boost the exports of handicrafts has launched a new programme called "Special Focus on Cottage sector and Handicrafts" keeping in view that the small sector forms 50% of India's exports. As part of this package, an initial amount of Rs. 5 crore has been earmarked for promoting cottage sector exports coming under the KVIC. Units in the handicrafts sector can also access funds on the Market Access Initiative Scheme, while under the Export Promotion Capital Goods (EPCG) scheme; these units will not be required to maintain average level of exports. These units are also entitled to the benefit of Export House status on achieving lower average export performance of Rs. 5 crores as against Rs. 15 crores for others and to duty free imports of specified items. The Exim Policy also recognizes the need to promote towns of export excellence. Towns like Moradabad, which are considered the hub of handicrafts as 40% of exports take place from here, should get encouragement under this new policy. Under the Market Access Initiative the Exim Policy recognizes the need to promote and faciliate direct access to major retail markets in focus countries for focus products. It also recognizes the need to develop the brand culture and promote branded products. An important thrust area in the new Exim Policy is to facilitate a greater involvement of State governments in export promotion. The impact of such policies needs to be further examined.

Intellectual Property Rights: The provisions of the TRIPS Agreement may pose challenges to the handicrafts. The need is to use the provisions of the TRIPS Agreement so that adequate protection could be provided to goods of origin in India.

An important IPR given in the TRIPS Agreement is Geographical Indication (GI). The protection of Geographical Indication, under the TRIPS Agreement, provides for the protection of the producers in those regions and countries that have already established the reputation of their geographical origin. In other words GI is a notice of a specific product having been produced in a particular place. An important question that needs some serious pondering is that how IPR laws like GI could be used to safeguard the handicrafts sector. In other words could GI be used to safeguard the chikan of Lucknow, or the silk of Banaras or any other handicraft that has built its reputation in terms of its geographical origin?

The TRIPS Agreement provides for situations where each nation is required to make its own law to protect and register its geographical indicia. India has the opportunity to formulate such laws and register by 2005, where it has to search its geographically specialized goods and register them. An important element of the TRIPS Agreement as regards GI is that it does not mandate any particular form of protection for geographical indication, and hence a considerable room is left to define the role to be played by the state. This has led to the enactment of The Geographical Indications of Goods (Registration and Protection) Act, 1999. The Act provides for the establishment of a Geographical Indications Registry. Under the Act, the registered proprietor of GI and the authorized user or users shall have the right to use the GI exclusively in relation to goods for which GI is registered. The enactment of this Act is a step in right direction. While the enactment is there, it is important to undertake scientific studies on crafts and to document them properly in order to protect the interests of the craftsmen.

MARKET FOR RURAL PRODUCTS

While rural industry in India has been perceived traditionally as catering to the local market, or at best, to a wider national market through limited formal channels, the reality of globalisation since 1990s introduced a new dimension to the market for such products. While on the one side, the public outlets lost their capability of providing marketing opportunities, on the other hand, the reality of the market itself became complex.

The issue of rural industrialization, therefore, needs to be looked from a new angle and on far more scientific lines. The core of a scientific approach to rural industrialization is to understand the market opportunities of rural products along with development priorities of the country and to chalk out a strategy where rural industries have an important role to play. It is often presumed that in the rural areas, industries form only a subsidiary occupation of the people. Most traditional industries are household-based and family labour-based. However, in an open economy, where materials and technology flow freely and markets are open and global in nature, production at the household level becomes rather difficult. This demands a change in the household organisation of production itself. For instance, household pottery is suitable for household production in terms of market, technology, and capital; but once a rise in income levels leads to a change in the demand pattern, the transformation of these units into Chinaware would be difficult on a household basis for reasons of technology, investment requirements and market size.

Many studies have indicated that, even for being an effective tool for rural development *per se,* the rural industries should enter as part of an overall industrialization process. The production structure and the consumption pattern of the rural areas, on the one hand, and the urban areas on the other, are characteristically distinct. With rising rural incomes, a shift both in the input structure of production and commodity structure of consumption in favour of the so-called urban products is inevitable. In order to take advantage of these changes, the rural industries need to have some dynamism relating to technology, product design and organizational structure. While before the globalisation era, the switch-over was relatively easy through supply-side interventions, under globalisation the situation has completely changed. While rural products are forced to become increasingly as part of global supply chains, these products need to adapt themselves, not only according to the changing tastes of the national market, but also according to changes in tastes in the international market. It is in this context that the importance of networking of enterprises becomes increasingly important.

The Fair Trade Movement

A significant international movement called the 'Fair Trade Movement' has been launched with the aim of projecting the most powerful responses to the problems facing the commodity producers. Fair Trade is a trading partnership, based on dialogue, transparency and respect, that seeks greater equity in international trade. The aim is to provide better trading conditions to the marginalized producers and workers especially in developing countries. It works through various national fair trade initiatives that are coordinated through an umbrella organization called Fairtrade Labelling Organisations International (FLO). The campaign has developed the concept of a 'Fairtrade mark' on the products, which guarantees the consumers, that farmers in developing countries get a fair deal for their products. At present different countries have different fairtrade marks. A central responsibility for FLO is to collect data and ensure the audit of all fairtrade-labelled products from the producers to the supermarket shelf. One of its aims is to see the introduction of a single international fairtrade-label. In Ghana, for instance, the fair trade campaign has changed the lives of cocoa producers in the Ashanti region. A local trade cooperative called the Kuapa Kokoo Cooperative is working with the fairtrade organizations and has helped 35,000 members to get their fair share of profits generated by cocoa. This cooperative sells its products to its fair trade partners in Europe who provide the cocoa producers a guaranteed minimum price as well as a 'social premium' which is utilized in building the social infrastructure like schools, hospitals and other basic amenities. This has brought about a huge transformation in the lives of those small producers who completely rely for their earnings on exports of cocoa.

Such a result could be achieved only because of the sustained pressure that has been created by the Make Trade

Fair campaign. Such campaigns ensure the effective implementation of the existing trade rules, and thus bring benefit to the small-scale producers of developing countries. It is worthwhile to explore the potential of such a model in the context of India's rural products as well. For example, the handicrafts producers who generally belong to the lower strata of the society firstly encounter problems in finding export markets and even if they find such markets they are not ensured of a fixed income. They are often subjected to the vagaries of international trade because of illegal anti-dumping and countervailing actions and of arbitrary quota restrictions. Therefore, the need is to initiate a trade fair campaign to ensure that the handicrafts producers are able to get proper return for their products.

CONCLUDING NOTE

Our discussion in the preceding pages leads us to the conclusion that, under globalisation the issue of sustainability of rural industries needs to be looked afresh. In a situation where the rules of the game are decided by market forces and the limits of the *nation state* to protect the interests of a particular pattern of industrial development increases, it is important to look at the prospects of rural industry from a new angle. A well-meaning government can at best be transparent enough, to come out openly with a clear statement of constraints in the area. Direct interventions by the government, in many cases, are not likely to be beneficial. On the other hand, there are four crucial areas in which it can play a positive role:

1. Scientific studies on international markets need to promoted.
2. Business demography should emerge as an important area of investigation, especially in the context of micro and rural enterprises.
3. Proper documentation of geographical indications should be initiatied so that, India does not lose from the IPR angle.

4. The international developments relating to Fair Trade Movement should be closely monitored and documented. Competent NGOs and people's organisations should be encouraged to enter into this area.

REFERENCES

Acs, Zoltan J. (2003), Public Policy on Small Industry in the Post-WTO Era: International Experience and Lessons for India (Cochin, Institute of Small Enterprises and Development (ISED).

Arora, R. C. (1978), Industry and Rural Development, New Delhi, S.Chand & Co.

Behari, Bepin (1976), Rural Industrialisation in India, New Delhi, Vikas Publishing House Pvt. Ltd.

Bhattacharya, S.N. (1980), Rural Industrialisation in India: Its Nature and Problems, New Delhi, B.R Publishing Corporation.

Bomley, R. and Chris Gerry (ed.), (1979), Casual Work and Poverty in Third World Cities, New York, John Wiley.

Rao, V. K. R. V, Industrialisation and Integrated Rural Development, *Man and Development*, Vol. 1, No. 2.

Chenery, Holis D., M. S. Ahluwalia, C. L. Jebell, John H. Duly (1974), Redistribution with Growth, London, Oxford University Press.

GOI (1955), Report of the Village and Small Industries Committee, New Delhi.

GOI (1958), Report of the Intensive Area Scheme of Rural Development, New Delhi, KVIC.

Government of India (1955), Report on Small Industries in India, New Delhi, Ministry of Commerce & Industry.

Government of India (2002), Report of the Committee on India-Vision 2020 (Chairman: S. P. Gupta), New Delhi, Planning Commission.

Government of India (2002): Report of the Special Group on Targeting Ten Million Employment Opportunities per year over the Tenth Plan Period (Chairman: S.P Gupta), New Delhi, Planning Commission.

Institute of Small Enterprises and Development (2002), Hand Book of Small Enterprises in Kerala, Cochin, ISED.

Joshi, Gopal (2003): Privatisation and Employment Opportunities (Cochin, Institute of Small Enterprises and Development, ISED.

Kamal Taori and Surendra Singh (1993), Rural Industrial: A Plan for the Future, New Delhi, Vikas Publishing House Pvt. Ltd.

Lewis, Arthur (1954), Economic Development with Unlimited Supply of Labour, London, The Manchester School.

Mathew P. M. (1999), Small Enterprises and Regional Development: Challenges and Choices, New Delhi, Kanishka Publishers, Distributors.

Mathew P. M. (2000), Small Enterprise Development: The Experience of the South and the North, New Delhi, Oxford.

Mathew P.M. (2003), Beyond Old Equations: Small Enterprise Experience and Perspectives in India, New Delhi, Kanishka Publishers, Distributors.

Pai Panandiker, V. A. and Arun Sud (1986), Rural Industrialisation, New Delhi, Oxford & IBH Publishing Co. Pvt. Ltd.

Papola, T. S. (1979), Rural Industrialisation: Issues and Evidence, Lucknow, Giri Institute of Development Studies.

Papola, T. S. (1982), Rural Industrialisation: Approaches and Potential, Bombay, Himalaya Publishing House.

Planning Commission (1956), Government of India, Second Five-Year Plan, New Delhi.

Rao, R.V. (1978), Rural Industrialization in India, New Delhi, Concept Publishing House.

Sigurdson, Jon (1977), Rural Industrialisation in China, Cambridge, Harward University Press.

Van Dijk, Mein Peter (2003), Innovation and Small Industry in the Globalisation Era, Cochin, Institute of Small Enterprises and Development (ISED).

Yawer, Duraid (1978), Rural Indistrialisation for Developing Countries, New Delhi, Chetana Publications.

Zuvekas, Clarence (1979), Economic Development: An Introduction (London, Macmillan).

3

MARKETING HOLDS THE FUTURE FOR RURAL INDUSTRIALISATION

B. Yerram Raju

A disturbing aspect of India's economic performance in recent years has been the slowdown in employment-generation in rural areas and the failure of the industrial/manufacturing sector to absorb the growing work force in the rural areas. Rural industrialization has immense potential as a development strategy to transform rural areas and ensure sustainable livelihoods for a growing work force further expanded by the backlog of unemployment. Several countries have followed such a strategy successfully. China is the best-known example of implementing a policy of accelerated rural industrialization (through Township and Village Enterprises–TVEs) that has helped to develop regions that were bypassed by the high-growth phase limited to the coastal regions of the country and also curbed the pressures of rural-urban migration.

India's industrial policies, which also impact the Rural Non-Farm Sector, have been shaped in a wide range of contexts. However, the broad policy thrust remains the same: to expand the capability of small and micro enterprises to generate employment, promote exports, further the process of rural industrialization, facilitate the development of appropriate technologies and new entrepreneurial skills. The six Industrial

Policy Resolutions, framed since 1948, set out guidelines for the country's industrial development with different degrees of emphasis on the main objectives. The Industries Development and Regulation Act of 1951 provided the basic framework for the post-independence industrialization strategy. Since the model for industrialization in the 1950s was based on capital-intensive heavy industries, employment generation required the development of widely dispersed, mass consumption-good producing, labour-intensive, small-scale industries. In the 1960s, a Rural Industrialisation Program was established. As the process of economic development led to changing priorities, the policy focus shifted to regional imbalances (1977), exports and dispersal in rural areas (1990) and then to small, tiny and village industries (1991).

The rural non-farm sector, a broader connotation of the rural industrial sector, today employs 40 million persons, at a wage rate higher than in agriculture and does so in lakh of dispersed villages in thousands of small towns, without making demands on the infrastructure and energy resources of large cities and metros. With policy neglect, employment in this sector grew at a rate of 5.4 per cent per annum in the 1987-1998 decade. If policy were more proactive and credit was provided in reasonable proportion of economic contribution of this sector, then, perhaps, at least in some pockets, India would have seen a significant transformation in its rural economy.

SLOWDOWN IN EMPLOYMENT GROWTH

The total labour force in the country increased from 381.94 million in 1993-94 to 406.05 million in 1999-2000. The growth rate of employment declined from 2.05 per cent during 1983-94 to 1.03 per cent in the period 1994-2000. The annual growth rate of employment in agriculture fell from 1.51 per cent to -0.34 per cent between the two periods (Planning Commission). The number of persons employed in agriculture has also declined for the first time from over 242 million in 1993-94 to 237.56 million in 1999-2000. (Economic Survey, 2001-02).

It is evident from the experience of the last few decades that economic growth has not reduced the problem of unemployment in both the urban and rural sectors. The growth of the labour force has outpaced the capacity of the manufacturing sector to absorb them. As a result there has been a deceleration in the growth of employment, particularly after the economic reforms. The growth of agricultural production was expected to lead to increased employment in the rural sector through expansion of farm and non-farm employment opportunities. Though the growth of the non-farm sector in more developed regions of the country such as Punjab and Haryana has led to such an outcome, such labour absorption has not occurred in other regions of the country.

Studies of agricultural employment pattern across States between 1987-88 and 1999-2000 have shown that in a significant majority of States there has been a substantial reduction in agricultural employment growth though the extent of deceleration varies from State to State. (Chandrashekhar and Ghosh, 2003).

The all India unemployment rate as a percentage of labour force has increased from 1.90 in 1993-94 to 2.23 in 1999-2000. The States with the highest unemployment rates in the country in 1999-2000 were Kerala (20.77%), West Bengal (14.95% and Tamil Nadu (12.05%). Assam (8.005) and Andhra Pradesh (7.94%) were in the intermediate range while the lowest unemployment rates were in Himachal Pradesh (2.93%), Punjab (4.15%), Uttar Pradesh (4.27%) and Karnataka (4.61%). (Planning Commission Report, 2001).

Distribution of Workers by category of employment shows that in 1999-2000, 56.0 per cent of workers in rural areas were self-employed as compared to 42.1 per cent in urban areas. Regular salaried employees constituted 6.7 per cent of workers in rural areas as against 40.1 per cent in urban areas. Casual workers were a sizeable proportion in rural areas with 37.3 per cent of workers in this category and 17.8 per cent in urban areas.

EMPLOYMENT GENERATION

Employment generation schemes initiated in recent years have included strategies to increase wage employment and self-employment. The former include the Jawahar Rozgar Yojana and the Swamjayanti Gram Swa Rozgar Yojana; and the latter operate through the Prime Minister's Rozgar Yojana and Khadi and Village Industries Commission. The total expenditure on these employment generation schemes doubled from Rs. 4121.33crore in 1990-91 to Rs.8697.63crore in 1999-2000.

Having witnessed a jobless growth during the past decade (1993-2003), with the eyes set on an 8% growth during the Tenth Five Year Plan, planners have turned their eyes again on rural industrialization.

The growth of rural industries in a particular region depends on the pace and pattern of agricultural development, the degree of commercialization in agriculture, the skills of the available work force, the breakdown of the artisan sector and the extent of landlessness, among other factors. The possibilities for agro-processing can provide an important thrust to the process of setting up rural industries.

A priority of development strategy has been to promote diversification of the rural workforce through productive employment generation. The policy of promoting rural industrialization aims to expand the non-farm sector based on appropriate technology-use, high productivity, high income-generating activity with greater demand for its products and strong forward linkages. The growth of this sector requires rising demand, efficient marketing, transportation network and proximity to urban/semi-urban centers.

A distinction needs to be made between static views of employment generation which takes a short term view to rapidly increase the number of those employed in rural areas even if in low productivity jobs at minimal levels of income merely aimed to discourage rural unemployed from migrating to urban areas. A dynamic policy on the other hand, aims at increasing income-earning potential and the asset-base of rural households and raising the level of future employment-generation though rural industrialization and technological upgradation of rural industries. In the present context where traditional rural industries such as pottery, bamboo basket weaving, toy making, etc. provide inadequate incomes for rural workers in these industries, a strategy of rural industrialized needs to be based on the expansion of modern non-traditional industries. The industries that are to be promoted in rural areas should have positive income elasticity for their products and greater technological flexibility to adapt to changing economic conditions.

RURAL ENTERPRISES

As per the Economic Census, 1998, there were a total of 17.71 million rural enterprises, of which 3.20 million or 18.1 per cent were engaged in agricultural activities such as livestock rearing (dairy, poultry, piggery), forestry, fishing and agricultural services such as custom hiring of tractors, and managing of irrigation systems. 3.52 mn enterprises are engaged in manufacturing activities qualifying for categorization as rural industries. We give below certain policy, product and procedural changes, which would improve the usefulness of existing banks and financial institutions and specialised new institutions focusing on this market segment.

The dramatic improvement in rural telecom connectivity should form a basis for a complete re-engineering of how financial services are delivered to rural producers. Thus, wireless and local loop and cell phone networks, broad band cable networks, low cost ATMs, credit cards, mobile vans with hand held computers, smart cards, STD PCOs and IT kiosks, and other emerging technologies must be pressed into service of the RNFS producers, so that they can get access to capital.

AGRO-PROCESSING

The size of our agricultural sector, diversity in crop production, large labour force in rural areas and changing demand patterns in domestic and global markets, offer considerable possibilities for development of food processing industries in rural areas. This would promote linkages between industry and agriculture, reduce wastage which presently amounts to 30-

40 per cent of horticultural production amounting to Rs.50, 000 crore, increase value addition to agricultural produce, attract investments by high-tech agro industries and promote incomes and export growth. Only 2 to 3 per cent of fruits and vegetables are processed in India compared to much higher figures of 30 to 70 per cent in other producing countries.

Agro-processing industry in India is critically placed in the economy as its development contributes not only to the value chain but also achieves a number of development objectives such as promoting rural-urban linkages and speeding up rural industrialization, raising farmers' incomes and increasing exports. For these reasons it has been estimated that the multiplier effect of the food processing industry on the wider economy - at 2.4 (with Rs. 100 crore generated in this sector leading to Rs.2400crores in the economy)-is the highest of any industry. Over the next ten years, the investment needed in the food processing sector has been estimated at Rs. 1, 40,000 crore.

There are several agricultural products that can serve as raw material for the food processing industry as a wide variety of processed products can be made with their input–rice, wheat, maize, sugarcane, soybean–are some of the products that can enter into the value addition chain. Several types of Fruits and vegetables have immense potential to be processed for domestic and global markets. Growth in demand is projected for: frozen/dehydrated/canned fruits and vegetables, Fruit juices/concentrates/pulps, Pickles, Jams, Jellies, Squashes, etc. apart from ready to eat vegetables. As mentioned earlier, a significant share of consumption in developed markets–almost 60 per cent in the US-is for fruits and vegetables in processed form. The number of fruit and vegetable processing licensed industries in India has gone up from 3,629 in 1990 to 4,132 by 1994. (Data Book, 2003).

Developing the agro-processing industry requires large investments in post-harvest equipment such as flour units, rice mills, maize shellers, oil expellers, etc. Projections for 2000 from the base year 1991 showed that the numbers for such equipment needed to be doubled during this period. The number of Maize shellers, for example, would have to increase from 65,000 to 1, 15,000 and Oil expellers from 2, 22,000 to 4,50,000 in order to keep pace with growing demand.

The Indian food processing industry worth US$20 billion ranks fifth in size in the world. It accounts for 14 per cent of the total industrial output and employs 1.6 million workers. Global food market is estimated at US$69,444 million and is expected to grow at a steady pace. Consumption of value added processed food is expected to treble to $62,500 million.

The Ministry of Food Processing Industries offers various incentives to private entrepreneurs for setting up, expansion/ modernization of units in various sectors including Fruit & Vegetable products, Milk products, Grain milling, Meat & Poultry products, Fishery products and Oilseeds processing. The grants offered by the Ministry for such schemes are up to 25%/33.3% of the capital cost & technical works with a maximum of Rs. 50/75 lakhs respectively.

The constraints that the farmer faces in the agro-processing link of the supply/value chain are related to lack of adequate information about the possibilities in agri-processing and, more important, the financial constraint as participation in this sector requires considerable amounts of investment.

CONTRACT FARMING

Contract farming has emerged as one option for farmers to enter agro-processing by availing the benefits and reducing the risks involved. While various models of contract farming have been put forward, and several controversies have been raised about its damaging effects on small farmers, it is important that the existing pattern of land ownership should not be threatened (by taking over lands owned by small farmers) in any scheme to involve the farmer in farming for the market. Under contract farming, a private company contracts to provide seeds and other inputs to the farmer for growing certain crops, which are then bought back by the farmer at a pre-fixed price. This model has the advantage of overcoming the input constraints of the farmer, assures him of a buyer and removes price uncertainty.

In order to promote backward linkages, one of the interventions by the Ministry of Food Processing is reimbursement to the Processors for contract farming @ 10% of the value of raw materials procured up to Rs. 10lakhs per year for 3 years. Processors have to provide best extension services/practices, technical know-how and physical inputs (like improved seed, fertilizer, pesticide, etc.) to the producers of the raw material and inform the Ministry in advance. However, the procedures for processing such proposals lack transparency and inordinate delays from six to nine months swallow the planned incentives.

For a strategy of agro-processing in rural areas to take off requires strengthening of the entire value chain from agricultural infrastructure (with emphasis on cold storage chains) to post-harvest technologies to quality enforcement through accredited laboratories, focus on marketing (auction houses, terminal markets, retail chain, etc.) and exports. Such a strategy has to put in place along with policies to diversify crop production (through crop shifts towards high value crops like fruits and vegetables, etc.) and raise agricultural productivity and competitive advantage for focus crops/ sectors. (Oilseeds, dairy products) The long-term objective should be to move to an optimized supply chain where production is in tune with consumer demand and where losses, costs and other inefficiencies are reduced. For this, it is necessary for coordinated policies for agricultural input providers, processing industries and marketing. (Agro-Fare 2000, on Agro and Food Processing Industry in Gujarat, CII)

MARKETING

The efforts of Rural Industrialization during the past five-and-a-half decades reflect anxiety on the part of policy makers to address Supply constraints on the presumption that demand would never pose a problem due to the following assumptions:

(i) Ever-increasing population with low purchasing power would pick up whatever is produced

(ii) Influence of external markets on the demand pattern would be very limited.

(iii) Tastes of people will be adjusted to production patterns.

Post-liberalization, the afore-mentioned assumptions proved to be fallacious. It is not the Supermarkets and Food Worlds that alone influenced the consumption pattern of the fast-moving consumer goods, most of which are capable of being produced in the rural areas, but, the vastly seen media advertisements on the TVs in the rural areas, changing advertisement scenarios, nuclear families with reduced family sizes, the revolution in the telecommunication systems, etc. have also contributed to a change in the complexion of demand for goods produced in the rural and cottage industries. Today, the demand constraints, therefore, are dictating supply patterns. Marketing, therefore, becomes extremely crucial for sustainable rural industrialization.

A comprehensive look at the marketing aspects for rural industrialization should start at the Agricultural Market Yards and the ways in which they need to be modernized to meet the food safety and quality standards to which we make a reference later.

AGRICULTURAL MARKET YARDS (AMY) AND INFORMATION TECHNOLOGY

The phenomenal increases in agricultural production and the compulsions of Agreement on Agriculture (AoA) and Market Access Provisions under the WTO demand a critical look at the capabilities of organized agricultural market yards in the country from the point of view of the farmer. Suicides of the farmers in some parts of the country, the distress sales of farm produce, large scale wastages of fruits and vegetables, are all portends to the gross inadequacies in the storage and post-harvest technologies on one side and the way the regulated market yards have been functioning in this country. Several Market Yards are yet to take full advantage of the Information Technology to provide the needed facilitation to the farmer in terms of cost-effective storage and remunerative prices.

The Central Marketing Act of 1935 was the guiding force for the States to enact the Market legislations for the regulation of agricultural produce markets. The regulated markets were established to regulate effectively sale and purchase of agricultural produce and establish market yards for marketing agricultural produce. The regulatory measures in India consist of two distinct sets, namely, (i) development and regulation of primary markets and (ii) regulation of market conduct through a series of legal instruments.

The number of wholesale markets increased to 7169 in 1998 from 150 in 1947. There are 27040 primary rural markets in the country, which cater to the vast majority of the small and marginal farmers. Agricultural commodities worth Rs .62000 crores were traded in wholesale markets during 1992-93 itself and now they crossed Rs.100000crs. Still, many of the AMY did not reach the level of maturity in terms of providing the targeted services like correct weightment, grading, packing, storage and cold storage, standard trading or auction platforms, provisions for comfortable overnight stay of the farmers who bring in produce, efficient payment mechanisms and transparent functioning. Handling losses in the market yards in this country are estimated to be of the order close to 20 per cent on average. Many State Governments are content with what they get statutorily from the farmers out of the declared sales and they are averse to adding more facilities at the Market Yards while those that have provided facilities still leave much to be desired.

There are a few States like Haryana and Punjab that have provided very good infrastructure in the Market yards in terms of proximity to the farmer, good roads, and reasonable storage although a lot needs to be done for the farmer. The traders have, by and large, benefited from the Market Committees more than the farmers. The government, by virtue of the provisions contained in the Marketing Acts, was happily collecting the Cess on whatever and wherever the sale of agricultural produce was being affected. There are States that are collecting a one-time payment for negotiating a procurement price with the Government of India for purchase by the FCI. Having stated the current position thus, where does the remedy lie? What needs to be done? The response to these questions lies in a series of measures.

Each market yard has to computerize its operations right from the entry of the farmer with his produce into the market. Each farmer getting produce can be given a SMART Card. Once the Gate Keeper swaps the card at the Gate, it should record simultaneously the stated quantity of the produce brought in by him and the mode of transport. It also records the handling, hamali and weighment charges payable by him on the declared quantity. Depending on the arrival time, the farmer gets an entry pass into the dormitory or lodging facility for overnight stay. The produce brought will be given a bin card and it is unloaded and kept at the weighing platform that should be attached to a computer. The computerized record of the weighment passes on through the network to the grading chamber where the produce moves to. After grading, the second weighment takes place in accordance with the grades and the prices determined on the trading or auction platform. This information again moves through the network to packing department. The graded produce appropriately gets packed and computerized labeling takes place. Then it moves to the cash counter where the farmer, on production of the SMART card, gets the payment after deducting all the service charges. All the charges for various services are to be displayed on the tariff board for the services. Tobacco Board is attempting to computerize the whole operations from such perspective.

COMMODITY FUTURES

Liberalization has opened the gates for trading in commodity futures. The government also regulates futures trading in agricultural commodities and initially permitted futures trading in commodities like pepper, gur, turmeric and hessian. The 'Kabra Committee' appointed by the government in 1993 to look into futures trading and suggest measures, recommended futures trading in 17 major agricultural commodities such as cotton kapas, jute and jute goods, all major oil seeds, and their oils and cakes, rice bran oil and coffee.

Trading sites or e-markets are springing up in a host of commodities, enabling sellers to post specifications and buyers to hunt among diverse suppliers to satisfy their exact needs.

Futures Markets require efficient connectivity with the financial markets. Currently, the futures Markets exist on six commodities: castor seed, hessian, gur, potatoes, turmeric, and pepper. The pepper exchange, which is at Cochin, is upgraded to the status of an "international pepper futures market" that will accept orders from all over the world. The Forwards Market Commission oversees these markets. A high level of interest exists for other market futures: basmati rice; cotton Kapas; raw jute and jute goods; groundnut, its oil and cake; cotton seed, its oil and cake; safflower, its oil and cake; copra, coconut oil and oil cake; soyabean, its oil and cake; ricebran oil; linseed and its oil; and onions. On the 4th December 1996, the Coffee Board decided to recommend that a domestic futures market for coffee should be set up and the recommendation was acted upon. On-line market information kiosks have to be set up with wide area network to ensure efficient functioning of markets if we define efficiency in terms of better prices for the farmers and fair margins for the trading intermediaries.

The Futures Markets are weak in a variety of issues: the use of modern market mechanisms (such as the electronic limit order book market), enforcement of contract standardization, dealing with heterogeneous grades, the counterparty guarantee of the clearing house, calculation and enforcement margins, and checks against market manipulation. The commodity markets can hardly tolerate a payment crisis. One serious weakness in India lies in the way individual commodity futures markets emerge as an outgrowth of trading on individual spot markets. Introducing cash-settlements derivatives on commodities is also extremely important. Using information technology and networking markets and providing on-line information on cultural practices, post-harvest operations and prices assume critical importance.

The success of strategies to promote horticulture through improved technologies for raising productivity and minimizing post-harvest waste is incomplete without adequate attention being given to marketing of the produce. Agro-Marketing is a vital link in the value chain that needs new approaches and innovative interventions.

Unlike other products, the marketing of fruit and vegetables does not involve either the producer or the retailer. Farmers in general operate in a *mandi* system, with powerful middlemen, as noted above–the commission agent and the wholesaler-as the key players. The commission for vegetables often varies from 3 per cent to 6 per cent, while for fruits; the commission fluctuates within a broader band of 4 to 12 per cent. Reshaping the marketing strategies for horticulture requires eliminating these intermediary margins in order to increase price realization for the farmer.

One of the major initiatives taken recently in the area of horticultural marketing is the entry of the Anand-based National Dairy Development Board (NDDB) into this sub-sector to replicate the Amul cooperative model nationally for fruits and vegetables by setting up an alternative horticultural produce marketing system in the country. As a start, NDDB will establish, own and operate auction markets for horticulture produce in Karmatala from November onwards. (*Business Standard,* 23/24-08-03). The project for wholesale marketing involves an outlay of Rs.150crore, and will cover 200 horticultural farmers associations and 50,000 grower members. The NDDB initiative is to be extended to the four metros in due course of time. With collection centers replacing village-level commission agents, the marketing system is expected to become more efficient and transparent. This system would also reduce post-harvest losses significantly as sorting, packaging; assembly and storage will be done at the collection centers.

Since Agricultural Marketing is a State subject, some legislative changes may be needed at the State level (as was done in Karnataka) to facilitate NDDB's entry into the auction market.

ROLE OF THE STATE

The State continues to play a very important role in the structural aspects of Agricultural Markets. They broadly relate to (a) development and regulation of primary markets and (b) regulation of market conduct through a series of legal instruments.

- Agricultural Produce (Grading and Marking) Act,
- Prevention of Food Adulteration Act, 1954, 1964, 1976, 1986
- Essential Commodities Act, 1955
- Solvent Extracted Oil, Deoiled Meal and Edible oil (Control) Order, 1967
- Meat Food Products Order, 1973
- Standards of weights and Measures Act, 1976
- Pulses, Edible oil seeds and edible oils storage control order, 1977.
- Vegetable oil products (control) order, 1977.
- Prevention of Black marketing and Maintenance of supply of essential commodities Act, 1980.
- The cold storage order, 964, 1980 (rescinded in 1997)
- Consumer Protection Act, 1986
- Bureau of Indian Standard Act, 1986
- Milk and Milk Products Order, 1992
- Fruit Products Order, 1955, 1997.

The provisions under the legal instruments, most being consumer protection measures are used to regulate the activities of traders and processors pertaining to trading, stocking maintenance of quality, grading, packing, processing, blending and movements. The future trading in agricultural commodities is also regulated by the Government. (Acharya, 1998).

The Financing institutions which lend against the primary security of stocks run the risk of non-compliance of the provisions of so many Acts by its borrowers. Since the penal provisions for non-compliance are administered by the respective regulatory authorities, the lender may not even know till news item appears or a noise is made, that the primary security has been taken possession of. Lender does not have recourse unless he collaterally secures such stocks. If the farmers are provided the marketing finance, they get into the shoes of a trader until the stocks are sold. The financing institution does not know the legal implications of financing marketing activity. Therefore, I would suggest that the NABARD brings out a compendium of such implications and the aspects that Banker should take note of during the course of monitoring such advances. Ignorance of law cannot be accepted as an excuse and the vicarious provisions of disciplinary action on the unintended provisions errors/ omissions will be applied when the Banks incur financial loss as a consequence, to the officials manning these advances. A secure environment for lending is very important and it needs to be created by the apex financing institution.

Enforcement has to be standardised and powerful and at the same time should have positive incentives for compliance. This would facilitate farmers converting their form steads into viable enterprises eligible for financing on their own merit.

Market places tend towards specification: e.g. Anakapalle (AP) for Jaggery, Guntur (AP), Palladam and Koduvai (Tamilnadu) for Tobacco; Adoni Guntakal(AP) Tirupur (Tamilnadu) for cotton, Avanashi for grain etc. They are enthusiastically welcomed as growth poles, benefiting from agglomeration economies derived from special infrastructure provision, concentration of the kind of information which facilitates innovation and market access via collective representation (Nadri & Schmitz, 1994). Such clusters have always attracted the attention of Bankers because of the availability of cross-functional information which itself acts as insurance for the risk capital.

When it comes to the question of financing diversified markets situated sometimes away from the hinterland of general financing activity, the field staff should have some appraisal system hands-on. (Raju 1999)

Effective marketing is one of the most important links in the supply chain from farm gate to the consumer. Global food chain is demand-driven. Marketing strategies need to identify global markets based on a stratified picture: i.e. those with high income consumers (per capita GNP of more than US$ 10,000 at PPP), middle-income consumers ($3500-$10,000) and low income consumers (less than $3500 per capital GNP). Market segmentation also needs analysis, as established markets and emerging markets have different penetration levels and growth prospects.

Domestic markets are expanding with rising incomes, more women in the work force and increasing demand for Convenience Foods. Retail chains are expanding though India has one of the lowest rates of adoption of modern retail compared to other countries in the South and East Asian region.

Two important aspects of supply chain management in food processing are food safety and quality standards.

QUALITY STANDARDS

The biggest challenge facing farmers who choose to diversify their agricultural production and cater to the growing domestic and global markets is ensuring product quality. Fruits and vegetables grown in the country have to meet the present stringent international standards where food safety is interlinked with quality expectations. Retailers in the EU expect their suppliers of agri/horticultural produce to be certified with EUROPGAP standards by January 2004. The increasing awareness worldwide about microbial and other contamination in farm produce and concerns over health issues combined with international norms (based on Codex Alimentarius Commission recommendations) for agricultural exports have made Quality Standards a focus of agricultural policy. The Hazard Analysis Critical Control Points (HACCP) framework is being used in this approach to food safety. The WTO Agreement on Sanitary and Phyto-Sanitary (SPS) standards lays down the guidelines in this area of international trade in agricultural products.

For units operating in the food processing sector that wish to upgrade to ISO/HACCP certificate, the Ministry of Food Processing, Government of India, offers a grant upto Rs. 10 lakhs/15 lakhs.

PACKAGING AND LABELING

Packaging is now regarded as a marketing tool and a symbol of value addition. This link in the value chain would depend on whether the agricultural produce is for the fresh produce market, or whether they are to be transported over long distances and/or exported. Prior to packaging, certain preliminary operations such as pre-sizing, sorting and grading have to be carried out. Special operations may also need to be carried out for some vegetables such as removal of unwanted leaves, stems and roots Washing the farm produce in the case of root vegetables and those grown close to the ground may also be necessary along with some disease prevention measures for the produce. Waxing (with approved food grade materials) is done on some fruits such as apples to prevent water loss (by more than one-third) and retain freshness.

Packing of agricultural produce can be done manually or by machines. Packaging material can consist of plastic/polythene material or fibre-boards or cardboard material of durable quality. The objective is ease of handling in loading and transit to the destination as well as minimizing loss or damage to the horticultural produce.

Labeling of several products is being made mandatory with growing concern over genetically-modified organisms in the food chain and concerns about threats to the environment through certain practices (marine food production, for example) as well as the right of consumers to make informed choices regarding food safety. A specific WTO Agreement–the Agreement on Technical Barriers to Trade (TBT)-deals with these issues and failure to meet the requirements set could have an adverse impact on exports of farm produce.

Use of Information and Communication Technologies (ICT) to Overcome Information Asymmetry for RNFS Producers:

One of the key reasons identified by us earlier in the paper as a cause of market distortions and failure is the lack of information, or more rigorously to use the economics phrase – information asymmetry, which means unequal access to information among the various actors involved in market transactions. This has been a difficult and persistent problem, particularly given the dispersed nature of rural India and of rural non-farm -enterprises, coupled with lack of literacy and access to the media among the producers. Over the last few years, however, there have been some exciting developments, which have the potential to reduce information asymmetry. The two main technologies, which can be used for this are cable television and the telecom network, including the internet.

There has been an explosive increase in the reach of television due to satellite channels, received in every small town and village through privately operated dish antennas. Of course, the information flow is one way but it does enhance the access to information about new products, opportunities, government programs and laws apart from news and events. In particular, programs about improved agriculture and allied activities are quite popular and serve as a means of extension. Similarly, SIDBI's TV programs on setting up small enterprises generated a massive response.

There are reportedly over 800,000 STD PCOs in India, with over half of them in small towns and villages. These STD PCOs are extensively used by farmers and other rural producers to exchange price and production information. Farmers are now able to talk to more than one agricultural markets and number of brokers. They are thus able to either defer their selling decision or send their produce to one of the markets offering them a better price. Similarly, weavers are able to check the availability and price of yarn from merchants before making a trip to the nearby town. Transporters are able to better schedule the usage of their vehicles, particularly reducing empty returns, by picking information about freight loads on the way back. Thus, telecom has been able to reduce transaction cost and improve margins.

There are a number of pilot projects in the country where telecom connections are being used for accessing the internet in rural areas and small towns. Some of these, such as Soya Choupal and i-Kisan are promoted by ITC and Nagarjuna Fertilizers respectively. Most of these sites offer information about commodity prices, volumes of market arrivals, the weather and about agronomic practices. There are also a few web sites put up by NGOs to promote handicraft products made by rural producers such as Kutch Mahila Vikas

Sangathan and ICICI Communities.org. Others, such as Gyandoot in Madhya Pradesh and Bhoomi in Karnataka are initiatives of state governments, providing a number of services, including land ownership and cultivation records, which are needed for various transactions including borrowing from formal institutions. There is also information about various government programs. Some sites also give information on employment opportunities. Though experimental and not yet widely used, many of these services have a great potential to reduce transaction costs as well as significantly do away with the information asymmetry which had kept rural producers at a disadvantage. (Mahajan & Raju 2002)

REFERENCE

Agro and Food Processing Industry in Gujarat, Agri-Fare 2000, CII.

Acharya, S. S. (1998), *Indian Journal of Agricultural Economics*, Vol. 53(3), pp. 3131-313

Banga, M. S. (2003), Food Revolution: A Win Win for Farmer and Consumer, Economic Times, 25th June

Chandrashekhar, C. P. and Jayati Ghosh (2003), Why is Farm Employment Generation Falling? *MacroScan, Business Line*, 22nd April.

Data Book 2003.

Economic Survey , 2001-02.

Mahajan, V. S. and Raju, B. Yerram (2002), Institutional Framework and Enabling Environment for the Rural Non-Farm Sector in India

Planning Commission Report, 2001.

4

POLICIES FOR REGIONAL DEVELOPMENT: THE CASE OF HANDLOOM TEXTILES, WITH REFERENCE TO ANDHRA PRADESH

Anne T. Kuriakose

INTRODUCTION

This paper is a preliminary reflection on policy constraints and opportunities in the handloom sector. The handloom sector was chosen the subject of study due to both its tremendous role in national employment, as well as its highly unique product characteristics, which cannot be replicated easily anywhere else in the world, and which therefore have the potential to command a premium price in both domestic and global markets, assuming sufficient design, production and marketing support. While reference will be made to handlooms at a national level, particular attention will be paid to the handloom scenario in the state of Andhra Pradesh (AP). My understanding of this sector is shaped by ongoing field research in Nalgonda District of AP, as well as by interviews with government, private and voluntary sector representatives active in handlooms, and review of secondary material. In places, I will make reference to specific institutions, programs and budget expenditures so that the day-to-day functioning of departmental support to the handloom sector can be put in context, amidst the wider socio-institutional setting of village handloom production and marketing.

The remainder of the paper is structured as follows. Section 2 provides an overview of the Indian textile industry, and the role of handlooms in both exports and employment. Section 3 examines the policy orientation and discourse around handloom policy in the country, particularly the use of 'schemes' and organizational instruments such as cooperatives. Section 4 looks at the literature on clusters and what this means for cluster development programs, and regional development more broadly. In Section 5, I expand the analysis to include a value chain approach and assess this against current efforts to develop textile and apparel parks, where the avowed aim is to leverage existing weaving skills. Section 6 concludes the paper by offering a number of principles for handloom policy and programming, along with some sample interventions.

PLACE OF HANDLOOMS IN THE CURRENT TEXTILE SCENARIO

Against the backdrop of economic reforms and trade liberalization, Government of India (GOI) has focused on the textile industry as a key sector, due both to its major contribution to export earnings as well as to national employment.[1] The Indian textile industry remains a key sector for the country and can even be considered a "propulsive industry", following Perroux's concept of an industry that dominates due to its size, market power or innovation capacity (see Bergman and Feser 2003). In 2000-01, the textile industry accounted for 14 per cent of industrial production, and for a full 27 per cent of total export earnings (Ministry of Textiles GOI 2002). Second only to agriculture as an employer, textiles provided work for 35 million persons in India in 2000-01 (ibid). Further, as the EXIM Bank observes, the handloom sector features: high labor intensity, low capital-output ratio, good export potential and 'negligible import content' (EXIM Bank 2000).

The textile industry exhibits a great deal of segmentation, however, and considerable growth variation can be seen across these sectors. Officially, the Indian textile industry is divided into the following four sectors: handloom; khadi; powerloom; and mill industries. Garments (apparel) are an additional related sub-sector which came into policy prominence only later. The industry's employment impact is most apparent in its more decentralized sectors, i.e. handloom (and khadi), and increasingly powerlooms, than in the formal mill sector which has experienced a severe contraction in recent decades. This paper focuses on the handloom sector (which uses mill-spun yarn in hand-woven production, in contrast to the khadi sector where the yarn itself is also handspun), though reference will also be made to other textile sub-sectors.

TRENDS IN INDIAN TEXTILE EXPORTS

I now turn to a brief review of the place of textiles in India's export portfolio. Table 1 presents a breakdown of the various sub-sector contributions to overall exports, with garments and cotton textiles taking the largest shares. Table 2 presents some export earnings data, showing that in recent global slowdown, silk textiles proved rather more resilient than either of the two big earners (garments and cotton textiles). Closer examination of such recession-proof sectors may prove important as India tries to boost its share in overseas markets. The majority of handloom production in India remains that of cotton. However, notably the share of all-cotton handloom products in total handloom production has been decreasing in the 1990s (from 98 per cent in 1985-86 to 88 per cent in 1996-97), with 100 per cent non-cotton handlooms (silk and wool?) rising over the same period (from 1 per cent to 12 per cent of all handloom fabric production) (Naik, Jain, and Singh 2001, p. 35).

As noted earlier, there is considerable diversity in the Indian textile sector. Some in the industry believe that there has been an artificial segmentation of the textile industry in India, following the lines set down by GOI policy over the years. They contrast the situation in India with that of China where all segments of the textile industry are taxed at the same rate rather than allowing for promotion of some sectors over others (Raghu 2003). With removal of these differential tax rates in India and the incoming ATC regime, these analysts forecast a doubling of Indian textile exports from the current level of USD$ 13 billion to within the range of $25-30 billion (ibid). The imposition of duties on hank yarn and the policy on CENVAT in the 2003-04 budget are expected to "rationalize" industry segmentation, in that the smaller mills for example will come under the excise net, thus reducing their previous exemption-based advantage over very large firms (Abraham 2003). The National Textile Policy of 2000 set a target of USD $50 billion in export earnings from textiles and garments (i.e. more than a third of total export earnings) by 2010, against a base of USD $11 billion in 2000 (Government of India 2000).

Table 1
Sector-wise Share of Total Textile Exports from India

	2001-02 (%)
Ready-made garments (RMG)	45.08
Cotton textiles incl handlooms	29.82
Man-made Fibre Textiles	10.27
Handicrafts	9.91
Silk Textiles	2.60
Jute	1.18
Coir	0.66
Woolen Textiles	0.48

Source: Annual Report 2001-02, Ministry of Textile GOI.

Table 2
Percentage Growth in Annual Textile Export Income by sub-sector

	1999-2000	*2000-2001*	*2001-2002*[2]	*Value of exports from Apr. to Oct. 2001(USD$ millions)*
Ready-made garments (RMG)	+9.2	+16.9	-15.6	2764.5
Silk textiles	+37.7	+30.0	-8.4	270.0
Man-made fibre textiles	+18.8	+28.1	-4.2	n.a.
Handicrafts	+11.7	-4.9	-22.4	n.a.
Cotton textiles incl handlooms	+10.2	+14.2	-12.0	1828.9
Coir	-38.7	+4.6	n.a.	40.6
Woolen textiles	-33.0	+27.6	-17.0	n.a.
Jute	-9.1	+62.1	-5.1	n.a.

Source: Annual Report 2001-02, Ministry of Textile GOI.

While from media accounts, there appears to be a large and growing garments market (and strong performance on the part of Indian manufacturers), global trade statistics tell a different story. Gereffi and Memedovic in a recent UNIDO paper trace garments (apparel) trade performance over time for countries around the world (Gereffi and Memedovic 2003). According to them, the total value of clothing imports by the US more than doubled from 1990 to 2000, from USD$25 billion to USD$64.4 billion (*ibid*). However, their analysis shows that for both the US and EU markets (the two biggest garment importers globally), India's share of the total apparel import market of each *did not change* between 1990 and 2000. This is particularly interesting given the policy context of economic liberalization in India during the same time period.

Crucially, all of India's South Asian competitors enhanced their share of the US apparel market, with Bangladesh and Sri Lanka reaching India's position of between 2-4% of the US market, and Pakistan also enhancing its share to 1-2% of the US market. In sum, while India's share did not decrease over the period, its competitors in the region, all enhanced their positions with two moving to positions equivalent to India's formerly dominant position. China, the oft-mentioned threat for Indian producers, did not shift its overall position (did not increase or decrease) but rather maintained its first-tier position of 10% or more of the US clothing import market (now also held by Mexico which has rapidly increased clothing exports to the US) (*ibid*). For the EU, which has a smaller overall clothing import market (of clothing coming from outside the EU) of USD$24.6 billion in 1990 rising to USD$53.6 billion in 2000, the story is similar (Gereffi and Memedovic 2003). There, India's position also remained stagnant (though at a higher share than in the US market, i.e. India held 4-5.9% of the EU clothing import market, double that of its share in the US market). However, once again its South Asian competitors increased their positions over the same period (particularly Bangladesh but also Sri Lanka), with Pakistan being the only exception of a South Asian country losing ground in the EU market from 1990-2000 (*ibid*). In terms of top tier countries, here Turkey and Hong Kong each share more than 10% of the EU clothing import market, while China now does the same having dramatically increased its share from 4-5-9% in 1990 to 10% or more in 2000 (*ibid*).

To sum up, in the global garments market, India is a fourth-tier player in the US market (along with a range of countries on nearly every continent), and a third-tier player in EU clothing imports. Such comparative analysis of relative place in the key garments markets as has been done by Gereffi and Memedovic is crucial in grounding any meaningful discussion of garment production and trade in India, as well as in discussions regarding promotion of particular sub-sectors in textiles, and/or integration of the industry as a whole.

Another interesting trend is the overall place of apparel in a country's export portfolio. Again, contrary to popular perception, garments have become less rather than more important for India as an export earner (see Table 3). While the period 1980-1990 saw apparel rising from 7.9% to 14.2% of total exports, the following decade saw apparel's place fall from 14.2% to 11.7% of total exports (Gereffi and Memedovic 2003). This is particularly important to note in the face of the performance of other South Asian countries (all of which saw consistent increases in the place of garments in their export basket) (ibid). Even China which showed a similar pattern to India in that the 1990s saw a drop in apparel's place in overall exports, did not experience the same degree of decrease. While this may be lauded in the case of India and China as successful diversification of the economy, it does not explain why the garment sector is still being promoted by state and national government as enthusiastically as is currently being done (see the discussion later in this paper on apparel and textile parks). One explanation is that India is widely expected to gain in garment and textile trade when existing quotas are removed with the Agreement on Trade and Textiles (ATC) coming into full force on 1 January, 2005. This is hoped for, even in the face of China's mammoth industry. However, some trade experts fear that protectionist measures may still be used by countries such as the US particularly in industries such as garments and textiles, though they may come in a different form such as more stringent industrial standards or labor standards (Kheir-el-Din 2002).

Table 3
Place of Apparel Exports in Select Asian Economies

	Total apparel exports (USD$ billion)			*Apparel as % oftotal exports*		
	1980	*1990*	*2000*	*1980*	*1990*	*2000*
India	0.6	2.6	5.6	7.9	14.2	11.7
Bangladesh	0.0	0.6	5.0	0.2	42.0	78.1
Sri Lanka	0.1	0.7	2.6	10.5	33.9	45.6
Pakistan	0.1	1.1	2.3	4.2	18.5	23.7
China	1.7	10.2	39.2	8.6	15.7	14.5
Indonesia	0.6	2.9	5.1	2.4	10.3	7.8

Source: Prepared with data from Gereffi and Memedovic 2003.

Given all this, where do handlooms stand in the textile scenario? Overall, handloom production as against other sectors has been fairly stable. Of total cloth production, handloom constitutes just 19 per cent but this rate has not varied much over the years, whereas the share of cloth production in the mill sector for example has been decreasing significantly since the 1980s (Niranjana and Vinayan 2001). Demand for handloom cloth must be decomposed into various product segments. Demand for niche market handloom products of high quality, including for home furnishings both domestically and abroad is strong. Handloom products constitute nearly 15% per cent of total fabric, made-ups and clothing exports from India textile exports from India (Nair n.d.). While powerlooms do well in production from synthetic fabrics, handlooms maintain a steady and growing share in cotton export markets. "Made-ups" are by far the main component of handloom exports. These include such items as bed linen, table linen and towels (as well as floor coverings, upholstery, and kitchen linen). Europe and the US constitute the main destinations for handloom products (46 per cent and 34 per cent of handloom exports respectively in 1999-2000). Crucially, buyer specifications (particularly of large chain stores in the West) require quality, color fastness, competitive pricing and improved supply chain management, as well as adherence to social codes of conduct such as non-use of child labor (EXIM Bank 2000). A particular challenge is the need for filling large orders with material of the same color, design et cetera. The handloom sector faces competition in some cheaper product ranges from the powerloom and mill sectors, however it is recognized that the unique characteristics of hand-woven materials (particularly in luxury fabrics such as silk, but increasingly cotton) cannot be duplicated by machine production. These characteristics include use of certain yarn types that automated machines cannot weave, as well as the production of particular area-specific loom-woven designs that are easily identified (Roy 1998).[3] In this way, the handloom market is a niche one. However, the boom in yarn exports in the 1990s has caused difficulties for handloom producers, causing a shortage in available yarn inputs (Roy 1998).

Table 4
Size of Textile Exports by India and Regional Competitors

Country	*USD$ (billions)*
China	54
India	13
Pakistan	10
Bangladesh	7.5

Source: Raghu 2003.

Review of Handloom Policy in India

The Indian government has promoted (and protected) the handloom sector as a key feature of its textile policy, due to a particular nationalist history of hand spinning, a desire to preserve a cultural heritage, and the employment implications of the sector. Since Independence in 1947, the Government has had a number of policies aimed at boosting the textile sector. India's first emphasis in handloom policy were the setting-up of village based production cooperatives, initiation of government product procurement and marketing, as well as government support to input supply. The first major set of changes to this government-driven approach came in 1985 when a series of textile reforms aimed at deregulation were announced. Still, some protective measures maintained such as a quota of yarn that mills must provide in hank form to the handloom sector, as well as an Act reserving certain garments for production only in the handloom sector (Liebl and Roy 2000). In 2000, the New Textile Policy (NTP) was announced. In it, readymade garment manufacture was de-reserved from the small-scale sector to any unit wishing to take up production, and financing schemes were offered for weaving and spinning machinery upgrading, there was relatively little offered to the handloom sector apart from some re-training for weavers (Liebl and Roy 2000). Liebl and Roy characterize the new policy stance towards handlooms as more a change in tone and expectation, i.e. the government was now highlighting the need for improved quality in the sector in order to meet international competition (particularly from China), and also pointed towards the coming shift in the environment when India as part of its WTO commitment began to liberalize textile imports (2000: 79). The government was making clear that it could no longer provide the sort of fiscal support to weavers that it had in the past, and that improved marketing approaches were required (ibid). The industry is only now starting to experience the deregulation that other industries have enjoyed since the early 1990s. Policy orientation is changing. In the Approach Paper to the Tenth Plan, the Textiles Working Group has recommended measures such as extending the CENVAT across the textile production chain, de-reserving the knitting sector from the list of small-scale industries; facilitating large-scale investments in technology through the Textile Upgradation Fund scheme (TUFS) (Ministry of Textiles GOI 2002). Notably, though these improvements are more oriented to large-scale formal sector textile firms, rather than the small firms that characterize the handloom sector. The theme is a scaling-up of production, as well as support to the previously-neglected powerloom sector. Garments have also been de-reserved from the SSI list (Government of India 2000).

As noted above, the government has had a policy entitled Hank Yarn Obligation which requires spinning mills to supply no less than 50 per cent of the total yarn they market in the form of hanks for use by the handloom sector (Kathuria and Bhardwaj 1998). This hank yarn is exempt from both excise and sales tax (ibid). However, recent studies suggest that between 30-40 per cent of the 571 million kgs of hank yarn intended for the handloom sector is diverted to the powerloom sector (NCAER 1998). Regarding product reservation, as of 2000, GOI had reserved 11 textile articles (down from 22 earlier) for exclusive production by the handloom sector (rather than by powerlooms or the mill sector) (Ministry of Textiles GOI 2002). Powerloom operations are inspected for breaking this act (over 140,000 inspections in 2001-02) though few were charged and convicted (25 persons in 2001-02) (ibid). De-reservation of items from the handloom sector has been slow despite the recommendations of the 1997 Abid Hussain Committee on Small-Scale Industry which called for such action (see Hussain 1997).

Employment Implications of the Handloom Sector, with Special Reference to Andhra Pradesh

In terms of sheer number of looms, India by far surpasses other nations. Fifty-eight per cent of looms in the world (3.5 million handlooms and 1.8 mil powerlooms) but technology remains basic (Government of India 2000). As noted above, the employment implications of the handloom sector in India are tremendous. Nationally, the handloom sector is second only to agriculture with regard to employment generated, employing 3 million weavers directly, and millions more who work in pre-loom processing, and related activities (EXIM Bank 2000). Hard figures are difficult to come by, but it appears that over the period 1940 to 1994-95, employment in handlooms shrank from 7.4 million to 6.5 million persons (when weavers and non-weavers such as assistants are considered) (Roy 1998: 898). Over the same period, loomage increased by nearly 50 per cent, implying an increase in productivity in the sector (more looms per worker).

The Indian state of Andhra Pradesh (AP) offers a very interesting setting in which to examine handloom sector employment. AP is one of the larger states for handlooms, both in terms of product output as well as percentage of workforce employed in the sector. The state also accounts for nearly half the handlooms in India producing for export (Mukund and Sundari 2001). State-wise data from the national Joint Census of Handlooms and Powerlooms 1995-96 show that handloom production in Andhra Pradesh is the fourth highest in the country at 23,746,604 linear metres per month, after the top handloom-producing states of West Bengal, Uttar Pradesh, Tamil Nadu (in that order) (NCAER 1998). The study also calculates a number of conversion ratios that highlight relative productivity in converting yarn to cloth (*ibid*). These are presented in the table below. The same survey shows that Andhra Pradesh is the third largest state in terms of workshed-based handloom production, hosting 11.28 per cent of all "non-household units" in India (NCAER 1998).[4] Andhra Pradesh also accounts for the third-largest share of yarn consumption by non-household units (11.83 per cent), as well as the highest fabric consumption by those units (13.82 per cent) (NCAER 1998). Nonetheless, handloom production in India, including Andhra Pradesh, remains overwhelmingly household-based in general, with the majority of full-time weavers in the country working from home (NCAER 1998).

Though located in the South of the country (typically rather more developed than much of the North), the state of Andhra Pradesh is one of the poorer states in India. Its performance on a range of human development indicators is weak. Illiteracy rates in AP are 67 per cent among rural workers, with a further 25 per cent educated only up to primary level (NSS Employment-Unemployment Survey data 1994-95). The proportion of rural households working as agricultural laborers is second in the country only to Tamil Nadu. AP also hosts the highest female work participation rate in India (i.e. 48 per cent, with 60 per cent of these working as agricultural laborers), as well as the highest child labor rates in India (34 per cent of rural children in AP aged 10-14 work–this is double the national average). Both rates reflect high levels of poverty within the state.

Table 5
Conversion Ratio Trends (1987-88 and 1995-96) for AP, Select States, and All-India

	Years	*Daily production per loom (linear metres)*	*Daily production per worker (linear metres)*	*Production per kg of yarn (linear metres)*
Andhra Pradesh	1987-88	3.60	1.71	n.a.
	1995-96	4.26	1.75	10.14
West Bengal	1987-88	6.50	2.99	n.a.
	1995-96	4.42	2.26	11.12
Uttar Pradesh	1987-88	7.84	3.16	n.a.
	1995-96	5.23	2.35	6.74
Tamil Nadu	1987-88	3.24	1.96	n.a.
	1995-96	3.55	2.42	9.98
All-India	1987-88	2.63	1.52	n.a.
	1995-96	2.49	1.33	8.86

Source: Report on Joint Census of Handlooms and Powerlooms 1995-96 (NCAER and Min. of Textiles).

Andhra Pradesh weavers are particularly dependent on weaving for a greater proportion of their total income than weavers in some other states. The NCAER Joint Census found that weaver households earned 83 per cent of their income from handloom production (with the remaining amount divided between non-agricultural income at 11 per cent, and agriculture at 6 per cent) (NCAER 1998). This stands in contrast to an all-India average (excluding the Northeast) of 72 per cent (ibid). This dependence on one activity for their livelihood has made weaver households particularly vulnerable to market downturns, resulting in destitution and in extreme cases, suicides, as well as the political pressure for the state that accompanies organization of weavers. Handloom production takes place in a variety of settings and under different modes of production, from home-based units to larger 'weaving sheds' or small factories (*karkhanas*) run by 'master weavers' (often, though not always, from the weaving caste themselves) who hire both regular and casual workers (including piece-rate outworkers). The NCAER Handloom Census in 1987-88 conducted for the MoT found that among full-time weavers, 54 per cent were 'independent', 20 per cent worked in cooperatives, 15 per cent were in putting-out relations with master weavers, and 11 per cent worked in private and public factories (cited in Roy 1993). The second round of the handloom census (conducted in 1995-96) shows a 15.2 per cent decline in the number of handloom units (household and non-household) from 1987-88 to 1995-96, from 3 million to 2.54 million, but a very slight increase in the number of workers from 6.54 million to 6.55 million (NCAER 1998).

The change in number of units at the Andhra Pradesh state level was very similar (a decline of 15.98 per cent i.e. from 172,970 in 1987-88 to 145,335 in 1995-96). In AP, a rise in the absolute number of workers was noted, however, as was also the case in Assam (these were the only two states where this occurred) (NCAER 1998).[5] At the all-India level, the number of persons engaged in handloom weaving and spinning declined between the two censuses by just 2.9 per cent (NCAER 1998). Also, the number of looms at the national level declined by 8 per cent over the same period which together with the other data suggests intensification or reorganization of the production process in that whereas in 1987-88 there was an average of 2.18 workers and 1.26 looms per unit, in 1995-96 these figures had increased to 2.58 and 1.37 respectively (NCAER 1998). The decline in looms in AP over the same period was comparable to the national average, and represented negative growth of 8.02 per cent (NCAER 1998). Table 6 shows intensification of production in the AP handloom sector, in contrast to the all-India situation.

Table 6
Handloom Employment in Andhra Pradesh

	Weavers [6]	*Preparatory Process Producers*[7]	*Hired Workers*[8]	*Other Producers*[9]
1987-88	252,157	200,797	16,132	n.a.
1995-96	228,007	147,244	30,540	84,825
% Change	-9.58	-26.67	89.31	n.a.

Source: NCAER Report on Joint Census of Handlooms and Powerlooms 1995-96.

Table 7
Trends in AP Handloom Sector

	1987-88	*1995-96*	*Percentage Changein AP*	*Percentage Change at all-India level*
Number of looms owned	219,715	202,100	-8.02	-7.73
Monthly production (in linear metres)	23,746,604	25,826,543	8.76	-12.77

Source: NCAER Report on Joint Census of Handlooms and Powerlooms 1995-96.

WELFARE VERSUS GROWTH: POLICY OBJECTIVES WITH REGARD TO HANDLOOMS

Having reviewed the place of handlooms in the textile industry, I now turn to a political economy approach to handloom policy design and implementation. Here I focus on the role of interest groups and the formation of political identities in the Indian polity.

There are a number of tropes, or misleading images, that remain relatively unexamined within the policy arena in relation to handlooms. The first is that of "the weaver" himself (sic)[10]. In the most simplistic version of the policy story, the weaver is assumed to be poor and unskilled. With the addition of a popular understanding of social and market relations, the weaver is also said to be "at the mercy of" the "master weaver". Missing here is an analysis of further layers of sub-contracting below the 'master weavers' (i.e. sub-contracting by sub-contractors, and even to an additional layer below), as well as consideration of the role of traders in handloom production and marketing. In other words, it is important to consider the labor status of weavers when designing and implementing schemes (both asset ownership, including loom/s owned, and employment arrangements such as shed-workers or sub-contractors or manufacturer-traders).[11] [In its more recent targeting efforts, the government has used other criteria to judge socio-economic exclusion particularly membership in cooperatives where non-members are assumed to be worse off. However this is far from always the case, as many better-off weavers cannot be bothered to participate in the failing cooperatives any longer]. Further, certain weaving castes including Padmasalis have a significant proportion of members who have managed to accumulate capital in a number of textile sectors, including powerlooms and through mill work in Maharashtra (Roy 1993). In addition to a lack of policy distinction about socio-economic classes of so-called weavers (by which I mean to include even those handloom traders who are weavers by caste but may not have owned looms in years), a similar lack of attention is paid to differences among regional weaving economies and the vulnerabilities that these dynamics may create for weavers, particularly those who have recently migrated from distressed handloom centers to more dynamic ones. In Andhra Pradesh for example, the Coastal region hosts much larger shed-based production centers, where piece rates for weavers are much lower than in the more decentralised Telangana production belt for example, thereby generating much migration to Telangana until very recently (and consequent re-training in place-specific skills such as tie and dye).

Given this all-pervasive official view of weavers as vulnerable persons without any significant poverty analysis to identify the more and less-vulnerable among the group, the policy response of a sector-specific ministry (i.e. Ministry of Textiles) has not been to identify strategic entry points along the value chain at which to help shift the entire industry up a notch, rather it has mainly chosen to deal in social welfare measures, whether stated as such or not. I believe this is doing an ultimate disservice to the sector as a whole, as growth requires investment in those economic levers that can support dynamism in the industry (such as product and design diversification, brand building, training and provision of information clearinghouse services). Instead, what we see is an emphasis on income transfers, working capital for loans (which could be better through rural non-banking financial institutions and other service providers), and such welfare measures as health services, borewell digging for drinking water, housing grants, and compensation to widows and other family members.

More specifically, Mooij lists four welfare schemes for handloom weavers: workshed cum housing scheme, thrift fund scheme, health package scheme and group insurance scheme (2002). The health package scheme include such components as medicine reimbursement, eye testing and spectacles provision, drinking water supply, maternity benefit, compensation for sterilization, and PHC infrastructure–none of which are directly related to handloom production. Of the handloom schemes listed by Niranjana, nearly half are social protection and welfare measures including insurance and thrift funds offered with little financial contribution from the weavers (Niranjana and Vinayan 2001). While some of these such as insurance or eye care may be seen to improve labor conditions and respond to workers' rights, the point is that the entire burden is on the government, even when the government is not the 'employer' as in the health measures extended to weavers who were not cooperative members. These measures, such as drinking water, housing loans, insurance and thrift services, et cetera can be provided through regular social programs (anti-poverty schemes) in place through the Department of Rural Development and others, rather than delivered through the Ministry of Textiles.

However, in the interest-group-driven political process easily observed in the country (see also (Mooij and Dev 2002), citizens are broken up into small groups for schemes that are duplicated across different ministries, e.g. different schemes for SC/ST, BCs, women, minorities, and so on. A similar thing is happening in the case of weavers, who are singled out as somehow more deserving than, for example, agricultural laborers, or construction workers. Means-testing is half-heartedly implemented. In addition, weavers recounted to me that in the case of housing loans a rather large self-deposit was required upfront to secure the grant amount, thereby excluding truly impoverished weavers. To sum up, I believe that as these schemes are essentially income transfers, they belong in the Department of Welfare or of Labor and not in the Department of Handlooms and Textiles which should be focusing on sectoral growth, product diversification, industry consolidation, and increasing national and international market share.

Does this mean that weaver households are to be abandoned, right at the time that globalization pressures are mounting (i.e. with further textile trade liberalization and the phasing-out of the Multi-Fibre Agreement after January 1, 2005?) Not at all. It is simply a call for closer analysis and disentangling of welfare and growth objectives. Anti-poverty measures for handloom workers (including poor independent weavers, shed workers in handlooms etc) should fall under the scope of the Ministry of Welfare (or at the least Labor), in the category of social protection measures. This would call for more targeting, and expansion of social protection itself (the subject of another paper). In fact, a most radical option would be see poor weavers just as poor persons, (or as poor rural persons, if that distinction must be maintained for regional convergence tracking). It is not clear to me that for the purposes of poverty alleviation, those weavers must be considered as a separate category (in a way that for example construction workers or agricultural laborers are not). There does appear to be something about the way the political system works that encourages the development of more and more special-interest groups (a close parallel here may be the "farmer", a category that remains dangerously aggregate, thereby leaving free farmers of all size plots, levels of irrigation, and degrees of local market development, to claim even more from the government in the form of subsidized inputs). Such blanket categorizations of occupational groups neither further sectoral development nor aid in poverty reduction.

What then is a possible explanation for such a narrow view taken by policymakers on what is possible within the handloom realm? Judith Tendler has identified a similar dynamic in policy support to 'small firms', particularly those in the informal sector (Tendler 2002). She notes that rather than working to improve efficiency, technological upgrading and market linkages, policymakers are often happy to simply keep them informal and unregistered, and not subject to tax, environmental or labor codes (*ibid*). There are also other sops offered to small industry, such as cheap credit and loan write-offs. This group of practices she calls the "devil's deal" between politicians and their constituents, including many small firm owners. It take place at the general level as a result of both "welfare" objectives on the part of governments, and at the specific level in response to lobbying efforts by various sector representative and their associations. Myriad examples can be found across industries in many different countries.

Recent GOI excise policy for textiles lends credence to Tendler's observation. The new GOI policy in place from 1 April 2003 states that yarn processors, powerlooms, hand processors, and power processors working on a jobwork basis need not register with excise authorities, nor maintain records or pay duty (PTI wire report 2003). Political pressure in the case of AP handlooms has proven to be quite effective in other ways also. In 2002, in response to a number of weaver suicides in the area, and the resultant joint strike by the weavers' organization and the master weavers' association (Tie and Dye Manufacturers Association) in Pochampally, APCO (the state handloom procurement organization) took the unprecedented step of lifting a very large amount of stock from not only the cooperative, but also from private traders. The combined purchases were worth 13.1 lakhs, according to the Department's records (Assistant Director-Handlooms and Textiles Nalgonda District 2003a).

As an example of a different route away from simple tax concessions and the like, Tendler notes a cases from Spain where rather than agreeing to such demands (often particularly strident when an industry is facing a particular crisis), the government instead offered its own alternative where the Planning Ministry agreed to facilitate a strategic process of problem-identification and action-planning by firms themselves, towards which it would then offer state funds. Such an adjustment of orientation on the part of both government and industry representatives, and reversal of their traditional roles as "giver" and "taker", "thinker" and "doer", allowed for a more dynamic and sustainable solution. Such a spirit of multi-actor co-planning and analysis is the essence of cluster development.

Table 8
Cooperative versus Private Sector Handloom Activity: Nalgonda District, AP

	Looms	*2002-03 Turnover (Rs. crores)*
Cooperatives (45 total)[12]	9,602	6.23
Private Sector	8,641	22.50

Source: Assistant Director, Handlooms and Textiles, Nalgonda District.

The second policy outcome stemming from a view of weavers as poor and vulnerable is what may be deemed the 'organizational response', namely that of developing the cooperative infrastructure. While local cooperatives may offer convenience in the promise of "services at the doorstep", still it appears that the economic viability of such decentralised production and marketing is questionable. To take the case of one district, Nalgonda, there are a total of 45 cooperatives (including 10 dormant ones, according to the government's own records) (see Table 8). Village-based cooperatives may also make them more prone to elite capture, though this is not to say that the same would not happen for area-based cooperatives, though perhaps in a more diffuse form. Still, handloom cooperatives have played important functions at different times and places, as nascent local industries grew and gained access to designs and training over the years. In the end however, rather than operating as businesses, their main function has been to serve as a delivery device for government schemes, (and in time of government procurement through state agency APCO to function as a supply channel for government buyers). Handloom textile policy is still so oriented towards cooperatives, despite widespread acknowledgement of their failures, that to date only one scheme has been designed for weavers who are not members of the cooperatives (despite the fact that these are the majority of weavers) see table below. This is the Deen Dayal scheme (DDHPY), introduced 50 years after the first cooperatives were started after Independence, and discussed below.

From April–December 2002, a total of Rs. 2694.68 lakhs was spent in Andhra Pradesh on the Deen Dayal Hathkargha Protsahan Yojana (DDHPY) scheme out of a total of Rs. 3201.32 for all handloom schemes (Department of Handlooms and Textiles GoAP 2003). While this new central scheme launched in 2000-01 was intended to strengthen the export capacity of the handloom sector for the post-MFA scene in 2005, in reality it is another mishmash of extension of working capital, some product development and marketing support. The DDHPY provides assistance from "basic inputs like looms and accessories, loans for working capital, product development, infrastructure and institutional support, training to weavers, supply of equipment and marketing support' (Ministry of Textiles GOI 2002 p. 10). However, one important difference from previous schemes is that this one targets weavers "outside the cooperative fold". While this was perhaps intended as a welfare measure (since for example loomless weavers generally cannot join the cooperatives), it also has the effect of including private-sector weavers (master weavers and those supplying to them as sub-contractors) in the purview of government policymakers. This shift from an over-reliance on the sole mechanism of the cooperative as the only way to implement handloom programs is welcome. DDHPY is run on a 50:50 cost-sharing basis between the Central and State governments. The DDHPY is designed to benefit individual weavers to the tune of Rs. 16550 each (Assistant Director-Handlooms and Textiles Nalgonda District 2003b). As it was explained by MAC members, weavers would receive Rs. 8000 at one time (50% grant), and then remaining money later after training had been completed. According to the program materials, the Rs 8000 is intended for "margin money" (i.e. working capital), while the remaining is intended for: (i) procurement of dobby attachment and loom accessories (Rs. 3000 and 2000 respectively), training (Rs. 2550) and design purchase (Rs. 1000) (Assistant Director-Handlooms and Textiles Nalgonda District 2003b). Again, the scheme can be understood to be an income transfer of some sort.

In practice, the laudable aim of reaching out to excluded weavers has been distorted by a new institutional wrinkle has appeared, known as the MAC. MACs (Mutually-Aided Cooperative Societies) are cooperatives formed by private individuals, in this case weavers who are not currently members of the existing government-organized cooperatives. However, because weavers learned of MACs through the government's representative (Assistant Director, DHT) and the existing cooperatives, and were told they could avail benefits (the DDHPY) only once a MAC had been formed, in practice, the MACS have become another shell, perhaps more empty in some places than others. In my fieldwork, I have come across MACs that consisted of just 6-7 members of an extended family of master weavers who are awaiting their amounts from the government, but also a MAC formed by around 200 migrant weavers who had previously been denied access to the existing village cooperative due to social exclusion.[13] While for them, the MAC might offer a chance to improve their position (currently working as suppliers to the sub-contractors of existing master weavers), they too are still mainly looking for the government's cash infusion, though training opportunities were also mentioned. My contention here is that over-involvement of the government in the handloom industry has conditioned weavers, of different classes and levels of organization, to expect government bailouts as their right in the face of "the weaver's plight".

Handloom production and marketing is based upon intricate social relations among pre-loom workers, weavers, and master weavers/traders, and different formal and informal organizations representing them. In more developed weaving centers it is common for master weavers to organize into associations, and for weavers also to do the same. The primary function of these associations is to negotiate piece rates for different woven products, on an annual or multi-year basis. I have observed weavers' associations in two different clusters. The first, located in a cluster which functioned as a central marketing node for the entire belt of clusters across two districts, was a formal organization which had recently taken part in a joint strike together with the master weavers' association in order to demand a number of concessions from the government. They were successful in most of the demands. I found a rather seamless united front of handloom sector organisations in this cluster, all oriented to government handouts. In the second cluster, a smaller one, where the coop was twenty years younger than the first (which had government intervention since the mid-1950s), a weavers' association also existed and conducted negotiations with the less formal master weavers' association every threeyears. Relations there were ordered but clearly there existed a more expected labor-capital tension than was present in the other cluster. The demands of the weavers association there were entirely directed to the master weavers' and wage and benefit conditions in the private sector, rather than expecting government to take care of every aspect of the handloom economy as was the case in the other cluster. It must also be said that this was not due to these weavers' lack of access to the district handloom official (Assistant Director), who they met with at different times, particularly in connection with setting up the MAC. Rather, the association was 'all about business', and had even recently decided not to align with any political parties as there had previously been political violence in the area.

Whereas weavers in the production-base cluster demanded only wage and condition improvements from master weavers (i.e. rise in piece rates for various products; a Rs. 125 bonus payment after every 6 months of work; a Rs. 75 monthly allowance for those weavers weaving in house rented from master weavers; and a general condition that should new designs arise, negotiations will have to be renewed to again decide rates), the demands of the weavers' association in the highly-politicized marketing node cluster were completely oriented to pressuring government for concessions, many of which mirrored government program guidelines exactly (see Table 9).

Table 9
Formal Demands of Weavers Associations in 2002 Negotiations in Pochampally

1. Government should pay Rs. 1 lakh to family members of those weavers who committed suicide.
2. The government must buy the stock from the cooperative.
3. The government must buy the stock from the master weavers.
4. The government (central and state) should secure the 22 designs [product reservations?] ordered by the Supreme Court for handlooms.
5. The printing of designs of tie and dye by powerlooms should be immediately stopped by the government
6. Handloom designs should be given a patent by the government
7. The government should supply yarn, zari, and dyes on a subsidized basis.
8. The government should establish an apparel park in Pochampally.
9. A handloom development bank should be established in Pochampally.
10. The government should provide a foreign market for tie and dye [products].
11. A pension of Rs. 250 should be given to weavers aged more than 60 years.
12. APCO losses should by supported through subsidy from the government.
13. A branch of NIFT (National Institute of Fashion Technology) should be established in Pochampally.
14. The weavers should be granted group insurance.
15. Cooperative society should be provided rebate facility 365 days a year.
16. Handloom cooperative membership should be provided to all weavers.

Source: Primary document from fieldwork (translated from Telugu).

CLUSTERS, REGIONAL PRODUCTION SYSTEMS AND VILLAGE AGGLOMERATIONS

For some time, both scholars and policymakers have been fascinated by industrial clusters and their offshoot, cluster development programs. Clusters have been studied throughout the developing and developed world, including the textile, footwear, furniture, surgical instruments, knitwear, automobile, electronics and software industries: (Schmitz 1995)

(Humphrey 1995) (Nadvi 1999) (Pietrobelli 1998) (Cawthorne 1995) (Tewari 1998) (Rabellotti 1999) (Knorringa 1999). Industrial clusters have been defined as: "sectoral and geographical concentrations of enterprises" (Humphrey and Schmitz 1996, p. 1861). The ideal variant is "industrial districts" which is a more all-encompassing concept, taking an institutional view and focusing on inter-firm relations and the presence of support institutions, particularly of a self-help nature, such as sectoral associations. With regard to the role of conscious joint action by firms within clusters, Humphrey and Schmitz note that "whether specialization and cooperation develop is ...a matter for empirical research and not subsumed in its definition" (*ibid*). Still, the mere presence of the concentration of firms is likely to engender external economies such as availability of skilled labor, raw materials suppliers, and trade and financial services catering to the sub-sector (*ibid*). I will more commonly employ the term "cluster" in this paper, implying that the level of joint action among firms in a particular place remains unknown until investigated. Industrial agglomerations, including clusters, are theorized to gain competitive advantage in part from their concentration of skilled labor locally, that is, from workers possessing 'tacit knowledge' gained in a socially-embedded 'industrial atmosphere'. An important concept within the cluster literature is that of *collective efficiency*. Collective efficiency has been defined as: "the competitive advantage derived from external economies and joint action" (Schmitz and Nadvi 1999, p. 1504). Unplanned external economies result from agglomeration effects such as easy access to raw material suppliers, machinery and labor, as well as more diffuse effects of technological innovation and diffusion processes, whereas joint action can take the form of establishment of business associations and producer consortia (Humphrey 1995).

Clusters are said to foster small-firm growth, enhance employment, and contribute to regional economic development. Indeed there is a large geographic component to the analysis of clusters, which requires a spatial perspective to understand fully. More recent value-chain driven critique of cluster analysis have noted the importance of identifying non-local demand and supply factors, in terms of markets and input flows that may cross geographic scales from state, to regional and national, and even global levels. Here the economic and the geographic meet again in an even deeper way. Following on from the discussion above on targeting and labor status, I would argue that a third axis is necessary in performing industry assessment towards promotion of sustainable regional growth, and that is the social. From micro-level understandings of how work is organized and assets gained by weavers households in the context of cluster economies, to broad intra- and inter-state study of temporary and permanent migration by sector workers, social analysis of economic activities is a key component in the preparation of any sector plan that holds poverty reduction as an ultimate goal (if not the immediate objective). The key distinction here is that of understanding distributional effects of growth (i.e. pro-poor growth), but privileging growth nonetheless as a necessary means of poverty reduction.

GOVERNMENT PROCUREMENT OF HANDLOOM PRODUCTS AND DESIGN DEVELOPMENT

A recent coup for the GoAP Department of Handlooms and Textiles (DHT) recently was the winning of a bid to produce saris for the Air India flight attendants. The deal signed in July 2003 was for 6,000 silk saris worth Rs. 2 crore (Anon. 2003). APCO the apex body of the AP handloom cooperatives negotiated the deal along with ACASH (the Association of Corporations and Apex Societies in Handlooms), while the design input and samples preparation was facilitated by NIFT (the National Institute of Fashion Technology). While this order represents an important opportunity in terms of sector visibility and product placement in the market, a crucial opportunity was lost by using only the name 'Pochampally' to refer to these saris which will actually be produced by 1000 weavers across cooperatives in 6 villages in the district (including for example, Puttapaka). While Pochampally already has name recognition at the state and even national level, other handloom centers could stand to have their name similarly promoted. Alternatively, if for strategic reasons the DHT wants to further strengthen the Pochampally 'brand', then this could be done by marketing the saris as from the "Pochampally region" comprising including Pochampally, Puttapaka, Veligonda, Mothkur (or whichever names it chose to promote). Whether such a debate took place within APCO's halls I am not sure, but at its worst the potential for a real branding opportunity could fall prey to being simply another case of government procurement.

One possible option is the use of trademarks in the form of geographical indications (see (Fink and Smarzynska 2002) (Penna and Visser 2002). While these legal protections for place-specific products have been in place for some time in the food and beverage industry in particular in the form of *origins d'appellation* laws (e.g. products labeled as Champagne must originate from the Champagne region in France, if they come from anywhere else such as California, Spain or even another region of France they must be labeled as 'sparkling wine'). These trade laws are upheld within countries and across international borders. Some are now looking into the possibility of using these laws in other industries, such as textiles (Maskus 2000). This may be an important area for policymakers in India to consider, e.g. the country would have to have both products as well as process patents in place. One caveat however is that given the costs associated with getting cases through the court system, the benefit to individual producers of such laws may be slow to materialize. Still, the deterrent effect might be of some use. Currently, handloom producers of silk tie and dye saris in Pochampally, Andhra Pradesh are facing much competition from powerloom producers in Surat and within the state who simply copy the tie and dye design, and print it on polyester saris which can be marketed at a fraction of the price of an original silk handloom sari. Were a trademark regime to be put in place, the protection of the Pochampally 'brand' would be strengthened. Look-alike saris might then have to be marketed as "Pochampally-style sari" or even just "tie and dye sari" depending on the provisions of the trademark. It might raise awareness among consumers and create more demand for the originals, particularly among those seeking the cachet of a handloom silk sari.

Of course, these provisions hit both ways as for example in the case of Pochampally designs where many so-called 'traditional' designs originated from Gujarat, West Bengal or Tamil Nadu originally (e.g. the Gujarati Pan Patola design). Where modifications are made to original designs however, as they are often are, these might be registered as new designs. Note though that there are two levels of protection: one to guarantee authenticity of place-specific production, and the other to protect trademark designs. The former may be more easily implemented (and have broader benefits) than the latter. Reichman goes as far as to say that "Trade dress protection" can be used which gives legal protection to not just the product, but the distinctive packaging: he advocated it for crafts in India as there is a strong national law for this, as well as TRIPs[14] provisions at the international level [cited in Penna, 2002 #1087]. (TC is trying to do this, with branded grading system and MRPs). Note also that the Policy Science Center is working with the Indian Commissioner for Handicrafts to develop a certification system for products labeled "handmade in India" (Penna and Visser 2002). The Pochampally Cluster Development Program of the Textiles Committee is following Reichman's suggestion in its own way (without legal protection), as it is working on developing a brand for saris jointly marketed by a group of Pochampally traders with a standard package, label, and grading system of A/B/C/D quality saris of various price points, with marked MRPs to aid in consumer trust.

Returning to the question of 'government as buyer' (and seller in this case!), it is possible to say this is not always a mis-step (see (Tendler and Amorim 1996) for the case of government procurement of school furniture by small producers in clusters. In the case of the Air India uniforms above, more positive externalities could be gained from sustaining a close, longer-term relationship complete with buyer feedback, rather than treating it as a one-off procurement order. Care must be taken to learning opportunities beyond the simple cash transaction; otherwise design preparations, buyer-supported upgrading and other such learning remain at the level of the broker (APCO and ACASH) rather than at the level of cluster producers. Tendler stresses the importance of the institutional relations among the purchasing departments; government agencies; the support agencies who work as brokers for the order (who should have a small financial stake in good supplier performance); the private sector association of firms and the individual firms themselves (Tendler and Amorim 1996). Longer-term buying relationships allow for development of 'sophisticated demand' (and adequate supplier responses) where small firms learn from buyer feedback. Tendler stresses there should be upfront deposits by buyers to allow for working capital, but that orders can and should be rejected if not up to the mark in terms of quality, cost and on-time delivery (1996).

In textiles, color and fabric preferences do change, and a large part of government efforts in the handloom sector is now concentrated on linking clusters to design inputs and market information. Quality improvements include the government-sponsored Handloom Export Promotion Council (HEPC)'s 'Computer-Aided Textile Design System' to improve design innovation and production of samples with new designs (EXIM Bank 2000). The Project Package Scheme funded equally by the Center and the State governments allowed for 40 freelance designers (with fine arts backgrounds) and textile technology specialists (often from weaving families themselves and most trained at IIHT) to develop new designs for use by coop producers (Chowdhury 2003). NIFT oversaw the project and offered technical input, and support with color forecasting etcetera. Designers were based in village cooperatives in all districts of the states (coops were vetted for their 'active' status). There designers tested designs and trained weavers, ensuring weavers could execute the designs which had been transferred from the CAD program to the more common graph paper format. Design innovations include use of vegetable dyes, fabric blending such as silk with chenille, and use of rarer fabrics such as jute. The 2-year scheme ended with a 2-day trade show in Hyderabad where 600 new designs were exhibited and it is expected that the program will be renewed for a second phase where the goal is to develop 6000 designs. It is already being replicated in Tamil Nadu.

Still government bodies such as APCO show a reluctance to step beyond government buyer-supply chains. The recent exhibition of the Design Development Scheme included only APCO buyers as invitees, rather than buyers from the private sector (who are expected for the next show). This fear of market competition is not warranted, particularly in this case where careful planning and sound technical and design inputs had been garnered as part of the program. In a even more telling instance, it was reported that buyers who do wish to purchase from specific cooperatives (as the designs were developed in concert with specific cooperatives to help ensure exclusivity and competitiveness, rather than splashed across the region) must go through APCO rather than negotiate directly with the cooperative. This is contrary to the greater spirit of self-sufficient economic viability that the government says it is trying to promote in the sector.

A recent listing of "Important Handloom Clusters in A.P." by the Directorate of Handlooms and Textiles of the Government of Andhra Pradesh (GoAP) identified no less than 73 'important' clusters. These so-called clusters cover 108,472 weavers owning 76,766 looms (note that loomless weavers are present). Of these totals, 55 per cent of looms are "outside the cooperative fold" while, 68 per cent of weavers are outside the coops, suggesting that loomless weavers in particular are not well-served by the cooperatives.

GOVERNANCE AND CLUSTER DEVELOPMENT

The Ministry of Textiles (MoT) through the Textiles Committee is implementing a Cluster Development Program (pre-dating DHT plans for such work), following the model successfully demonstrated by UNIDO across India including garment clusters such as Ludhiana and Tiruppur. The Textiles Committee initiated an India-wide program, targeting 23 textile clusters in the country, of which only a quarter are handloom clusters, and others are in garments, spinning mills, and powerlooms. In Andhra Pradesh, the handloom cluster of Pochampally has also been targeted, as have Guntur and Nagari for other textile sub-sectors (e.g. spinning mill). Planned activities include training on export development; also branding and joint marketing activities (Kopresachari n.d.). The important thing here is the process, starting with a diagnostic/problem identification and formation of action plan with cluster participants (rather than a centrally-design blueprint). This is in stark contrast to the ways most government programs are run. While the Textiles Committee's program is certainly a more strategic approach, there are some additional measures that can be taken, chief among these would be the awareness and program-planning for a more regional approach (rather than village level). Again, clusters are not simply village agglomerations, but particularly in a program like this, clusters should be selected for the key backward and forward linkage functions they are already performing in the regional sector-based economy. Pochampally for example is a key marketing node for the belt of handloom clusters in Nalgonda and even Warangal districts, however, there are other key actors in the belt who would not be based at Pochampally but who would have important contributions to make in a regional development program. While definitional questions always remain about the 'correct' boundaries of a cluster, it is instructive the many different cluster configurations identified by Guerrieri and Pietrobelli (i.e. hub and spoke; satellite) which clearly point to the livelihood of a cluster's working area as beyond any single village (Guerrieri and Pietrobelli 2001). These are points to keep in mind as cluster development programs are designed, either by the Textiles Committee, or by the DHT which is planning its own cluster development program.

VALUE CHAINS AND THE CASE OF APPAREL AND TEXTILE PARKS

The value chain literature continues in the tradition of work on global commodity chains (GCC) as elaborated by Gary

Gereffi (see Gereffi and Korzeniewicz 1994) (Gereffi 1996). Following on from commodity chain literature (both buyer-driven and producer-driven chains) (Gereffi 1996) (Frenkel 1999), cluster theorists are now examining the role of external linkages, such as foreign buyers, extra-local kin/ethnic investors in cluster upgrading (Schmitz and Nadvi 1999), (see also Helmsing 2001). Kaplinsky has also introduced the concept of the 'extended value chain', defined as all inter-related industries and sub-sectors participating in bringing a product or service from conception through production and delivery to the final consumer and then to disposal of the product (Kaplinsky and Morris 2001). There is a debate as to whether the long-term survival of firms requires that they move up the value chain, or whether competent upgrading of products and processes for production at lower ends of the chain is one route to increasing one's staying power (Ernst *et al.* 2001).

There is an important line of thinking within the literature on upgrading that talk about the learning inherent in close buyer-supplier relationships, in sectors from electronics and computer hardware to clothing. As an extension of this thinking, sub-contracting is considered not just a form of market guarantee but a relationship in which buyers are sufficiently 'invested' to make improving supplier capacity worth their while. Nadvi and Schmitz note the importance of user-producer interactions to enhance learning and responsive technical innovation (Nadvi and Schmitz 1998). This however is not unique to clusters and can be found in those firms we think of as 'customer-oriented', as well as buyer-driven supply chains which must respond quickly to changing tastes, as in the apparel industry for example with its six seasons per year and turnaround times of just several weeks (Gereffi 1996).[15] Value chain characteristics, such as product definition by buyers, or large competence differentials between producers and buyers, also tend to make it more likely that user-producer interactions will be structured to facilitate upgrading (Humphrey and Schmitz 2000). As an example of the use of a value chain approach within the cluster literature, Knorringa's study of the Agra footwear industry identifies the different segments of footwear producers, according to their market channels and final markets (1996). The majority of firms suffer in 'direct sales' (cheap local retail markets including auctions), while others: (i) take orders from domestic traders (mainly as sub-contractors, though a few as high-end producers for boutiques); (ii) engage in direct exports; (iii) take orders from large Indian corporations, iv. engage in indirect exports; or (v) engage in relations with larger enterprise groups in India (producing branded shoes) (Knorringa 1996). Crucially, it is only in the direct export and premium domestic markets that producers receive direct feedback on designs and make suggestions themselves (*ibid*).

It is important to recognize here that firm size growth does not guarantee improved quality of production, or a learning approach. Similarly, engagement with 'bigger' buyers such as trade houses also does not imply upgrading necessarily, as buyers may be seeking only the cheapest producers with the lowest price points among a range of substitutable suppliers. Rather, it is quality of the final product, its niche characteristics, and specifically their final markets that matter. Knorringa found that premium domestic and export buyers are in one sense dependent on quality products for their own business reputations, and thus are willing to invest in a more time-intensive learning-oriented supplier relationship (see Knorringa 1996).

As an example of projects aiming to capture gains along the textile value chain, we have the case of apparel and textile parks, now being promoted by GOI through state governments. The Andhra Pradesh state government is now actively promoting the installation of 'apparel export parks under the Centrally sponsored scheme 'Apparel Parks for Exports Scheme'. GOI is spending Rs. 320 crores on this from 2000-04 (Ministry of Textiles GOI 2002). A separate scheme for textile parks (called the Textile Centres Infrastructure Development Scheme TCIDS) is intended to upgrade infrastructure facilities at "important textile centers' (Ministry of Textiles GOI 2002) and Rs. 170 crores will be spent over the same period. This both follows from its own plans stemming from Vision 2020 planning document which calls for use of the garments and textile sector as a "growth engine" for the state, and also from central government incentives in the form of matching funding. As of August 2003, work was underway for parks at Gundla Pochampally in Nalgonda District (where 63 slots were reported to have been taken by entrepreneurs including many from the Middle East) as well as two more parks in Rayalaseema and Coastal Andhra. (Staff reporter 2003). Investment in apparel firms has been made more attractive for foreign firms as the government has allowed 100% foreign equity participation through the automatic route (with the exception of knitwear reserved for SSI) (Ministry of Textiles GOI 2002). A number of textile and apparel parks have already been sanctioned and one is also being built in Nalgonda District (though not in Pochampally itself as many had lobbied for). The apparel parks (a separate scheme) are intended to being employment to 20,000 persons (provided state governments loosen labor requirements!) and are funded on a 75-25% basis where the Center pays the majority of costs (Ministry of Textiles GOI n.d.-a). The emphasis in the parks is on infrastructure development and FDI although the National Textile Policy of 2000 does suggest that for the garment sector there be the "setting up of strong domestic retail chains to ensure easy availability of branded Indian products" (Government of India 2000, p. 11). Textile parks are to be funded by the Textile Centre Infrastructure Development scheme on a fast- track basis, outside of the regular GOI annual planning process. 'Critical components' (common effluent treatment plant, water supply and drainage, and crèche buildings for apparel units) are fully funded by the central government while the remaining items are funded on a 75-25 basis for the Center and the state respectively (Ministry of Textiles GOI n.d.-b). The stated aim of the textile parks is to "to improve infrastructure facilities at potential textile growth centers" and thus remove export bottlenecks to achieving the NTP target of US $50 billion in exports by 2010 (*ibid*). Vision 2020 seeks to employ 20 million persons in the garment industry by that date and grow textile exports to Rs. 5000 crores by 2005 and Rs. 15,000 crores by

2020 (APITCO Ltd 2002), p. 2. The 13 investment headings include just 4 that are not purely infrastructure such as roads, ports, power and water are the following: facilities for human resource development, design centers, quality testing facilities, and an exhibition hall–though these may in fact be just buildings perhaps (Ministry of Textiles GOI n.d.-b). The textile parks are intended to cover 'traditional textile centers' (as well as 'emerging powerloom clusters') across the country but interestingly of the 24 places named as examples, AP locales are not on the list.

The proposal for the textile park near Pochampally gives all the right signals, stating:

> *"The ...park will.. leverage the weaving skills...unique to handloom weavers of Pochampally-Koyyalagudem cluster and contribute to stabilizing the market for end products. [It] will focus on attracting private investment to set up value-added manufacturing facilities for readymade garments, dress materials, made-ups, furnishings and bed linens based on the handloom fabrics emanating from the weavers in the cluster"*. (APITCO Ltd. 2002), p. 1.

The wording about leveraging is particularly welcome in that it values indigenous skills, rather than casting the sector as "backward". The document also displays a regional sensibility, by listing all the clusters in the Pochampally belt that are expected to benefit from the park's demand for labor and products. In contrast, the Vision 2020 document does not talk about handlooms, but rather garments (despite AP's preeminent role in handlooms in the country). Further, the first parks in the state to be set up were apparel parks rather than the textile park now coming up in Nalgonda District.

The above discussion has focused on inter-sectoral links in the textile value chain. That said, how important is upgrading to cluster competitiveness? There is a consensus that to maintain its place in an industry over time (or improve it), a cluster must engage in continuous upgrading, at least at the process and product levels. Four different types of upgrading can be distinguished. These are: (i) process upgrading; (ii) product upgrading; (iii) functional upgrading;

and (iv) chain upgrading (Humphrey and Schmitz 2000) (Kaplinsky and Morris 2001). *Process upgrading* refers to more efficient transformation of inputs into outputs (e.g. through production system reorganization or the introduction of improved technology), while *product upgrading* involves entry into more sophisticated product lines, holding increased unit values, or improvements to existing products (ibid). *Functional upgrading* refers to firms acquiring new functions in the value chain (i.e. higher value-added activities), such as design and marketing (*ibid*).[16] *Chain upgrading* (the rarest form) involves moving to a new value chain, with the Taiwanese example of moving from radio and TV manufacture to that of laptops and cell phones (Kaplinsky and Morris 2001).

As noted earlier, value chain theorists have criticized the cluster literature for underemphasizing factors external to the cluster shaping cluster trajectories (such as input supply relations and demand conditions), and also for lack of attention to upgrading. Other authors have criticized earlier cluster studies for paying insufficient attention to learning processes (Bell and Albu 1999), or for under-emphasis of the place of clusters in international trade (see also Helmsing 2001). An attention to value chains in the handloom sector and particularly to the location of key marketer and exporter concentrations is important. Currently, handloom exporters are concentrated in the states of Tamil Nadu and to a lesser extent Delhi and Haryana. Particularly for that key production state such as Andhra Pradesh and West Bengal which have ambitious export targets, it is clear that greater emphasis must be placed on developing local export capacity, perhaps through use of exporter fora, partnership programs or even tax incentives. (Handloom Export Promotion Council (HEPC) n.d.). Gains in export capacity are a crucial step for such states to take in order to participate in functional upgrading as described earlier.

This is the sort of role the learning region approach envisions for government. Based on the learning and innovation systems research of the last decade, policy impacts have been growing since then. Formal policy efforts that seek to encourage innovation abound, in both developed and to a lesser extent developing, country contexts. A *learning region* is defined formally as a region "with an economy embedded in 'institutional thickness' and characterized by innovative activity based on localized, interactive learning and cooperation" (Asheim 1998). The learning region builds on both the idea of networks, themselves an implicit element of industrial clusters and industrial districts, in the form of worker and firm relations, as well as that of evolutionary economics, with its focus on technical and organizational innovation (Morgan 1997). Crucially, innovation is not viewed as occurring in a linear fashion but rather is interactive, social and reflective (Asheim 1998). Local and national governments then can facilitate cluster development by: (i) encouraging technological diffusion and spillover effects; (ii) training suppliers; (iii) establishing science and technology centers; and (iv) fostering "technology clubs" (sectoral combinations of users, producers, researchers and regulators who engage in collaborative learning as facilitated by public agencies) (Morgan 1997).

CONCLUSION AND POLICY IMPLICATIONS

This paper has drawn attention to some of the challenges and opportunities faced by handloom producers, their representative organizations, and government and other promoters trying to support both the sector and local economic development. A number of principles can be drawn from the discussion above. I also discuss below some illustrative policy and program interventions that might follow from these principles.

The first theme is the importance of *segregating social welfare objectives from those of growth-enhancement* for the handloom sector. In practice, this may mean a reallocation of welfare schemes to Departments such as Welfare or Labor, and a considered expansion of social policy and social protection measures for the working poor, rather than for particular occupations. Poverty analysis, including attention to labor relations and employment status is key. The second lesson is the importance of *considering the region* as a whole entity. Piecemeal approaches which divide regional sector-based economies into non-viable village units (through cooperatives, or more recently the use of MACs and sometimes even so-called 'cluster' development programs must be discarded in favor of spatial approaches which are sensitive to scale and flows along the value chain. Particular attention is drawn here to the importance of considering whether 'belts' of handloom (or other) clusters are in existence in particular regions of the state. Strategic interventions at nodal points (e.g. marketing centers) may be a better use of government resources, in contrast to valiant attempts to cover all districts with a new intervention simultaneously and thereby diluting the quality of the intervention at any one place.[17]

Thirdly, it is important to *look outside the state* apparatus by considering the range of possible non-state actors and allies. Administrative solutions should be used with extreme caution as these are most likely to fade as soon as the funds do. Networked approaches and greater integration with the private sector in particular may be attempted instead. Notably, this approach is supported in the National Textile Policy of 2000 document itself which calls for government actors to ensure "Active cooperation and partnership of the State governments, financial institutions, entrepreneurs, farmers and NGOs' in fulfilling NTP objectives, but use of such non-state actors to date has been limited (Government of India 2000, p. 3). Here I would also emphasize the importance of working with those cluster actors outside the cooperative such as master weavers' associations and especially weavers' associations (these are also sometimes federated at the area, district or state level). These voluntary and functioning bodies play important roles in the clusters of norm-setting and dispute resolution. In this context, it is also important to recognize the potential role of MACs which unfortunately to date is already becoming sullied and politicized, perhaps inevitably as they are a public funds-dispersal (and product procurement) mechanism. Further, revision of MAC implementation guidelines may be called for. In this vein of considering non-state actors, I also draw attention to the importance of working with private buyers to understand market trends, and perhaps conduct joint market surveys.

Finally, there is a need to look at the *longer-term integration of the textile and garment industry* in India, and to support synergies across the various sub-sectors and up and down the value chain. The model should not be one of 'modernization and industrialization' wherein traditional technologies such as the handloom are expected to disappear eventually. Rather, strategic upgradation can be supported (for example in pre-loom process machinery such as warping machines that reduce women's work and double the speed of that pre-loom processing stage; or use of CAD design). Design inputs remain critical for the sector, as do institutional means of accessing new designs (whether through development of local information clearinghouses, provision of training or other methods). The IIHT training program (3-year diplomas on handloom technology offered on scholarship to weavers' children) have been particularly successful in imparting skills, access to employment in other sectors of the textile industry, and the return of skills and market links to the home cluster. Further use might be made of such groups of local IIHT graduates in the form of regular networking fora, as well as arrangement for formal information sharing and para-training in the clusters themselves. Marketing innovations, such as branding, product diversification (e.g. the case in Tamil Nadu where consumers can design and order their own saris for purchase with the help of CAD software) will remain key.

The common theme here is that universal, one-size-fits-all solutions are not solutions at all. Linkages and synergistic effects are not guaranteed simply through fund allocation and expenditure. Rather, in a learning region approach, local actors and the government must work together for custom-made and institutionalized responses to the growing challenges facing textile producers in a global market place.

NOTES

1. The national Planning Commission commissioned a study on the Growth and Prospects of the Handloom Sector, which focused on Andhra Pradesh state (Niranjana and Vinayan 2001). Further, the Export-Import Bank of India recently conducted a study on

the Indian handloom sector (see EXIM Bank 2000). This interest in a "low-technology" sector stands in contrast to the other sectors chosen for EXIM Bank attention which have all been in the realm of high technology, such as software.

2. Negative trends here are explained by the MoT as a decline in demand from importing countries such as the US and EU due to economic slowdown.
3. The bordered sari in particular is made using several shuttles simultaneously during production, a process which would slow down powerlooms should they try to replicate it (Liebl and Roy 2000). In addition, there are several hand-woven features of handloom products that are also unique to that production process, such as the "tie and dye" technique where hanks of yarn are banded by elastics, dyed in multiple colors to form patterns, and then woven by hand to form geometric shapes on the cloth with each individual thread painstakingly adjusted (in the case of weft designs) after each shuttle throw until the pre-dyed portion edges line up to form sharp borders for each pattern.
4. Tamil Nadu and West Bengal came first and second with regard to commercial production, with 22.54 per cent and 14.82 per cent of non-household units respectively (NCAER 1998).
5. Notably, the Report on the Joint Census of Handlooms and Textiles notes that overall handloom productivity at the national level has decreased (despite most individual states registering increases) because the three chief handloom states (i.e. Uttar Pradesh, West Bengal and Tamil Nadu which accounted for 57 per cent of handloom production in 1987-88) have reduced their production levels by 29 per cent in 1995-96 (NCAER 1998).
6. Engaged in weaving directly on the loom.
7. Engaged in yarn winding for warp; winding of pirns for weft; weft preparation on the loom; and sizing of yarn
8. From both household and non-household units (other categories refer only to household units).
9. Engaged in yarn dyeing; post-loom activities; made-up production etc.
10. While most weavers in AP are male (in contrast say to the Northeast of the country), women's labor in the handloom sector (as pre-loom process workers, working the same number of hours as men) has been overlooked by many policymakers. Even in

AP, there is considerable variation among regions, with Coastal Andhra said to have more women weaving on the loom. In addition to gender considerations, I observed age differences, where young men for example are preferred for both waged weaving jobs in-house and the remunerative training in tie and dye work (marking of warp etc). Weavers interviewed noted that age plays a particularly important role in access to work in cotton handlooms (more than silk) as more physical strength is required to move the shuttle and frame is more in cotton weaving.

11. Standing has elaborated a range of gradations of labor status (from slave to employer) with varied levels of both control over resources, and effect of labor control (including economic and extra-economic forces, both direct and indirect nature) (2000). The resources ("aspects") over which one may have greater or lesser degrees of control include the following: land; tools; labor power (self); work (time, effort, intensity); raw materials; output; proceeds of output; and skills (Standing 2000: p. 11). He notes that while various labor statuses can be arranged in a rough order of desirability, such as where individuals are less subject to negative economic and extra-economic forces, and have greater control over resources (including e.g. own labor power, work time, output and its proceeds, and skills), most gradations of labor status still combine positive and negative conditions. Standing's typology identifies approximately 20 main categories of labor status, with "artisan", "outworker", "wage worker", "family worker", "apprentice", "cooperative worker", "merchant", and "employer" being the most applicable to the handloom sector (2000).

12. Cooperative figures include 35 working cooperatives and 10 dormant ones.

13. Tellingly when this large group of 'new' settlers (some who had been there for as long as 20 years) tried to form a separate cooperative (in cotton, as they could not form a second silk cooperative in the same village), the cooperative application was opposed at the village level and then blocked by DHT administrators I was told. [The MAC was their third, and finally successful, attempt to join/form a cooperative and found 200 members paying their share capital and joining. In the first attempt to join the local silk coop, 30 members were joined en masse through the pressure of a local Communist party representative, the remainder (who had paid a deposit to join) were summarily blocked].

14. Trade-Related Aspects of Intellectual Property Rights (a WTO trade agreement).
15. Taking a longer-term horizon, however, the interests of the producer households (owner-operated firms, or what is known in India as own-account enterprises or OAEs) and the cluster converge again down the road in that those clusters that do not upgrade eventually decline and even fail, leading to firm closure and job loss.
16. In the handloom sector, the relevant functions in the value chain include yarn preparation (carding, washing, dyeing, sizing, reeling, gumming); warping (twisting thread); weaving; finishing; freight/handling; design; wholesaling; marketing and advertising; and retailing).
17. An interesting initiative in Andhra Pradesh by Oxfam GB should be mentioned here as it combines both attention to the region, and to links along the value chain. Recognizing that yarn supply is a major expenditure and bottleneck for poor producers and that AP while a very large cotton-producing state currently gets most of its cotton spun in mills outside the state (thereby raising cotton yarn prices), Oxfam is working with organic cotton farmers, a local appropriate technology spinning machine group, and weavers and buyers interested in organic materials (including vegetable dyed products) to create a continuous localized supply and marketing chain (Nishant Pandey, personal communication).

REFERENCES

Abraham, Thomas P. (2003), Baleing Out? And How. *Economic Times,* 16 April.

Anon (2003), Air Hostesses to Don Designs from APCO. *BusinessLine India,* July 24.

APITCO Ltd. (2002), *Project Report on Textile Park at Pochampalle-Nalgonda District Andhra Pradesh-Prepared for Development Commissioner Apparel Export Parks (Government of Andhra Pradesh).* Hyderabad: APITCO Ltd.

Asheim, Bjorn, and P. Cooke (1999), Local Learning and Interactive Innovation Networks in a Global Economy. In *Making Connections: Technological Learning and Regional Economic Change,* edited by E. Malecki and P. Oinas. Aldershot UK: Ashgate Publishing.

Asheim, Bjorn T. (1998), Learning Regions as Development Coalitions: Partnerships as Governance in European Workfare States? Paper presented at the Second European Urban and Regional Studies Conference on 'Culture, Place and Space in Contemporary Europe', University of Durham UK, Sept. 17-20.

Assistant Director-Handlooms and Textiles Nalgonda District. 2003a. *Developmental and Welfare Measures Taken Up by the Government to Solve the Problems of the Handloom and Powerloom Weavers of Nalgonda District During 2002-03*. Nalgonda-AP India,: Department of Handlooms and Textiles GoAP.

Assistant Director-Handlooms and Textiles Nalgonda District. 2003b. *Impact of Deen Dayal Hathkargha Prostahana Yojana on Ikkat Handlooms in Nalgonda*. Nalgonda-AP India: Department of Handlooms and Textiles GoAP.

Assomull, Sujata (2003), Under the Hammer. *Business India*, 138-9.

Bell, Martin, and Michael Albu (1999), Knowledge Systems and Technological Dynamism in Industrial Clusters in Developing Countries. *World Development*, 27 (9):1715-1734.

Cawthorne, Pamela M. (1995), Of Networks and Markets: the Rise and Fall of a South India Form: the Example of Tirrupur's Cotton Knitwear Industry. *World Development*, 23 (1):43-56.

Chowdhury, Souvik (2003), Crafting a New Face. *The Hindu*, 24 June.

Cooke, Philip and Kevin Morgan (1998), *The Associational Economy: Firms, Regions and Innovation*. Oxford: Oxford UP.

Department of Handlooms and Textiles GoAP (2003), *Performance Budget of Handlooms and Textiles Department,*. Hyderabad, India: GoAP.

Ernst, Dieter (2000), *Global Production Networks and the Changing Geography of Innovation Systems: Implications for Developing Countries*. Vol. No. 9, November, *East -West Center Working Paper (Economic Series)*. Honolulu: East-West Center.

Ernst, Dieter, Paolo Guerrieri, Simona Iammarino, and Carlo Pietrobelli (2001), New Challenges for Industrial Clusters and Districts: Global Production Networks and Knowledge Diffusion. In *Global Challenge to Industrial Districts: Small and Medium-Sized Enterprises in Italy and Taiwan*, edited by P. Guerrieri, S. Iammarino and C. Pietrobelli. Cheltenham UK: Edward Elgar.

EXIM Bank (2000), *Indian Handloom: A Sector Study*. Vol. 79, *Occasional Paper*.

Fink, Carsten, and Beata K. Smarzynska (2002), Trademarks, Geographical Indications and Developing Countries. In *Development, Trade and the WTO: A Handbook*, edited by B. Hoekman, A. Mattoo and P. English. Washington DC: World Bank.

Frenkel, Stephen J. (1999), Globalization, Athletic Footwear Commodity Chains and Employment Relations in Southern China.

Gereffi, Gary (1996), Global Commodity Chains: New Forms of Coordination and Control Among Nations and Firms in International Industries. *Competition and Change*, 4:427-439.

Gereffi, Gary, and M. Korzeniewicz, eds. (1994), *Commodity Chains and Global Capitalism*. London: Praeger Publishing.

Gereffi, Gary, and Olga Memedovic (2003), *The Global Apparel Value Chain: What Prospects for Upgrading by Developing Countries?* Vienna: United Nations Industrial Development Organization (UNIDO).

Government of India (2000), *National Textile Policy 2000*. New Delhi, GOI.

Guerrieri, Paolo, and Carlo Pietrobelli (2001), Models of Industrial Clusters' Evolution and Changes in Technological Regimes. In *The Global Challenge to Industrial Districts: Small and Medium-Sized Enterprises in Italy*, edited by P. Guerrieri, S. Iammarino and C. Pietrobelli. Cheltenham UK: Edward Elgar.

Handloom Export Promotion Council (HEPC). n.d. *Status Report of Cotton Handloom Exports and Strategy for Improving Cotton Handloom Exports*,. Chennai India,: HEPC.

Helmsing, A.H.J. (2001), Externalities, Learning and Governance: New Perspectives on Local Economic Development. *Development and Change*, 32:277-308.

Humphrey, John (1995), Industrial Reorganization in Developing Countries: From Models to Trajectories. *World Development*, 23 (1):149-162.

Humphrey, John, and Hubert Schmitz (1996), The Triple C Approach to Local Industrial Policy. *World Development* 24 (12):1859-1877.

Humphrey, John, and Hubert Schmitz (2000), *Governance and Upgrading: Linking Industrial Cluster and Global Value Chain Research*. Vol. 120, *IDS Working Paper*. Brighton UK: IDS Sussex.

Hussain, Abid (1997), *Report of the Expert Committee on Small Enterprises*. New Delhi, Ministry of Industry, Government of India

NCAER.

Kaplinsky, .Raphael and Mike Morris (2001), *A Handbook for Value Chain Research*. Brighton UK: IDS Sussex.

Kathuria, Sanjay and Anjali Bhardwaj (1998), *Export Quotas and Policy Constraints in the Indian Textile and Garment Industries*. Vol. WPS 2012, *Policy Research Working Paper*. Washington DC: World Bank.

Kheir-el-Din, Hanaa (2002), Implementing the Agreement on Textiles and Clothing. In *Development, Trade and the WTO: A Handbook*, edited by B. Hoekman, A. Mattoo and P. English. Washington DC: World Bank.

Knorringa, Peter (1999), Agra: An Old Cluster Facing the New Competition. *World Development* 27 (9):1587-1604.

Kopresachari, H. (n.d.), *Action Plan for Capacity-Building of Handloom Textile SMEs in Pochampally Cluster, National Programme for Capacity Building of Textile SMEs: A Cluster-Based Approach*. Hyderabad: Textiles Committee-GOI Ministry of Textiles.

Lanjouw, Peter (1999), *The Rural Non-Farm Sector: A Note on Policy Options-(Draft)*. Washington DC: World Bank.

Liebl, Maureen and Tirthankar Roy (2002), *Handmade in India: Preliminary Analysis of Crafts Producers and Crafts Production in India: Issues, Initiatives, Interventions: A Report prepared for the Policy Sciences Center, Inc. as part of the "Multi-Country Crafts Study" Project* World Bank, 2000 [cited 21 December 2002]. Available from *www.worldbank.org*.

Lundvall, Bengt-Ake, ed. (1992), *National Systems of Innovation: Towards a Theory of Innovation and Interactive Learning*. London: Pinter Publishers.

Maskus, Keith (2000), Strengthening Intellectual Property Rights in Lebanon. In *Catching Up With the Competition: Trade Opportunities and Challenges for Arab Countries*, edited by B. Hoekman and J. Zarrouk. Ann Arbor: University of Michigan Press.

Ministry of Textiles GOI (2002), *Annual Report 2001-02*. New Delhi, GOI.

Ministry of Textiles GOI (n.d.-a), *Guidelines for Establishment of Apparel Parks for Exports*. New Delhi, GOI.

Ministry of Textiles GOI. (n.d.-b), *Guidelines for Establishment of the Revised Textile Centres Infrastructure Development Scheme (TCIDS)*, New Delhi, GOI.

Mooij, Jos, and S. Mahendra Dev (2002), *Social Sector Priorities: An Analysis of Budgets and Expenditures in India in the 1990s*. Vol. 164, *IDS Working Paper*, Brighton: IDS Sussex.

Morgan, Kevin (1997), The Learning Region: Institutions, Innovation and Regional Renewal. *Regional Studies*, 31 (5):491-503.

Mukund, Kanakalatha, and B. Syama Sundari (2001), *Traditional Industry in the New Market Economy: The Cotton Handlooms of Andhra Pradesh*. New Delhi, Sage Publications.

Nadvi, Khalid (1999), Collective Efficiency and Collective Failure: the Response of the Sialkot Surgical Instrument Industry Cluster to Global Quality Pressures. *World Development*, 27 (9):1605-1626.

Nadvi, Khalid, and Hubert Schmitz (1998), Industrial Clusters in Less Developed Countries: Review of Experiences and Research Agenda. In *Decentralized Production in India: Industrial Districts, Flexible Specialization and Employment*, edited by P. Cadene and M. Holmstrom. New Delhi, Sage Publications.

Naik, Gopal, Sudhir Kumar Jain, and Santosh Kumar Singh (2001), *Econometric Modelling of the Indian Cotton Textile Industry*. New Delhi: Oxford and IBH Publishing Co.

Nair, K. Rajendran (n.d), *Handloom Exports Beyond 2002*. Chennai, India: Handloom Export Promotion Council (HEPC)-Ministry of Textiles Government of India.

NCAER (1998), *Report of Joint Census of Handlooms and Powerlooms 1995 sponsored by Development Commissioner (Handlooms)-Ministry of Textiles*. New Delhi, NCAER and Ministry of Textiles.

Niranjana, Seemanthani, and Soumya Vinayan (2001), *Report on the Growth and Prospects of the Handloom Industry: Study Commissioned by the Planning Commission*. Edited by Planning Commission GOI. New Delhi: Government of India (GOI),.

Penna, Frank J., and Coenraad J. Visser (2002), Cultural Industries and Intellectual Property Rights. In *Development, Trade and the WTO: A Handbook*, edited by B. Hoekman, A. Mattoo and P. English. Washington DC: World Bank.

Pietrobelli, Carlo (1998), The Socio-Economic Foundations of Competitiveness: An Econometric Analysis of Italian Industrial Districts. *Industry and Innovation*, 5 (2):139-155.

PTI Wire Report (2003), Textile Sector's Excise Norms Simplified. *Economic Times*, 4 April.

Rabellotti, Roberta (1999), Recovery of a Mexican Cluster: Devaluation Bonanza or Collective Efficiency? *World Development*, 27 (9):1571-1585.

Raghu, Sunil (2003), Interview-Sanjay Lalbhai-India Can Dominate the Textile Market. *Economic Times*, 22 April.

Roy, Tirthankar (1998), Development or Distortion: Powerlooms in India 1950-1997. *Economic and Political Weekly*, 33 (16).

Schmitz, Hubert (1995), Small Shoemakers and Fordist Giants: Tales of a Supercluster. *World Development*, 23 (1):9-28.

Schmitz, Hubert and Khalid Nadvi (1999), Clustering and Industrialization: An Introduction. *World Development*, 27 (9):1503-1514.

Staff Reporter (2003), Two More Apparel Export Parks to be Set Up. *The Hindu*, 9 August.

Storper, Michael (1995), The Resurgence of Regional Economics, Ten Years Later: The Region as a Nexus of Untraded Interdependencies. *European Urban and Regional Studies*, 2 (3):191-221.

Tendler, Judith (2002), Small Firms, the Informal Sector, and the Devil's Deal. *IDS Bulletin*, 33 (3).

Tendler, Judith, and Monica Amorim (1996), Small Firms and Their Helpers: Lessons in Demand. *World Development*, 24 (3):407-426.

Tewari, Meenu (1998), The State and the Shaping of the Conditions of Accumulation in Ludhiana's Industrial Regime: An Historical Interpretation. In *Decentralized Production in India: Industrial Districts, Flexible Specialization and Employment*, edited by P. Cadene and M. Holmstrom. New Delhi, Sage Publications.

5

ENTREPRENEURSHIP DEVELOPMENT THROUGH COOPERATIVES:AN EXPERIENCE OF WOMEN DAIRY PROJECT IN RAJASTHAN

V. M. Rao

STATUS OF WOMEN

The hand that rocks the cradle rules the world is a famous saying that speaks volumes about the strength and capabilities of women. They constitute half of global population, and 1/3rd of labour force, but receive only 1/10th of world income, and own less than 1% of the world's property. As per 2001 census, women account for 495.74 millions, and represent 48.3% of India's total population. Thus, they are a vital part of our economy too constituting one-third of the national labour force. Despite progress in several key indicators, a gender analysis demonstrates that women continue to be relatively disadvantaged in matters of survival, health, nutrition, literacy, and productivity. Further, more than 90% of rural women are unskilled, restricting them to low paid occupations. Women generally have no control over land and other productive assets, which largely excludes them from access to institutional credit. Further, agricultural wages for women are, on an average, 30-50% less than those for men. Though they work for longer hours under inhospitable conditions, their participation in decision making process is less than desirable.

INTERVENTIONS BY THE GOVERNMENT

Bringing women out of house and enabling them to join main stream of national life was certainly a difficult task before independence. Government of India has realized existing disparities and a number of initiatives were taken up for emancipation of women. Some of the steps worth mentioning include setting up of CSWB (1953), declaring 1975-85 as women's decade, DWCRA (1982), Department of Women and Child Development (1985), National Commission for Women (1992), declaring 2001 as women's empowerment year, and drafting a national policy for empowerment of women (2001).

Based on the prescriptions of national policy for empowerment for women, Tenth Five Year Plan (2002-07) proposed to adopt a sector specific three fold strategy for empowering women. They include (a) social empowerment to create an enabling environment through various affirmative developmental policies and programs for development of women besides providing them easy and equal access to all the basic minimum services so as to enable them to realize their full potentials, (b) economic empowerment to ensure provision of training, employment and income generation activities with both forward and backward linkages with the ultimate objective of making all potential women economically independent and self reliant, and (c) gender justice to eliminate all forms of gender discrimination and thus, allow women to enjoy not only the de-jure but also the de-facto rights and fundamental freedom on par with men in all spheres (political, economic, social, civil, cultural, etc.) (Planning commission, 2003).

WOMEN IN DAIRYING

Cattle rearing and dairying are vocations that have been traditionally centered on women, with the latter, estimated to account for as much as 85% of India's animal husbandry. On an average, a woman with a milch animal spends more than two-and-a half hours daily in its feeding, watering, cleaning, milking, and grazing, often the responsibility of children under their mother's keen supervision, consumes additional time and energy (Rao, 2000, Rao, 2003, Rao, 2003 a, 2003 b, and 2003 c). The country's 77000 DCSs pump in over Rs. 3500 crores every year to its 10 million odd farmer members, but only 20% of these members comprise women (NDDB, 2003). Women dairy project (WDP) was launched in 1986 as part of the Support to Training and Employment Program for women (STEP) under the Department of Women and Child Development, Ministry of Human Resources Development, Government of India. It aims at increasing self reliance and autonomy of women by enhancing productivity and enabling them to take up income generation activities. Target group covered under STEP[1] program includes marginalized, asset less rural women, and urban poor (for more details on STEP, see Rao 2003). An attempt is made in this paper (a) to provide a brief review of progress of WDP in Rajasthan[2], (b) to evaluate performance of WDCSs *vis-à-vis* mixed gender dairy cooperative societies (GDCSs), and (c) to document life histories of few women entrepreneurs.

METHODOLOGY

Animal husbandry has been an integral part of Rajasthan's economy. The state has been a major beneficiary under WDP. Phase I of WDP was implemented in Ajmer, Banswara, Bharatpur, Bikaner, Jaipur, Jodhpur, and Pali. Six WDCSs/milk unions were selected on the basis of membership, pourers, procurement, input services provided, involvement of women in society's activities, etc. Thus, in all 42 WDCSs were randomly drawn from the above milk unions. Equal number of GDCSs was also selected with similar age, socio-economic background, and agro-climatic conditions so as to make meaningful comparisons. Mean differences were tested with "T' statistics. Secondary data were also collected from RCDF, and concerned milk unions during October-December, 2002.

PROGRESS OF WDP IN RAJASTHAN

Rajasthan Cooperative Dairy Federation (RCDF) is the nodal agency for planning and implementation of dairy cooperatives on Anand pattern in the state. Since its inception in 1977, RCDF contributed substantially for the growth of dairying by providing both backward and forward linkages. It has 16 milk unions with over 3000 functional DCSs, and 3.70 producer members. Average procurement of federation is 4.2 lakh kgs./ day with over 50% capacity utilization (for more details, see Rao, 2003). Like other dairy federations, RCDF too submitted a proposal to implement women dairy project in 1990. The project mainly aimed at overall development of rural women by way of income generation through dairy cooperatives, literacy, rural health, and sanitation, awareness generation through training and education. Specific objectives of the project, among others, were (a) to bring about economic equality and social justice by focussing attention on and directing training towards poor women, (b) to enable active participation of poor SC/ST rural women in their own village economy, (c) to provide employment for poor rural women through activities linked with income generation, (d) to generate grassroot level leadership, and (e) to empower women to be able to move into positions of decision making and power (RCDF, 1990).

As mentioned earlier, WDP (phase I) was taken up in Ajmer, Banswara, Bharatpur, Bikaner, Jaipur, Jodhpur, and Pali, and was sanctioned in February, 1991 for three years (1991-92 to 1993-94). Subsequently, Government of India sanctioned five more phases of WDP in the state. Financial support was provided for (1) organisation of WDCSs, (2) support to women members, (3) animal health cover and breeding, (4) fodder production, (5) field organisation, (6) training, (7) general awareness, cooperative education, motivation, and literacy, (8) supervision, monitoring and administration, (9) propulsion, MIS, and office automisation, and (10) workshops and information dissemination.

Table 1 provides details on phase-wise unions covered, money received from ministry, and contribution of RCDF. A close examination of above tables reveals that (a) there are wide variations between amounts sanctioned and released by ministry, (b) federation and unions failed to expend the entire amount released by ministry on time, and (c) contribution of

Table 1
Expenditure (Rs. crores) on Various Phases of WDP in Rajasthan

Phase	Period	Unions covered	Government of India			
			Sanctioned	*Released*	*Expenditure*	*Contribution of RCDF*
I	1992-94	Ajmer, Banswara, Bharatpur, Bikaner, Jaipur, Jodhpur and Pali	4.57	4.09	3.22	0.71
II	1993-95	Ajmer, Banswara, Bharatpur, Bikaner, Jaipur, Jodhpur, and Pali	5.48	3.15	1.58	
			0.67			
III	1994-96	Bilwara, and Sikar	3.45	1.54	1.20	0.26
IV	1995-97	Udaipur	0.62	0.19	0.42	0.01
V	1995-97	Churu	0.62	0.19	01.6	0.06
VI	1996-98	Ajmer, Banswara, Sriganganagar, Bikaner, Jaipur, Jodhpur, and Pali	6.08	5.26	4.47	0.96

Source: Records of RCDF.

link agency (RCDF and unions) is much higher than what was proposed in the ministry's circular. In all, against a sanctioned amount of Rs. 22.80 crore, ministry released Rs. 14.42 crore. As a result of the efforts made by federation, unions, and ministry, WDCSs organized in the state increased from 362 in 1994-95 to 1163 by 2001-02, and that of women membership increased from 0.34 lakh to 0.80 lakh. These WDCSs constitute 20% of total DCSs, and contribute 19% of total milk procurement of RCDF (2002).

A COMPARISON OF WDCSS AND GDCSS

Performance of a commercial organisation is generally measured in terms of financial indicators, growth, well being of staff, system viability and adoptability, and good corporate citizenship (Steers, 1975). However, organisations working primarily for the welfare of rural people like dairy cooperatives cannot be evaluated using these criteria alone. Shah (1990) identified service to members, financial indicators, autonomy and self reliance, impact on member incomes, strategies for viability and growth, and leadership and management as parameters of success. More details on evaluation of dairy cooperatives can be seen from Rao (2000). In the light of above facts, performance of WDCSs and GDCSs is evaluated (Table 2). Both average membership/DCS, and pourers are significantly higher in WDCSs. Average membership, at the state level, is worked out as 48 of which 32 are pourers. Procurement, amount paid to producers, and net profits are much higher in WDCSs compared to GDCSs. Net profit as percentage of amount paid to producers is almost two times higher in WDCSs. On the top of it, quantity of savour[3] milk supplied is on higher side in GDCSs. High percentage of pourers, net profit, and relatively less quantity of savour milk indicate women members' loyalty towards society. All the indicators identified, except membership, are significant at 1% level of significance. Thus, WDCSs relatively performed well and established their superiority over GDCSs[4]. Apart from procurement and regular payment, these societies provide number of technical inputs (Table 3). They include cattle feed,

Table 2
Physical and Financial Performance of Selected Dairy Societies, 2000-02

Indicator	*WDCSs (n=42)*	*GDCSs (n=42)*	*Overall (n=84)*	*'t' value*
Membership	52	43	48	1.86 *
Pourers	41	22	32	6.53 **
Procurement(lakh litres/year)	29319	13456	21388	15.78 **
Amount paid to producers (Rs. lakhs)	2.49	1.08	1.79	22.54 **
Sour milk (litres/year)	205	528	367	17.35 **
Net profit (Rs./annum)	8731	2035	5383	32.15 **

*significant at 5% level ,**significant at 1% level.

Source: Records of the societies.

Table 3
Progress in Technical Inputs Supplied by Selected Dairy Societies, 2000-02

Indicator	*WDCSs*	*GDCSs*	*Overall*	*'t' value*
Cattle feed (tonnes/annum)	6.22	2.10	4.16	46.78 **
AIs performed	554	325	440	20.96 **
Animals conceived	299	140	220	23.42 **
First aid cases treated	356	285	321	8.75 **
Mineral mixture (kgs.)	845	256	551	35.44 **
Fodder seeds (kgs.)	36	24	30	03.25 **
Members trained	34	5	20	96.44 **

**significant at 1% level,

Source: Records of the societies.

artificial insemination, health care, mineral mixture, fodder seeds, and training to members. WDCS once again re-affirmed their superiority over GDCSs. There has been a provision in the STEP to provide training programs both at village and training centre for ordinary members, committee members, secretary, tester, etc. (Table 4). Approximately 20% of the total budget is spent on training programs. As evident from Table 3 about 34 members, on an average, were trained in WDCSs while it is 5 in GDCSs. Distribution of economic returns/litre of milk supplied is provided in Table 5. Average base price is Rs. 8.49/litre in WDCSs, and Rs. 8.03/litre in GDCSs. This difference in base price could be due to quality of milk supplied in terms of fat and SNF. Apart from the base price, union also ploughs back a portion of its profit to members as 'union's price difference' which is same (11 paise/litre) in both categories. Apart from the union's price difference, societies also pay a portion of their profits in the form of 'society's price difference'. As expected, GDCSs paid 41% of WDCSs price difference. In all, WDCSs paid Rs. 8.90/litre of milk while GDCSs paid Rs. 8.28. Thus, once again WDCSs performed better than GDCSs.

Table 4
Training Programs Organised Under STEP

At the training centre	*At field level*
• Managing committee training program	• Women education program
• Secretary training on society management	• Health awareness program
• AI worker training	• Legal literacy program
• First aid training	• Male orientation program
• Dairy and animal management training	• Women MC members seminar
• Training on AH and fodder development	• Chairpersons orientation program
• Farmer induction program	• Medium functionaries training/ workshop
	• Trainers training program
	• Health worker (mid-wife) crèche management training
	• Dairy animal management program
	• Women education program
	• Women farmers induction program
	• Women farmers orientation program
	• Program on income generation activities

Source: Records of the societies.

Based on Tables 2 to 5, an attempt is made to calculate productivity indicators (% of pourers to total members, procurement/pourer member/annum, savour milk as percentage of total procurement, cattle feed sold/litre milk procured, rate of conception in AI, etc) for both categories of societies under observation (Table 6). GDCSs, once again, under performed in all the indicators studied. Except cost of procurement[5], all productivity measures studied are significant at 1 % level. Member's participation in society's activities too provided similar picture (Table 7). Invariably, women participated more compared to their counterparts in GDCSs. Above findings have shown that WDCSs have consistently and significantly performed better than GDCSs.

Table 5
Distribution of Returns/litre of Milk (Rupees), 2000-02

Indicator	*WDCSs*	*GDCSs*	*Overall*
Average base price	8.49	8.03	8.26
Union's price difference	0.11	0.11	0.11
Society's price difference	0.22	0.09	0.15
Bonus	0.08	0.05	0.07
Total returns	8.90	8.28	8.59

Source: Records of the societies.

Table 6
Productivity of Selected Dairy Societies, 2000-02

Particulars	*WDCSs*	*GDCSs*	*Overall*	*"t" value*
% of pourers	79	51	67	5.36 **
Procurement/ pourer member/ annum (litres)	715	611	663	5.78 **
Sour milk as % of total procurement	0.70	3.92	2.31	15.39 **
Cost of procurement (Rs./litre)	0.42	0.54	0.48	01.54
Net returns (Rs./litre)	8.90	8.28	8.59	2.05 **
Cattle feed sold/litre of milk procured (grams)	212	156	184	3.23 **
Rate of conception in AI (%)	54	43	49	2.75 **

**significant at 1% level
Source: Records of the societies.

Table 7
Members Participation in Society's Activities, 2000-02

Indicator	*WDSs*	*GDCSs*	*Overall*
AGMs conducted	3	2	2.5
Attendance in AGMs (%)	62	45	53
Committee meetings conducted/annum	8	4	6
Attendance in committee meetings (%)	77.8	55.6	66.7
Members purchased cattle feed (%)	85	78	81
Members availed AI (%)	82	72	77
Members availed mineral mixture (%)	25	15	20

Source: Records of the societies.

LIFE HISTORIES

Brief histories of three women entrepreneurs[6] are provided in following section. Selection is based on responses during interviews, intensity of problems faced, family background, level of awareness, involvement in society's activities, etc. Such brief histories would enable us to understand socio-economic background of respondents, and transformation taken place due to WDCSs.

SMT. BHAURI DEVI

Frail, fair complexioned, wizened, and illiterate Bhauri Devi belongs to Ajmer union. She hails from a conservative Rajput community. Prior to organising WDCS in the village, she had no opportunity to interact with neighbors. When attempts were made to have WDCS, Bhauri Devi's husband took interest and mobilized women. Being a land lord in the village, her name was proposed for chairperson. She had neither interest nor inclination for this. However, due to husband's pressure, she reluctantly accepted. Soon after taking charge, she attended two orientation programs at the village followed by farmers induction program at Anand. Being a chairperson, she was forced to interact with route supervisor, women extension worker, veterinary doctor, and other officials of the union. Over a period of five years, Bhauri Devi developed expertise in management of WDCS. With increased popularity, she contested for ward member, and now aiming at panchayat president. During long tenure as chairperson, Bhauri mobilised women and brought pressure on district collector to stop transfer of a school teacher from their village. She also took lead in approaching RDO for vacating land occupied by a villager, and the same was used for construction of society building. These women also made fair price shop dealer to open shop regularly and distribute prescribed quantities. Due to these actions, she is popularly known as 'Netaji' in the village. According to her 'a strong leader must discriminate between right and wrong before taking any action. Being woman in a male dominated society, she has had its strange moments. She opined that 'it is unrealistic not to expect obstacles, but stick to fight when hardest hit. There is always a better way to do something. It is up to you to explore the possibilities', asserts the lady. During one of the training programs attended, Bhauri Devi came to know about degradation of soil caused by excessive usage of chemical fertilizers, and toxic effects of pesticides. Since then she has been planning to go for organic farming, and vermi-composting.

SMT. JAYANTI DEVI

Mother of two and wife to a farmer cum petty trader, Jayanti Devi hails from Pali district. She studied upto 10th standard and married at the age of 15. Like any other Indian rural woman, she is orthodox and God fearing with purdha. She had just come to her husband's house when villagers were planning to organize WDCS. In-laws discouraged her to take up a job of secretary. However, encouraged by husband she attended a 30 days training program in testing, and maintenance of records at Jaipur. There were difficulties initially for a new bride to work openly in the village. However, due to passage of time villagers internalized the facts. Jayanti is considered to be an efficient secretary in the district and has been maintaining all the dozen records regularly on her own. She promptly conducts monthly management committee meetings. Apart from procuring milk, she also sells cattle feed, ghee, and fodder seeds which contributed to salary.

Recognizing need for provision shop in the village, Jayanti Devi started a grocery. She provides items on credit to members and deducts the same from their milk bills. Her husband has been supportive in all these efforts. She attends all milk route meetings, and brings to the notice of officials regarding difference in quantity, fat, and SNF. Differences, if any, are attended to by the officials on time. She has a saving of Rs. 23500 in SBI. According to her, 'initiative knows no gender. All it takes is imagination backed by positivity'. Forty-two years old lady secretary is one such initiator. She believes that 'women are better equipped to deal with rough times. Management and decision making skills come naturally to a women. After all, women is the one who keeps home together, and looks into every member's welfare'.

SMT. BHANWARI DEVI

Smt. Bhanwari belongs to backward caste community, and studied up to 9th standard. She has a son and daughter, and currently staying in her natal village due to sudden demise of husband. Her husband worked as a mechanic in a nearby town, and encouraged her to be a lady inseminator. In those days, lady inseminator was unheard and unthinkable. She had undergone a training program for 35 days in first aid, and artificial insemination. She performs, on an average, 65 AIs, and 25 first aid cases and earns about Rs. 2000/month. Interactions with union's officials, outsiders, and villagers increased her awareness. Her social status too increased. Society accepted her services and is popularly known as doctor. Rate of conception is 50 to 60% which is high by any standard. She has a moped, telephone, and doing reasonably good business. Smt. Bhanwari was also instrumental in starting a SHG.

SUMMARY AND CONCLUSIONS

Progress of WDP in Rajasthan, performance of selected WDCSs, and three live examples described above show that seeds of success are available everywhere. Real need is to provide water, fertilizer, devotion, and cultivation of personal attention. Women would not have succeeded in such risky activities if they had not been clever entrepreneurs. A new breed of women entrepreneurs is emerging from rural India, and they are breaking gender stereo-typing. Women overcame male dominance, suppression, and intimidation. Their priorities and views are now considered, and given due attention in the village. WDCSs are acting as stepping stone to women for climbing political ladder.

NOTES

1. The author has been associated with conducting evaluation of WDPs organised under STEP in the states of Andhra Pradesh, Bihar, Karnataka, Orissa, and Rajasthan.

2. A number of state level dairy federations have been organising WDCSs with the help of assistance received from the ministry. Rajasthan Cooperative Dairy Federation (RCDF) is one among them. RCDF so far implemented six phases of WDP in the state (more details on progress of WDP in Rajasthan are provided in the ensuing section).
3. Milk is highly perishable and spoils fast due to ambient temperature. Milk can also get spoiled when malpractices are followed by members in the form of adding preservatives, supplying previous day's milk, pouring newly calved animal's milk, pouring milk of sick animals etc.
4. There is no rationale for giving a blanket statement that 'women entrepreneurs are better than their counterparts'. However, it appears that given enabling environment and institutional support, they are inferior to none.
5. It is calculated by dividing total cost incurred (salaries to employees, stationary, detergents, chemicals, electricity, rent, traveling expenses, audit fees, entertainment expenses, contributions to village amenities, etc.) By quantity of milk procured during a year.
6. Entrepreneurs are persons who initiate, organise, manage and control affairs of a business that combines factors of production to supply goods and services. It is a life moving force behind any economy.

REFERENCES

N.D.D.B. (2003), Women's Dairy Cooperative Leadership Program (mimeo), N.D.D.B, Anand.

Planning Commission (2003), Tenth Five Year Plan (2002-07), Volume II, Government of India, New Delhi, pp. 217-278.

Rao, V. M. (2000), Developing Agro-enterprises among Farm Women: A Case of Amul, Regency Publications, New Delhi.

Rao, V. M. (2003), Evaluation of Women Dairy Project in Rajasthan, Regency Publications, New Delhi.

Rao, V. M. (2003 a), Empowering Farm Women Through Dairy Cooperatives: A Study in Andhra Pradesh and Karnataka, Anmol Publications (in press), New Delhi.

Rao, V. M. (2003 b), Evaluation of Women Dairy Project (Phase 3) in Rajasthan (mimeo), VMNICM, Pune.

Rao, V. M. (2003 c), Evaluation of women dairy project (Phases 1, 3, and 4) in Orissa (mimeo), VMNICM, Pune.

Shah, T. (1990), Repporteur's Report on Learning from Success: Analytical Review of Successful Farmers and Farmer's Cooperatives, *Indian Journal of Agricultural Economics*, 45(3):419-431.

Steers, R. M. (1975), Problems in the Measurement of Organizational Effectiveness, *Administrative Science Quarterly*, 20:546-558.

6

RURAL INDUSTRY THAT THRIVE ON NIMBLE FINGERS CASE OF MATCH INDUSTRY IN TAMIL NADU

R. Vidyasagar

Sivakasi region in Tamil Nadu has the pride of being noted as *"Kutty Japan"* (Mini Japan), as it provides full employment, year round, for the local population. Sivakasi region is not only known for hand made match industry but also for manufacture of fire works and Printing industry with most modern technology. However, match industry is a classic case where the primitive technology of production prevailed over modern technology. In 1945 it was reported that nearly six or seven factories belonging to a single combine, namely, the Western India Match Company (WIMCO) using most up-to-date machinery contributed 80% of the production. (Deshpande, 1945, p. 35). And now the hand-made match sector concentrated in the match belt of Sivakasi accounts for 85% of India's match production. Hand made match industry thrives only in the match belt of Sivakasi region. During 1997-98 the hand made match sector in the Sivakasi region contributed Rs. 47 million as excise duty to the Central Excise department[1]. How did this happen? The hand made match industry has traversed an arduous path to attain its current position. The use of child labour in the hand made match industry is closely associated with this. Thus it is essential to look at the evolution of match industry.

GROWTH AND DEVELOPMENT OF HAND MADE MATCH INDUSTRY IN SIVAKASI REGION

The growth of hand made match industry has been slow in the early years but rapid subsequently. The emerging composition of the industry is important because, with demand having been relatively buoyant-between 1920 ad 1970 the rate of growth of demand rose sharply so that match consumption in India doubled first in 40 years, then in 20 years and then again in 8 years. During the 1970s growth averaged 8 per cent compound per annum, but subsequently came down to 4 per cent during the 1980s. At the turn of the decade the average Indian consumed five matches a day, with three-quarters of the demand attributable to smokers (ITCOT, 1992, 15).

The units in match industry are classified into four categories viz. A, B, C, D sectors, by the excise department. Any unit using power for the match manufacturing process is defined as part of the mechanised 'A' sector. WIMCO is the only production unit classified under this. If any one of the complementary processes is produced with the use of power and if the total value of the capital invested in the unit does not exceed Rs. 2 million the unit is treated as part of the semi-mechanised 'B' sector. In the case of Sivakasi 'B' sector units have mechanised the highly labour-intensive frame filling operation. It loses out because it manufactures and uses short-length wax sticks, which involve an additional cost of around 10 paise per box compared with hand made sector. 'C' and 'D' sectors are completely hand made sectors. 'C' sector units are defined as units not using power in any of the production processes. These are also called as middle sector units that form the core of match production. These units generally employ more than 20 workers in each unit and are to be registered as factories under the Factories Act and subjected to enforcement under relevant acts. If the unit does not use power and produce within the ceiling limit of 120 million match sticks in a year these are defined as 'D' sector units. Given the ceiling on production limits these units cannot employ more than 20 workers. These units are not needed to register under the Factories Act. These are also called tiny sector units. Apart from these four categories there are traders involved in lending working capital and supply of raw materials to the tiny 'D' sector units and arrange to market their produce. These are locally known as trading companies in the Sivakasi region. Most of the 'D' sector units are totally dependent on these trading companies. There is a kind of putting out relationship exists between the trading companies and the tiny sector match units. In addition to these production and trading units, veneer box making (both inner and outer box making) is done at home in thousands of households in this region. Agents of the factories distribute raw materials to houses and collect the finished product by paying piece rate wages.

Despite being characterised by 4 different categories of units, with differing technical combinations in production, domestic market has been catered by a geographically relatively concentrated set of hand made producers located in around the Sivakasi-Sattur-Kovilpatti belt in Tamil Nadu. At present around 15 per cent of total match production in the country occurs in the five units of WIMCO, and the remaining 85 per cent in the semi- and non-mechanised sector. Of the output produced by units other than those of WIMCO, an overwhelming proportion around 85 per cent comes from the 5 taluks that constitute the match belt in Virudhunagar and Tutucorin districts of Tamil Nadu. (There are hand made match units in Quilon district of Kerala state and in a few other districts in Tamil Nadu. However, production from these areas is negligible in the total production of the hand made industry). The market share of hand made match sector in Tamil Nadu rose from 24 per cent in 1953 to 40 per cent in 1971/72 and 55 per cent during 1976-79, (Moulik and Purushotham, 1982) and at present over 80 per cent. Out of the 85 per cent of matches produced by units other than those under the WIMCO umbrella, only one per cent is accounted for by the 'B' or semi-mechanised sector

CURRENT PROFILE OF HAND MADE MATCH INDUSTRY IN THE SIVAKASI REGION

According to information provided by the Factory Inspectorate there is nearly 6000 'D' sector units and 400 'C' sector units. There are a few 'B' sector units. But in practice a few decision-making agents control these units. While the 'C' sector is dominated by less than 20 families (Harbans Singh Committee Report, 1976), 'D' sector units are either benami units of those who control the 'C' sector units or controlled by a few trading companies. Many of the 'C' sector owners have vertically integrated their operations to include splint and veneer production, chlorate manufacture, transportation and other such activities, as well as diversified into related areas like printing and fireworks manufacture. Even in terms of scale, these empires are, reportedly, extremely large. The biggest of them, through its many match units belonging to different members of the family, produces three times as much as a single WIMCO factory. They have a strong industry association, which lobbies for state concessions. Thus there is a sort of oligopolistic domination of relatively large trading and industrial capital in the hand made match industry (Chandrasekher, 1997).

FACTORS BEHIND GEOGRAPHICAL CONCENTRATION

The industry became concentrated in the match belt area because of pioneering entrepreneurship, close knit caste co-operation among entrepreneurs, availability of timber from nearby Kerala, drought in the area leading to supply of cheap labour, arid climate facilitating natural drying of match sticks and boxes and low levels of literacy and organisation among labour. This heavy concentration has been facilitated by availability of labour, especially child labour and there are signs of the industry spreading radially outwards of the core match belt, because of the felt labour shortage (ITCOT, 1992a). The match belt has been expanding to a few pockets in the neighbouring Tutucorin district and the new areas are contiguous to the match belt. During the first half of the 20th century there were hand made match units in Bombay suburbs,

Calcutta City, Baroda and Assam. But they all died down probably because of growth of other industries and shortage of cheap labour.

Earlier studies done on the match industry concluded that cheap labour is the corner stone of this industry (Vidyasagar 1991 & 1994, Government of Tamil Nadu, 1993, Raja, D.V.P., 1993, Kothari, 1983, Daniel C. 1995, Tiyabji, 1985, ITCOT, 1992a, Government of India, 1979, Harbans Singh, 1976, Hari Bhasker, 1985). This has made possible the extraordinary growth of the handmade sector. Though substantive excise preference is given to the hand made sector, it is a recent phenomenon. More important is the factor of labour cost advantage over the capital servicing cost of mechanisation, which has been the bedrock of this industry. Further expansion of labour supply has been made possible by increased use of child labour, bussing in of labour over long distances, inward migration of families, spread of 'D' sector to villages and some outward spread of 'C' units. However, Chandrasekhar (1997) has characterised the concentration of match units in this region as irrational clustering. According to him the extremely low investment costs required for creating capacity in the non-mechanised segment of the industry suggests that entry must be relatively free. A 'D' sector producer using rented premises, with a high share of intermediaries bought out or produced in households on a putting out basis, would need working capital support from the trade to the tune of Rs.25000. To achieve a turnover of a magnitude similar to such a unit, a 'C' sector producer with a greater degree of 'internalisation' of production would need to invest around Rs. 50, 000. Since sums of this magnitude are not large, one can expect that easy entry would ensure an extremely competitive environment that drives down profits. However, the evidence does not appear to suggest that returns are low in this segment of the industry. According to one estimate, in 1991 a 'D' sector manufacturer of the kind referred to above would have earned a profit-cum-wage of Rs. 12000 a year, while the trader supporting him with working capital could have garnered up to Rs. 15000 per annum after costs, amounting to a return of 60 per cent. In the case of C sector units annual surplus could have amounted to upwards of 80 per cent on investment. (ITCOT 1992a, p. 74).

While the cheap labour and low capital requirement may keep production cost low, it requires access to a suitable trade network, and raises working capital requirements and trading costs and margins as the industry from this region caters to the entire nation. In fact, if trading costs and margins are considered, the concentration of the industry is irrational. One study found that transportation costs and trade margins together accounted for more rapid than the growth of manufactories in the C-sector. With the oligopolistic control over production, the industry is able to more than neutralise the cost disadvantage in distribution associated with handmade production aimed at the national market, with a cost advantage in production stemming in large part from the "decentralised" organisation of the industry (that pervades even household activity) and it consequent ability to access large volumes of cheap labour. Relocating the industry nearer to markets will lead to emergence of new competitors. With advantage of access to large volumes of cheap labour the industry is able to manage the disadvantages of distribution costs. "Thus, irrational clustering is not the reflection of any geographical advantages or "economies" in production, but results from large capital using backward forms of organisation in combination with cheap labour to virtually foreclose competition and "protect" its manufacturing and trading margins at the expense of labour. The strength of that process in an otherwise modernising environment lies not in directly squeezing the money and real wage of labourers who are considered "main earners", but of resorting to the more "acceptable" wage discrimination against women and children, who bear the costs of the irrational concentration of handmade production for a national market characteristic of this industry". Labour cost is estimated to be only around 10 per cent of the total cost of production. (Chandrasekher, 1997). A census survey conducted during December 1994 revealed that 33 per cent of the labour force in match production were children of less than 14 years old (21 per cent female children and 12 per cent male children) and 55 per cent female adults. Thus women and children constitute about 88 per cent of the total labour force in the hand made match industry. (Vidyasagar, 1994). They constitute a docile labour force involved in labour intensive processes in the hand made match industry.

LABOUR IN MATCH INDUSTRY

As already mentioned, this region being a draught prone area, the mainstay of occupation for people in this region is the three industries, viz., match, fireworks and printing, for their livelihood. A door to door Census survey conducted during 1994 (Vidyasagar, 1994), revealed that only around 28 per cent of the total workers were involved in agriculture as their full time occupation in Virudhunagar district. All the rest were involved in secondary and tertiary sectors (including match works, fireworks, printing industry and other associated services). All 'C' sector match units would employ more than 20 persons, and consequently, most of them are registered factories. In the C sector, it is not uncommon to find that only 30% of the labour employed is shown on the books. It is observed during the fieldwork that children are continued to be employed in 'C' sector units though there is a clear prohibition through the CLPR Act of 1986. 'D' sector units are non-factories and do not provide any long - term benefits. They consider themselves exempted from all labour laws and official visitations, even though they would come under the Minimum Wages Act. Unlike the 'C' sector where specified timings are observed, in the 'D' sector units in villages, workers choose their own working time and place of work. It is usual to find in many villages that women work from 3 am to 6 am, go home to cook, then come back at 8.30 am and continue to work till 3 p.m., after which, they go home to attend to housework, sometimes carrying frames to home for filling. Employment in this industry has several pre-industrial characteristics. One such is the practice of `advances' to workers. These advances usually range from a couple of hundred rupees to a thousand rupees, taken at the commencement of employment-and sometimes increased later-as interest free loans; the worker cannot stop away without repaying the advance. This practice serves the need for social loans to workers-or for discharging earlier loans-and gives a reasonable assurance of labour continuity to the employer. This would not amount to bondage, as the `advanced' worker is not paid discriminatory wages and had the option-and reasonable feasibility-of transferring to any other unit repaying his employer by taking an advance from the new employer. Bondage does, however, creep in when the advances taken are for larger amounts such as Rs. 2000 or Rs. 3000, and mobility gets restricted by the inability to find another employer willing to advance such sums. More open - and physical - restrictions are placed on migrant labour who are brought in as families and housed near the units on assurances of minimum productivity. In some cases they'll have to take permission to move out of the village and even have to take an escort to go to movies in nearby towns.

CHILD LABOUR IN MATCH INDUSTRY

The issue of child labour in match industry is as old as that of the hand made match industry[2]. Cheap labour, especially of children's, is the corner stone of handmade match sector in the Sivakasi region.

To arrive at the actual number of children working in the match belt, a door-to-door survey of the main match and feeder blocks which are spread over Kamarajar (now renamed Virudhunagar) and V.O. Chidambaranar (now renamed Tutucorin) districts was commissioned by the Department of Social Welfare in August 1993 with UNICEF support (Vidyasagar, 1994).

This survey covered a population of nearly 200,000 households of seven blocks and four municipalities of Virudhunagar district and 5 blocks and one municipality of Tutucorin district. Key findings of the survey are:

- In the areas surveyed, there are a total of 80,221 working children in the age group of 6-14 in all occupations: matches, fireworks, printing, agriculture and different service sectors. Of these 44% are boys and 56% are girls.

- Out of 80,221 working children, 53,479 are full-time workers and 26,742 are part time workers.
- In the surveyed blocks of Kamarajar (Virudhunagar) district, children account for 12% of the work force, and in V.O.C. (Tutucorin) district it is 8%. The average proportion of child workers to total work force in Tamil Nadu state is (2.4%)(1991 Census). Thus there are many more children working in these two districts than in other districts.
- In the match manufacturing, children constitute 33% (21% girls and 12% boys) of the total work force in Virudhunagar district and 21% (18% girls and 9% boys) in Tutucorin district. The concentration of child labour in match industry is found in the Sattur and Sivakasi blocks of Virudhunagar and Kovilpatty block in Tutucorin districts.
- In match manufacturing women and girl children constitute 76% of work force in Virudhunagar district and 80% in Tutucorin district.
- There are 65,908 children working in the match industry; accounting for 82% of the total child work force. Of these 40% are boys and 60% are girls. In the match industry girls out number boys, *the problem of child labour is also a manifestation of the problem of girl child.*
- Of these child workers, 40,974 are full time workers (37% are boys and 57% are girls) and 24,934 are part time workers (45% are boys and 55% are girls). 77% of the children working full time and 93% of children working part time are concentrated in the match industry.
- The survey found 5,176 children working in the fireworks industry. Of these 48% are boys and 52% are girls. There are 3,368 full time workers (51% boys

and 49% girls) and 1,808 part-time workers (43% boys and 57% girls). The main area of child labour in the fireworks industry is in Vembakottai block of Virudhunagar district.

- In the surveyed blocks of Virudhunagar district, 76% of the boys and 70% of girls in the 6-11 age group are enrolled in school, while 15% of the boys and 19% of the girls are working full time. 9% of boys and 11% of girls are neither in school nor in work.
- In the 12-14 year age group, 59% of the boys and 46% of girls are enrolled in school while 36% of the boys and 48% of the girls are working full time. About 5% of boys and 6% of girls are neither working nor in school.
- In the surveyed blocks of Tutucorin district, 81% of the boys and 77% of girls in the 6-11 age group are enrolled in school while 8.5% of the boys and 12.3% of the girls in the same age group are working full time. About 11% of both boys and girls are neither in school nor in work.
- In the 12-14 age groups, 64% of the boys and 52% of the girls are in school while 30% of boys and 42% of *girls are working full time.* 6% of both boys and girls are neither in work nor in school.
- It is critical to note that in both districts about 10% of the children in the age group of 6-11 are neither in school nor in work. This section may eventually join the work force. In 12-14 age groups the proportion of children of this category is much less compared to 6-11 years showing that many children who are not enrolled in primary schools join the work force eventually.
- In Virudhunagar district, of the full time working children, 16% of boys and 24% girls were never enrolled in schools, while 56% of both boys and girls dropped out at the primary school level.

- In Tutucorin district, of the full time working children, 16% of the boys and 19% of girls were never enrolled in schools, while 57% of the boys and 60% of female children dropped out at primary schools.

Another survey on Child Labour conducted during 1997 under the directions of the Supreme Court of India has identified in all only 1124-working children in the district. (Of these 760 were in match works, 75 in fire works, 88 in textile mills, 218 in printing press and 36 in other occupations). However this is a gross underestimation of the reality as the survey teams faced the hostile attitude of the employers while conducting the survey (The Hindu, 12th April 1997). Moreover, this survey was based on establishments. Working children can be easily driven away before the survey takes place.

Employers often argue that they are not demanding child labour. They always say that the parents force them to employ their children in order to survive. From employers' point of view, they are the benefactors of working children and their families. However, our field survey has revealed that the employers are luring children into work by providing certain incentives. There are various forms of incentives.

INCENTIVE TO LURE CHILDREN

If children finish filling 10 frames within one hour, they are awarded incentives like ribbon, soap, soapboxes, hair clips etc. Though these children are paid on piece rate basis the above incentive is to drive them work fast. The employers very well know that filling ten frames in one hour is just not possible. Rarely some children achieve this and it motivates other children to work fast. Those who complete 180 frames in a week of six working days (an average of 30 frames per day) will be awarded some stainless steel utility articles. The average productivity of a teen-age child (who is experienced for at least 2-3 years) is about 25 frames per day (of 10-12 hours of work). In order to make children not feel the drudgery of labour; popular cinema music is played through out the day in the factories through stereo. Generally, the employers transport children from the villages to factories. But, if children in nearby villages opt for walking the distance they are given an incentive of Rs. Two per day. It is called "Nadai Kasu" in Tamil, meaning compensation for walking. This extra money motivates children to walk to the factory and work instead of using factory transport. The employers also use certain forms of cultural trappings as an incentive for the workers. For example the employers perform *"Kuthu Vilakku pooja"* (worshipping lit brass lamp), inviting all girl children and women to participate. During these sessions those who have regular attendance to work are presented with a brass lamp. They also organise Rangoli competitions (making patterns on the floor with colour powders) for the girls. All working children are given sugar cane, jaggery and fruits or a cash prize of Rs. 25 during pongal festival. Annual picnics are organised for the workers to near by tourist spots at the expense of the employers. Another feature of employment relations that weans the workers away from any organisation is the kind of patron-client relationship between the employer and employee. While being highly exploitative, the employers use the trappings of a patron client relationship, with all its emotional overtones. For example, most workers address their employers as "Annachi" (elder brother) and the "Annachi" attends all the functions in the workers' families. This relationship is reinforced every year during "Panguni Pongal" (a festival specific to this area) when the employers give gifts and pay new advances, (social loans) settling old accounts. These trappings, whether monetarily beneficial to the workers are not, creates a kind of social bond between the employers and the employees. It also weans the workers away from getting organised as workers. This bond is handy not only for the employers to continue their exploitation of cheap labour but also for winning over the support of these people when the industry in trouble because of law enforcement. To cite an example, when the Supreme Court of India ordered a survey of child labour in hazardous industries in the country during 1996, the survey was undertaken in match industry also. The employers not only closed their units to protest against the survey, claiming that the survey is "false and malicious", but called for a 'bandh' (general strike) in the area. The local people en masse supported the bandh and it was a total success (The Hindu, April 12, 1997).

WORKERS' ORGANISATION

Workers' organisations are very weak in this area for a number of reasons. Primary among them are that the work arrangement between the employers in match units and the workers is very informal in nature. Most of the labourers are not registered labourers and hence not entitled for legal benefits (though all the workers, including children, are paid statutory minimum bonus of 8.33 per cent per annum based on the total piece rate wages they received in the relevant year). Even for those registered workers, the preponderance of child labour (in all the three main industries) acts as a check against any trade union activities. There is a general feeling among the people in this arid region that but for match and fireworks industries they would be starving. As all the family members, including children, are working in any one of the three industries, the total family earnings is sufficient for stave them off from poverty. (In terms of household economic levels, this area is much better compared to even Thanjavur district–the once rice bowl of Tamil Nadu–where abject poverty of agricultural labourers during off-season is very severe). Thus, on the one hand subsistence not being a threat and the kind of social relations that exist between the employers and workers on the other prevent the emergence of any strong workers organisation in this region. Even prominent central trade unions in the country have only some kind of general workers union (not unit based as in the case of other industries) in Sivakasi region and take up occasional and isolated complaints from victimised workers. This being the situation of labour in match industry what is the role of state with regard to ending child labour in match industry?

GOVERNMENT'S RESPONSE–COMMITTEES AFTER COMMITTEES

The issue of child labour in Sivakasi area has for long agitated policy makers and thinkers inside and outside the government.

Way back in 1976 a committee under the chairmanship of Mr.Harbans Singh, a member of the revenue board then, was appointed by the State Government, to suggest measures for the eradication of the unfair labour practice of employing children and to explore the possibilities of their working from home with a facility to attend school at least in one shift. After taking into account the appalling conditions of working children the committee recommended that the problem should be tackled without causing hardship to the families of the child labourers and also without upsetting the industries which have created employment. The committee observed that "The stoppage of child labour is likely to create more problems than it will solve," threatening the existence of the industry and creating extreme hardship to the people. Thus the committee suggested certain ameliorative steps to enhance the wages for children with reduced working hours and part time schooling.

Notwithstanding these recommendations the issue continued to persist and in 1981, a survey conducted by the Area Development Programme (UNICEF) found that there are 45000 children working full time in the match industry alone. Owing to public pressure and the intervention of the Supreme Court of India another committee under the chairmanship of Mr.Hari Bhasker, Commissioner of Land Reforms then, was appointed to study the implementation of the recommendations of Harbans Singh Committee. The Hari Bhasker Committee suggested certain measures as to how to effectively implement Harbans Singh Committee's unimplemented recommendations.

Despite these committees and intervention by the highest court of the country and the enactment of Child Labour Prohibition and Regulation Act of 1986, the problem continues and, in fact, has been increasing keeping in pace with the in match production (at the rate of 4% per annum). Again in April 1992, the issue of child labour in Sivakasi was in focus with the formation of a Special Inter-Departmental Committee by the government of Tamil Nadu, under the Chairmanship of the Secretary, Labour and Employment, to develop a strategic plan for total elimination of child labour, in the match belt. A Sub-Committee was subsequently formed to undertake an in-depth study of the problem and prepare a strategy framework. This Sub-Committee submitted its report in March 1993. The sub-committee has recommended a comprehensive action plan involving various aspects of the issue of child labour. With regard to industry the sub-committee has recommended improving the adult wage levels and gradually replacing the piece rate system of wages and encouraging the spread of industry into the neighbouring labour surplus areas. The sub-committee has also taken note of state of genuine 'D' sector units which are tied to the trading companies and are forced to employ cheap labour to get a reasonable margin. It is suggested to federate these units into co-operatives with professional managerial assistance and state aid for running of the units. Thus there was a suggestion to change the structure and concentration of the industry.

There is a general fear that the industry will collapse if child labour is withdrawn. But a study commissioned by the sub-committee revealed that the industry will not be affected in the event of child labour being withdrawn (ITCOT, 1992a).

On Withdrawal of Child Labour

- An important reason for the use of child labour in the match industry is that the industry is concentrated in a narrow area. This has resulted in not merely utilising the available surplus labour in the area - including children - but also inward migration of families and bussing in of children.
- The phenomenon of 'Nimble fingers' is considered significant and hence increased productivity is attributed to children. This is supposed to result in more productive use of the floor space occupied by a worker and reduced supervision cost. It is true that in the 11-14 age group are generally more productive than adults, but smaller children are less productive. On average, *child productivity, if anything, will be equal to or marginally lower than adult productivity.* There is hardly any direct labour cost advantage in using child labour, since the child and the adult are paid the same wages for a given quantity of production. The somewhat higher productivity of children

above the age of 10 or 11 would be balanced out by the lower productivity of children below that age.

- However, use of a substantial number of child labourers result in indirect labour cost saving by depressing the general wage level in the area and by making a large part of the labour pliant and docile. On this account, it can be said that withdrawal of children from the labour force would make labour more scarce and costlier. However, there are limits to the extent it can go up given that the cost of labour has general tendency to level with other predominant occupations in the area.
- The adult wage level in the match belt is likely to increase compared to neighbouring areas in the event of the withdrawal of children from the work force. However, this differential cannot be large, as the feasibility of a radial spread to low wage and drought stricken areas makes the cost of relocation affordable for this industry.
- Based on the above considerations, it is unlikely that the labour cost would substantially increase if child labour is withdrawn. Even the modest increase in labour cost that could result will not in any way affect the competitiveness of the hand-made match sector.

In support of the above conclusions, another quick study commissioned by the sub-committee to study the absence of child labour in hand made match industry in neighbouring Kerala state has revealed the socio-economic factors behind non-use of child labour (ITCOT, 1992b).

ABSENCE OF CHILD LABOUR IN KERALA MATCH INDUSTRY

There are 800 match-producing units in Kerala, mostly concentrated in Quilon district. All labour used is adult, and labourers work shorter hours (by two to three hours) in Kerala compared to Sivakasi but earn 50% more on average. The piece rates are higher by 20% to 100% and in addition the workers get paid Dearness allowance and bonus. Absence of child labour in the match industry is part of a picture in which child labour is not used in any industry in the state.

The additional labour and material costs compared to Tamil Nadu are passed on to the consumer in Kerala as all production sold within the State. Even within Kerala, the units control only half of the market and yield the other half to Sivakasi and WIMCO.

The reasons attributed for non-use of child labour are:

- A socio-political environment which discourages child labour use.
- A higher level of general wages, and consequently, of family income.
- A better standard of living of the poor because of better availability of social services such as public distribution, health, education, housing and implementation of land reforms.
- Smaller family size because of more successful family planning programme.
- Heightened awareness among all parents, and in society as a whole, because of higher level of literacy among parents and higher aspiration on their part for their children.
- A very good educational infrastructure, adequate for meeting the needs of the entire population and a low drop out rate.
- A vigilant trade union, political and NGO system ensuring legal enforcement relating to labour.

It is thus clear that absence of child labour in Kerala is the result of many interrelated factors, with probably high literacy as a connecting thread.

The preceding account clearly shows that the hand made match industry in Sivakasi region thrives because of its ability to garner plenty of cheap labour available in the region, mainly of women and children. The oligopolistic nature of control over the industry in this region provides a premier position for the industry. While explaining the prevalence of child labour, Chandrasekher (1997) has concluded that it exists because of the demand side factors that create a selective market for cheap child labour, which is then serviced by poorer, but not necessarily poverty-stricken households (*ibid* p. 6).

While it is true that given the nature of organisation of production in the hand made match industry and the comparative cost advantage on labour that the industry has, the demand side factors play a primary role for persistence of child labour, supply side factors also provide a fertile ground for the demand for cheap labour to grow and the industry to expand and get agglomerated. Chapter 4 is devoted to an understanding of supply side factors based on the field study.

NOTES

1. Central Excise Commissionarate, Madurai, Match Production and Revenue Reports, April 97 to March 98. The average for previous five years is over Rs. 45 million per annum. Sivakasi region also produces over 90 per cent of total production of fireworks in the country and is one of the important printing centres in the country.
2. Deshpande (1945, p. 19) has reported that "It was impossible to make an intensive survey into the working conditions in all these factories but a good few both at Sattur and Shivakasi were personally inspected. A most remarkable sight was that on arrival it was found that young persons of about the age of 8 or 10, particularly girls, ran helter-skelter with trays on their heads. It was explained to me by the Factory inspector that this was an usual sight when he visited these factories. The meaning of it all was that these youngsters were all uncertified children working in the factories who were trained to pretend, on the appearance of the factory Inspector or any other visitor, that they were only carrying the trays etc. to their homes for the work to be done by their elders in their homes. In these factories were also found working many children who were obviously under 12 years of age although they seemed to be in the possession of badges showing that they were certified... There are complaints that many of the workers in these factories are made to work for about ten hours a day without being paid any over-time allowance." The unskilled labour in these factories consists mostly of women and children. They are usually engaged in frame filling, box making, box filling, banderoling and labeling. Also see Government of India, 1965-66, & 1979, Harbans Singh, 1976.

REFERENCES

All India Chamber of Match Industries, Sivakasi (AICMI) (1983), Note Submitted to the Minister of Labour, Tamil Nadu, Sivakasi, AICMI, mimeo.

All India Chamber of Match Industries, Sivakasi (AICMI) (1985), Note on Child Employment in Match Industry, Sivakasi, AICMI, mimeo.

All India Chamber of Match Industries, Sivakasi (AICMI) (1980(a)), "Handmade Safety Matches Industry in India", AICMI, Sivakasi.

All India Chamber of Match Industries, Sivakasi (AICMI) (1980(b)), "Sivakasi Where Light & Sound Are Packaged–A Panorama of the Match, Fireworks and Printing Industries of South India" (A reproduction of a series of articles published in the "Business Standard", "*Economic Times*" and "*Financial Express*"), AICMI, T.T. Press, Sivakasi.

Chandrasekhar, C. P. (1997), "The Economic Consequences of the Abolition of Child Labour: An Indian Study", *Journal of Peasant Studies*, 24(3), April, p. 13.

Daniel C. & Peace Trust (1995), "A Study of Child Labour in Match Factories in Kovilpatti", (A Handout of lecture delivered to the Participants of Orientation Programme for Voluntary Organisation on Child Labour held at the National Labour Institute), mimeo.

Deshpande S. R. (1945), Labour Investigation Committee, Government of India, "Report on An Enquiry Into Conditions of Labour in the Match Industry in India", Government of India Press, Simla.

Government of India (1979), "Report of the Committee on Child Labour", Ministry of Labour, New Delhi.

Government of India, Ministry of Labour, 1979, Report on the working and living conditions of workers in the match industry in and around Sivakasi, Tamil Nadu", Labour Bureau, Chandigarh, 1979.

7

ARTISAN FOOTWEAR INDUSTRY–IMPACT OF TECHNOLOGY TRANSFER AND GLOBALIZATION

Giriyappa Kollannavar,
D. Chandramouli and B. Krishnama Naidu

INTRODUCTION

Leather processing is one of the ancient and traditional professions in India. This was carried out by certain communities who developed excellent skills over the years to produce various leather products to meet local needs. Collecting hides from dead animals and converting them into useful products by the leather artisans was adopted as a traditional occupation and source of their livelihood. Footwear is the major item produced from leather.

The traditional artisans engaged in the leather vocation can be grouped into three categories viz. (1) Flayers (2) Tanners and (3) Cobblers

(1) *Flayers:* The main work of the flayers is to collect the dead animals and transport them to the outskirts of the village/ town for recovery of hide from the dead animal and this leather is a major economic value for their service. Flayed hides are neither sold to local tanners or in certain cases flayers themselves process these hides into finished leathers and then convert them into footwear.

(2) *Tanners:* Tanners process the raw hide into finished leather which again converted into products. If one looks back into the history of the leather industry, the tanners are the initiators of the rural leather industry as the art of tanning was invented by them. The attempt to render soft skin convenient to wear might be the foundation for the art of tanning. Later the art and skill of tanning of hides with natural ingredients such as bark, leaves, fruits, and nuts was developed. The traditional tanning vocation with a few modification and improvements in the processing of hides has been practiced in certain pockets of the country.

(3) *Cobblers:* Cobblers (footwear manufacturers) produce footwear for local use by utilizing traditional skills. Tanned leather, which is processed by the traditional tanners, was the main source of raw material for manufacture of the leather footwear. However, gradual decline in the availability of tanned leather has affected large number of cobblers (footwear manufacturers) in the countryside. These cobblers have been manufacturing and supplying footwear to the local people using their traditional skills. The skills are transferred from father to son and use of machine and modern tools is absent in their footwear manufacture.

Self Sustenance in Rural Set Up: Involvement of a few communities in traditional vocations in the ancient society was based on social stratification, where certain occupations are attached with communities. However, the division of work among the communities has created continuous source of livelihood and work. Dependence of artisans on each other for their requirements was the main feature of the society. It was a rural industrial scenario where micro enterprises were dominant. Participation of the entire family in the production process helped to maintain unity and integrity among them. The rural traditional leather artisans were never aspired for mechanization except expansion of the marketing opportunities.

Change and Continuity of Footwear Industry: Leather industry in Indian society has undergone a sea-change during the last three decades. There was a spurt in the mechanization of the product sector. Value addition to the raw material and exports increased phenomenally. Automation and mechanization in the production of footwear was introduced to meet the growing export demand. During 2002-03, India exported Rs. 2813 crore worth of footwear to various countries. However, the demand for artisan products particularly for leather footwear has declined due to the introduction of non leather footwear into the domestic market at competitive prices. Organized sector of the footwear (leather) industry has emerged as a major foreign exchange earner for the country with various supportive measures initiated by the Government. Similar encouragement and timely support was not extended to the decentralized sector, resulting in an unabated declining trend in their activity.

CONSUMPTION AND PRODUCTION

India is one of the major countries for large consumption of footwear in the world. Footwear is a widely used consumer item and has attained a product of prominence for trade and employment generation. The study conducted by Central Leather Research Institute (CLRI: 1997) reveals that the annual demand for footwear is nearly 1800 million pairs with a per capita demand of 1.8 pairs in India. Further, the domestic market for footwear is growing at an annual rate of 10%. According to the Tenth Five Year Plan document on leather and leather goods industry, the projected demand for footwear by 2010 will be 2500 million pairs and in this 800 million pairs constitute leather[1]. It is a fact that nearly 80% of the total footwear produced in the country is originating from the artisan sector as half of the total manufacturing units are located in rural areas.

At global level industrialized countries are the major consumers of leather products particularly footwear. USA, Germany, France, UK, Italy, Netherlands are the major countries with per capita footwear ranging 4-5 pairs per annum.

The footwear production in India is the main source of livelihood for 1.2 million artisans who carry the family occupation over generations. The level of employment and criticality of the incomes for their footwear work are the vital factors for the socio-economic development process of the artisans.

Proportion of leather and non-leather footwear: Of the total consumption of 1800 million pairs of footwear in India, leather footwear accounts for 30% and the rest is non-leather footwear. Leather footwear comprises full leather and part-leather in equal proportions and large proportions of this segment is chappals and sandals. While the leather footwear produced by the organized sector goes for export, footwear produced by the decentralized sector units meets the domestic demand. In the case of non-leather footwear, there are numerous categories and varieties such as plastic, rubber etc., The segment of rubber (Hawai) has a major share with 300 million pairs in the total non-leather footwear production. In other words, low cost non-leather footwear segment is playing an important role in the domestic market. Since the manufacture of leather and non-leather footwear continue in the small and tiny household units, the level of employment and incomes are critical for their progress.

Free market and its impact: Under the new economic policy of globalization and liberalization, the world trade is open to all countries. Import and export of goods are free from the trade barriers. Under changed global trade circumstances import of footwear into the country is under consideration and is likely to cause an imbalance in the small and tiny scale manufacturers' business.

The import of footwear into the country has to be seen from two angles. In the case of leather footwear, import surge may not be significant. It is likely that globally reputed few brands may capture the premium market which is considered a small portion in the Indian market. Such market is confined to high income groups. However, liberal import of footwear with low price is to be viewed cautiously.

China is the major competitor and a real threat to the large number of tiny footwear manufacturers in India as it is capable of producing low cost footwear. Apart from China, Indonesia, Vietnam, Thailand are the other countries that are producing low cost non-leather footwear.

Low cost inputs, large capacities of the plants in those countries would really pose a threat to Indian manufacturers. Indian market for leather and non-leather footwear is price sensitive and imported products may find favour if they are cheaper. The footwear sector has to improve its competitive strength with technology and scale of operation in order to sustain in the business. The important component in this aspect is rationalization of input pricing in India. Reduction in production cost, technological up gradation and strengthening of skills are other major concerns to be addressed urgently. These measures will help to improve the ability of competitiveness of Indian firms. At the same time India has to closely monitor the product pricing systems in China and Vietnam so as to be vigilant on dumping (If a country sells a product below its cost of production is treated as dumping). World Trade Organization (WTO) norms provide remedial measures for such dumping. If dumping is proved, counter measures are allowed in the form of imposing duties. However, imposing/raising duties in the pretext of protecting the domestic industry may not hold good for long time. India needs to harmonize its trade policies in tune with WTO norms.

Economic reforms, free trade, globalization etc., are the emerging realities of the global economy. Building competitive strength among the domestic producers is essential for the survival in global trade.

SWOT ANALYSIS OF INDIAN ARTISAN FOOTWEAR SECTOR

SWOT analysis will highlight the strength, weakness, opportunities and threats existing to regain its market share in the country.

Strengths

(a) Strong traditional skill base

(b) Involvement of whole family and division of labour, assured employment to each member in the family.

(c) Of the total leather footwear produced, 80% originated from artisan sector.

(d) Promotes rural industries.
(e) Use of environmental friendly material i.e. leather is a bio degradable material.
(f) Backward linkage of rural tanners-another avenue for continuation of traditional vocation.
(g) Increased or growing demand for leather footwear.
(h) Production of ethnic brands only by hand tools.
(i) Saves foreign exchange as import of leather footwear, is negligible for domestic consumption.

Weakness

(a) Use of primitive tools in the manufacture of footwear
(b) Lack of innovative designs.
(c) Lack of quality consciousness
(d) Lack of training facilities.
(e) Limited market accessibility
(f) Use of inferior quality raw materials and accessories.
(g) Illiteracy and lack of representatives in decision making at Govt. level.

Opportunities

(a) Innovative and New designs to attract customers.
(b) Constant growing demand for leather footwear.
(c) Strengthening of skills through training.
(d) Exploitation of global market by stamping as ethnic footwear.
(e) Could be marketed worldwide
(f) Employment generation through micro entrepreneurship
(g) Preservation of Indian cultural heritage

Threats

(a) Losing market to plastic and rubber footwear.
(b) Low cost footwear import from China

(c) High cost of raw materials
(d) Increase in cost of production
(e) High cost of training
(f) Resistance of new generation to continue in the occupation.
(g) Being in decentralized sector, financial institutions not coming forward to extend loan facilities.

STRENGTHENING ARTISAN FOOTWEAR INDUSTRY

As has been mentioned that 80% of the leather footwear produced in India is originating from the decentralized sector, the artisans with traditional background dominate in the manufacture of footwear. Dependence of whole family is crucial and make them to compete in the changing marketing scenario is essential. Competitiveness will emerge after strengthening the skills of the footwear artisans. Following are the important measures suggested for strengthening the skills of footwear artisans.

- Initiation of Nationwide intensive training programme among the footwear artisans on quality conscious and cost effective production system.
- Establishment of exclusive footwear complexes.
- Creation of more ethnic brand names.
- Creation/stamping of a brand name 'artisan product' or 'only leather' footwear.
- Publicity on the Indian artisan products (footwear) at global level.
- Use of bag tanned leather in the footwear manufacture.
- Identification of new market (countries).
- Develop use of 'swadesh' wave among the customers.
- Ensuring the availability of low cost non-leather accessories.

NEED FOR INITIATION OF NATIONWIDE INTENSIVE TRAINING

Among the measures suggested above for strengthening the skills of the footwear artisan through intensive training programme, the Central Leather Research Institute (CLRI) and Footwear Design Development Institute (FDDI) can initiate such programme as they have the expertise with required technology and infrastructure facilities. In fact CLRI has taken up an intensive programme, to preserve and upgrade the skills of footwear artisans in Belgaum district in Karnataka. CLRI selected a few enthusiastic footwear artisans from Athani, Nippani, Shiraguppi, Chikhodi and Madhubavi and trained them at CLRI on a wide range of innovative designs, quality maintenance and business skills. During training, varieties of leathers were used as upper of the Kolhapuri footwear to enhance its appearance. The idea was to provide the artisans a window to global market. Further the artisans were encouraged to participate in the footwear trade fairs at national and international level. Exposure tours undertaken for the benefit of artisans to visit large scale footwear producing units have created an awakening among them. For the artisans, the tour was an eye opener as they witnessed a new world of footwear production system.

It was a new experience for the artisans to enter into global market through export of Kolhapuri footwear. During 2001-02 export of Kolhapuri and similar type of footwear was recorded at Rs.90 million[2]. The footwear artisans of Belgaum District of Karnataka are proud of the initiatives taken by CLRI for intervening in improving the quality and expansion of marketing base of their product.

CONCLUSION

The development programme initiated by CLRI is a tip of an ice-berg. Large Scale institutional intervention and similar Athani model of intensive training programmes are needed in the artisan concentrated clusters in the country to strengthen the skills of footwear artisans in view of emerging free trade scenario under WTO. It is a crucial juncture for the policy makers to utilize the available 1.2 million skilled labour for the competitive global market. They are the invisible force in the domestic market producing annually Rs.135000 million worth of footwear to meet domestic demand. China may take away such a huge market potential with its invasion of cheap footwear at any moment under the WTO agreement. Hence, planned approach through careful implementation of strengthening the skills of the artisans through various programmes is necessary as the proposed intervention would be a better solution under the swift changing global scenario.

NOTES AND REFERENCES

1. Report of the Working Group on Leather and Leather Goods Industry for the Tenth Five Year Plan 2002-2007, Vol. I., Govt. of India, Planning Commission, October 2001.

2. Monthly Statistics of Foreign Trade of India (Annual Number for 2001-02) Vol. I, Exports & Re-exports. Directorate-General of Commercial Intelligence & Statistics, Ministry of Commerce, Govt. of India, pp. 1829-30.

8

TEXTILE POLICY AND HANDLOOM SECTOR

K. Srinivasulu

The national textile policy (2000) proposes a major policy shift for the textile industry comprising of the handlooms, power looms and mills. Given the significance of the handloom sector in the Indian economy as a major employer next only to agriculture and severe crises it experienced during the last decade and half, it would be instructive to examine the implications of the textile policy for the handloom sector.

The need for a new textile policy, it is stated, is necessitated by the fact that it is a decade and half since the last policy came into effect and lot of changes have occurred since then. Significant among them are the reforms initiated in the Indian economy and the new world trade regime being initiated by the World Trade Organization (WTO). A textile policy suitable to meet the requirements and challenges of the changed environment there is stated to be the need of the hour. In this essay we propose to examine the possible implications of this to the handlooms.

What is crucial to the formulation of the 2000 textile policy is the report of the Satyam committee, constituted by the Government of India in July 1998 specifically to make recommendations for this purpose. The report, going by the available details, seems to envisage an entirely different textile scenario; far-reaching, without exaggeration, are the recommendations pertaining to the handloom sector.

The principal objective of the policy, in the view of this committee, is one of coping up with the competition in the international market. The handloom weavers, it is stated, need market. While suggesting the government to support the weavers in this by devising special schemes, the committee did not hesitate to recommend the scrapping of the Reservation Act and Hank Yarn Obligation which despite their ineffective implementation has been two crucial legal measures meant to protect the interests of the handlooms weavers.

Crucial to the understanding of the recommendations of the Satyam committee pertaining to the handloom sector is the classification of the handloom weavers. The categorization of weaves on the basis of organization of production into co-operative, master-weaver and independent weaver segments has been a fairly well accepted method followed to analyze the internal differentiation in the handloom sector and to appreciate the problems of the weavers therein.

Deviating from this, the report sought to differentiate the weavers into three tiers on the basis of the 'quality' of cloth produced. In the first tier are grouped the weavers "producing unique, exclusive, high value added items" in the second tier producers of "medium priced fabrics and made up articles from not-so-fine counts of yarn" and in the third tier those producing "plains and low cost textile items".

There is no evidence to believe that the committee has made any attempt to justify why it has chosen to view the handloom industry in terms of product quality as against the systems of production. Nor has there been any attempt to estimate the proportion of weavers in each tier either in terms of production of fabric or the volume of employment. On the contrary, it is simply assumed that the third tier comprises the bulk of weavers producing coarse fabric and by implication the less skilled lot of the handloom weavers!

Thus follows from this perception the most significant of the recommendations of the committee to shift the weavers of the third tier to other tiers of handlooms, power looms and other occupations. For the 'least painful conversion' the first tier of power loom and handloom sectors are identified as 'alternative avenues of livelihood'. The Government is suggested to take steps in this direction by providing the weavers with semi-automatic looms and requisite training.

The poor and inadequate data base on handlooms, which the committee acknowledges, has not deterred it from making far-reaching recommendations. Needless to say, such a callous exercise would be disastrous to the vulnerable weavers who belong predominantly to the backward class, dalit, tribal and minority communities. For one of the major and unexamined assumptions of this exercise is that the weavers in the third tier are not only unskilled but produce cloth that has no market demand!

It would be appropriate to see to what extent the state policy, which is presumed to have facilitated the survival of the handlooms, has really been supportive to the handloom sector. To appreciate this it would be useful to examine the changes in the handloom sector since the late 1960s and especially in the post-1985 textile policy period seen in relation to the macro economic policy changes witnessed especially since the early 1990s.

II

The handloom sector had begun to witness remarkable changes in the nature and structure of production, technology and marketing since the late 1960s in response to the changes in the textile production and marketing, albeit with regional and local specificities. Equally significant are the changes that have occurred in the social life of the weaver communities shaping their survival responses.

The factor that contributed immensely to this change is the phenomenal growth of the power looms which recorded an unprecedented increase from 1.5 lakh in 1963 to 3.09 lakh in 1975. The direct impact of the power loom growth on the handlooms can be gauged from the assessment of the high-powered committee of the Planning Commission [GOI, 1974] headed by Shivaraman, according to which the addition of the power loom resulted in the displacement of six handlooms. The impact of the power loom proliferation could clearly be seen in the gradual and visible displacement of the weavers, decline of their economic well-being and loss of their independence in the production process.

To appreciate this process it may be useful to examine the changes in the organisational structure and the relations of production in the handloom industry. On the basis of this the handloom sector can be divided into (i) Independent weaver, (ii) Co-operative, and (iii) Master-weaver sectors.

Independent weavers are those who carry on production of cloth on their own, i.e., own the instruments of production purchase raw materials from the market and produce fabric with family labour and sell the products in the local market or to traders.

With the proliferation of the power loom sector since the Sixties, and the low priced power loom products penetrating the market, especially in the countryside, the handlooms had to face stiff competition from the former. Further, the rising prices of cotton hank yarn and dyes rendered the handlooms vulnerable. The most effected by this were the independent weavers and small master-weavers-cum-traders owning few looms and employing wage labourers. The displacement of the independent weavers led to growth of the major urban power loom and handloom centers under the master-weavers: with men weavers migrating to them and women weavers shifting to beedi making. In the urban areas where alternative employment opportunities are relatively better, we find the young weavers taking up job of shop assistants and also shifting to construction work, auto rickshaw driving, etc., as the skilled handloom weaving is found to be less attractive due to low wages and continual insecurity. The handloom co-operatives are a major segment accounting for a large proportion of weavers, next to the master-weaver segment. The co-operative movement, which was initiated with the objective of protecting the weavers from the dominant intermediaries like master-weavers and traders, has a record of achievements in certain states like Andhra Pradesh. If the entry of vested interests, and their increasing use as channels of political ascendancy by the community elite drifted the handloom co-operatives away from their true purpose, then the increasing political and governmental interference, development of bureaucratic tendencies and corruption hampered their autonomous functioning. Further, the ineffectiveness of the co-operatives in ensuring regular supply of they raw materials and the inordinate delay in the payment of wages, has forced the average weaver to prefer to work for the master-weaver. As a consequence of this, a number of co-operatives, which once had successful record, have been rendered non-functional. The bogus co-operatives, floated by influential master-weavers/traders/local politicians (and also the power loom owners) to corner the public funds and marketing facilities extended by the state apex handloom co-operative bodies, have not only robbed the genuine co-operatives of their due share but also contributed to the credibility crisis of the co-operatives movement. The third and the most important system of production is the master-weaver system. In this system the master-weaver or the entrepreneur, by employing wage labour produces cloth. Either he directly markets the product or sells it to traders. Here two kinds of production practices can be notices: (a) Put-out system, the weaver works at his home on his own loom using the raw materials supplied by the master-weaver for a piece-wise wage. The entire family of the weaver is involved in the production process–with the adult members engaged in weaving and the aged and children helping in the preparation of accessories. In the *kharkhana* system, the weavers work on the looms provided by the master weaves under one roof. This system is prevalent in the handloom centres where migrant weavers are dominant like Mangalagiri in Guntur and Koyalagudem in Nalgonda district in Andhra Pradesh. With the decline of the independent weavers and the marginalization of the co-operative sector, the master-weaver sector has emerged as the dominant system by attracting the displaced weavers. It accounts for a major share in the handloom production. The 1985 Textile Policy introduced by the Rajiv Gandhi government has to be appreciated against this background. It made a decisive departure from the earlier policy regime by visualizing an entirely different textile scenario. While the earlier policy framework viewed the textile industry in terms of its employment potential and therefore accorded a prime place to handlooms *vis-à-vis* the other two sectors (i.e., power looms and mills), the 1985 policy marked a departure from this by emphasizing productivity as the chief objective. In accordance with the shift of emphasis form employment to production the 1985 policy announced a shift from a sectoral view (the three sectors being the handlooms, power looms and mills) to a process view (the important processes being spinning, weaving and product processing) of the textile industry. Stating the sectoral orientation to the textile industry, without much justification, as leading to the "structural rigidities" in the industry it considered the prioritization of processes to be contributing to a 'comprehensive view' of the industry and thereby eliminating its rigidities. Accordingly it promised to provide "fuller flexibility in t use of various fibers" and "pragmatic policies regarding creation or contraction of capabilities by units to increase competition and promote healthy growth" [GOI 1985: 1, 2]. The process view of the industry by overlooking the specificities of each of the sectors in terms of the requirement of raw materials and capital, labour conditions, production and marketing structure and consumer demand pattern, etc, - the relative strengths/ weaknesses or advantages/disadvantages of the different sectors sought to treat all the sectors to be equal in their ability to compete in the market. Thus by emphasizing productivity as the main objective and insisting on the process view of the industry, the 1985 policy aimed at creating a level playing field in the industrial. This policy perspective, needless to say, was clearly to the disadvantage of the handloom sector as the crisis in the already vulnerable handlooms in the late 1980s and early 1990s amply demonstrated. In spite of this shift, the 1985 policy continued to promise support to the handlooms. A major move in this direction was the Handloom (Reservation of articles for Production) Act, 1985 reserving 22 varieties of articles for exclusive production in the handloom, sector.

Though it was promised that this act "shall be strictly enforced and the machinery for doing so shall be suitable strengthened" [GOI, 1985: 4] the fate of this act clearly illustrated how whatever limited legal safeguards the handloom weavers are promised with are diluted and rendered ineffective by the powers-that-be. Challenged by the powerful power loom and mill owner lobbies it remained *sub judice* for eight years till the Supreme Court upheld it in 1993. With whatever limited legal restrictions removed, the aggressive power looms proliferated and encroached on the handlooms without any hindrance. It is important to note that in the subsequent period the government instead of creating the necessary institutional mechanism to implement the act as the high powered committee headed by Abid Hussain also recommended taking serious view of the ground realities, the government issued an order reducing the reserved items to mere eleven. If the 1985 policy could be seen as an important initial move towards the liberalization of the textile industry, then the macro-economic reforms initiated in 1991 pushed it further. The most important and immediate consequence of this was the relaxation of the export of yarn and dyes. As a result of the trade liberalization there has been a sudden increase in the export of yarn and within this the proportion of hank yarn especially in the counts of 20s and 40s used by the majority of handloom weavers, has increased phenomenally. [K. Srinivasulu, 1996]. Critical to the crisis in the handloom industry has been the rise in the prices of yarn and dyes. It is important to note that the Abid Hussain committee reviewing the 1985 policy emphasized the "high and fluctuating prices of yarn" imposing great hardship on the handloom weavers". It further noted that the "handloom yarn for their requirements" on account of the violation of Hank Yarn Obligation order by the spinning mills requiring to produce 50 per cent of their yarn output in hank yarn form [GOI, 1990: 11].

The trade liberalisation initiated as part of the economic reforms had further compounded the problem by allowing exports. In 1991, as the experience of the weavers in Andhra Pradesh showed, with the master-weavers disinclined to continue production, thus finding them out of work, the weavers were pushed into starvation and suicides.

What had been the policy response of government to the crisis of the handloom weavers? Two specific schemes meant to address this may be mentioned. They were Mill Gate Price Scheme (MGPS) and Hank Yarn Price Subsidy Scheme. While the per annum requirement of the hank yarn is assessed to be around 460 to 480 million kgs, the hank yarn target under the MGPS was 10 million kgs and that under the HYPSS was f20 million kgs (with a subsidy of rupees 15 per kg) to the weavers in the cooperative sector.

If the above schemes were inadequate to address the magnitude of the problem, then the introduction of the 'Loom to the Loom- less Weavers' scheme in the midst of the crisis showed the callousness of the governmental response. This scheme launched with a budget of 523.20 crore (with one-fourth as subsidy component) and phased over three years from 1993-94 with a target of 1.09 lakh looms per year [Compendium of Handloom Schemes, pp. 23-44] meant unpredictable rise of hank yarn prices it is shocking to note that the government should come out with this scheme and allocate a whopping sum of 523.20 crore to it as against a mere 30 crore to HYPSS. Further, on the ground when there were only weaver less looms an imagined 'loom less' weaver was accorded priority. As a matter of factor, the loom-lessness and loom idleness are two aspects of the displacement and marginalization of handloom weavers: when a weaver displaced from work leaves his native village he becomes loom less and his loom back at home idle. The migrant weaver working on the loom provided by the master-weaver in fact does not need loom as much as he needs yarn at reasonable process to continue to be employed. This basic fact, which undoubtedly was within the knowledge of the policy makers, has been ignored.

III

Even though, the 1985 policy moved away from the earlier policy commitments and prioritised productivity, efficiency and competition (which are seen to be lacking in handlooms) as against employment (seen as the only consideration for the support to handlooms), it, as discussed above, continued to talk about providing reservations and hank yarn obligation to the handlooms. The proposed policy, if the recommendations of the Satyam committee are any indication, may undo all this. The Satyam committee as a matter of fact is a continuation of the Mira Seth committee. In view of the non-availability of the detailed report of the former it would perhaps be instructive to recall the recommendations of the Seth committee, a high-powered handloom and make recommendations for the revamping of this sector [K. Srinivasulu, 1997.] The Mira Seth report mirrors the official thinking on the future of the handlooms. The principal thrust of the report has been on reorienting the handlooms to meet the challenges of the globalization process, which is presumed to be inevitable. In its View the strength of the handlooms lies in its "ability to commercially produce the goods in small volumes, quick switchover to new designs and creation of exquisite designs which cannot be made on the power looms." For this it recommended that the support to "develop new designs, new fabrics and new products having market acceptance and commercial viability... which may not be easily replicated on power looms." [GOI, 1996: 39] As a matter of fact all those designs which have specific mark of handloom and identified with well-known handloom production centers, in the absence of any legal safeguards to protect the rights of the handloom weaver-designers of these centers and the gross violation of the reservation act, have been very freely replicated in the power looms and mills. The Seth report, making an oblique reference to this, seems to be taking this as something unavoidable. The Mira Seth report, on the basis of the above perception, recommended an export growth strategy for the handloom survival. What the Satyam committee has done in essence is only to concretize their recommendation of the Seth report. In other words, it has sought t remove whatever ambiguities were present in the latter: while Seth recommended export strategy for the handlooms in general terms Satyam committee through its classification scheme sought to impress upon the policy makers that only the upper crust of the weaver community could attempt to survive the ensuing competition, while the bulk of the weavers have to simply give up their occupation. The anti-handloom dispensation of the latter becomes amply clear from its statement that "generally the handloom weavers remain tradition bound and are averse to change... For more than five decades, the poor handloom weavers remained spoon-fed through Government Schemes and they continue to look up the Government for anything and everything". This is the premise, though parades as a conclusion, which in fact served as the basis of the Satyam committee recommendations. What is striking about these reports is their conspicuous silence on the local markets. The handloom sector presents a quite complex picture of diversity; in fact, the strength of the handlooms has been the regional specificity and specialty of their products determined by the historically inherited community skills, techniques and designs and tuned to the local traditions, cultural practices and community needs. Ignoring this reality, if the fashionable prescription of the official policy makers to the handlooms to go 'global' were to be accepted and followed, the end to the handlooms weavers would not be very far away. The future of the handlooms depends on the organized struggles of the weavers against the anti-handloom policy dispensation of the rulers. Undoubtedly, this has to be part of a broader people's movement building up in the country as a resistance to the neo-liberal globalisation agenda.

REFERENCES

Government of India (GOI) (1974), 'Report of the High Powered study Team on the Problems of handloom Industry', Ministry of Commerce, July.

——(1985), 'Statement on Textile Policy: June 1985', Ministry of Supply and Textiles, Department of Textiles.

——(1990), 'The Textile Industry in the 1990s: Restructuring with a Human Face', Report of the Committee to Review the Progress of Implementation of Textile Policy of June 1985, New Delhi, January.

——(1996), 'Report of the High Powered Committee on Handlooms', Ministry of Textiles, Office of the Development Commissioner for Handlooms.

——(n.d.), Compendium on Handloom Schemes, Development Commissioner for Handlooms, Ministry of Textiles, New Delhi.

Srinivasulu, K (1996), '1985 Textile Policy and Handloom Industry: Policy, Promises and performance,' *Economic and Political Weekly*, December 7.

Srinivasulu, K. (1997), 'High-Powered Committee, Low Voltage Report: Mira Seth Report on handlooms', *Economic and Political Weekly*, June 14.

9

HANDLOOMS–A MODEL OF SUSTAINABLE RURAL INDUSTRY

Dastkar Andhra

Dastkar Andhra began in 1989, as a small group dedicated to providing support to artisan industries in Andhra Pradesh. Why artisan industries? We felt that the basic problem facing people was how to earn a living, and this imperative was forcing them to become part of the large commercial system, which in fact was what was destroying their lives. For example, the bamboo artisans in areas around the paper mills such as Sirpur in Adilabad, are the ones who cut the bamboo that is needed by the mills, whose predatory use of bamboo is destroying the bamboo forests. In other words, artisans often unwittingly become partners in their own exploitation, feeling that there is no alternative.

DA's work has to be seen against this background, of the issues facing artisan industries today. India is the only country in the world where crafts are a way of life for literally millions of people – handloom weavers alone are 12 million – producing goods for everyday use by every section of society. These industries can provide sustainable alternatives to much of the industrial production that is devastating our environment today. Our involvement of the last 10 years has led us to understand that traditional technologies and industries are not only sustainable in terms of products, but also in terms of processes, which provide stable livelihoods to vast numbers of people.

PUTTING TRADITIONAL TECHNOLOGY/INDUSTRY IN PERSPECTIVE

The sweeping discourse of modernization has tended to demarcate certain areas/industries as traditional, and hence in need of modernization or improvement in techniques of production, or put more simply, in terms of technological up gradation. In this perception, all that is urban-based or western is technologically advanced, whereas all that is rural is backward or traditional, and hence seen as in need of development. Rather than accept this viewpoint, we could well turn to rural areas as offering models for learning. Historically, it is clear that there were several kinds of industries flourishing in India.

WHAT ACTUALLY WERE THESE INDUSTRIES? A PRELIMINARY LIST WOULD INCLUDE

Iron and steel making, paper, building and masonry, sugar, distillation, textiles of silk and cotton, leather, wood, metal, bamboo, stone, glass, ceramics, ship building, musical instruments, tools, transport vehicles, precious metals and stones, lacs, adhesives and paints, food preservation, dyeing, printing, painting and sophisticated tools for all this. There was a continuous process of technology transfer upgradation and exchange of skills within the producing and trading communities.

WHAT ARE THE SIGNIFICANT FEATURES OF TRADITIONAL TECHNOLOGIES?

The significant aspects of traditional technologies are that they are low capital intensive, suited to the environment (soil, water, and seasons), use local raw materials and renewable energies, and with large quantities of output from large numbers of small dispersed units. The technological skills involve large numbers of people and are easily propagated. These technologies are embedded in their societal context, with in-built systems for skill dissemination. Taken together, these characteristics ensure that traditional industries can be sustained over millennia, without creating social upheavals or environmental degradation.

THE HANDLOOM INDUSTRY

We offer below a perspective on the potential and needs of a traditional, rural production system–namely the handloom industry–as a possible model for sustainable rural development incorporating traditional skills.

The handloom sector is the largest occupation in the country after agriculture even today. The sector produces around 18% of the country's total textile output. (The mill segment produces 5% of the total textile production, while powerlooms produce close to 60% of the total). Markets for the products of the handloom sector are found both in urban and rural areas. Most often, handlooms are in the news because of the problems of the handloom weaver, the low earnings, even the suicides when times get really bad. While it is true that the handloom weaver is in dire straits, these problems cannot be tackled through welfare measures alone. First of all, we need to understand and work on the potential and strengths of the handloom industry.

These are the *charactertisitcs of the handloom industry* today, which also contribute to its strengths:

1. *It is extremely diversified in nature, in terms of product and relations of production.* From weaving coarse cloth for local needs to producing a range of medium and fine fabrics for a larger (usually urban) market, the varieties of cloth produced on handlooms are indeed vast. Each region is known for a specific product that is unique in design and style. The modes and relations of production are also very diverse. There are independent weavers, weavers organized into co-operatives and those working under master weavers. While a few areas may be characterized by one clear-cut mode of production, a combination of types and a multiplicity of relations of production are usually found elsewhere.

2. *It is capable of flexibility in processes and products. It is capable of great flexibility in processes, products and geographical shifts.* Alterations in the production process and innovations in product are fairly easily achieved. Unlike land resources that root an individual to a given place, a weaver is limited only by his skill and, being mobile, could shift from one production base to another.

3. *It is decentralized, located in clusters in rural areas and also some urban areas.* Handloom weaving as an economic activity predates modern industrialization. Within the village economy that obtained in the past, weavers catered primarily to local needs and was one of the service castes. Thus every village, or every cluster of villages, would have a number of weaving families. Running parallel to this was also market-oriented production, located largely in weaving centres near port towns, where master traders organized weaving for export. Sometimes, these were organized as karkhanas, or weaving 'factories', but by and large, unlike the highly centralized mill sector, handloom weaving today continues to be dispersed and decentralized in nature.

4. *It is largely home-based, with labour inputs form the entire family.* The second sense in which the handloom industry is decentralized is that it is largely household-based. While weaving sheds do exist occasionally, more widespread is the weaver weaving at home, drawing on the labour of all the family members. In each stage of the production process, whether it is pre-loom processing, weaving or finishing–every member of the household has a clear role to play. In many ways, it is similar to the subsistence agricultural household that engages in the self-exploitation of labour in order to remain at the subsistence level.

This household-based industry, with its low capital and energy requirements and its ability to provide livelihoods to a large number of people, has immense economic potential. In the present economic climate, where dependency of the domestic industries on foreign collaborations and capital is increasing, this sector, which is free of foreign raw material, capital or know-how, and which is closely integrated to the domestic markets, has the potential to become the backbone of sustainable industrial production in the domestic sector. Its advantages lie in the facts of:

1. A large pool of highly skilled manpower
2. Minimum capital requirement, no foreign exchange component
3. Zero energy input
4. Economy of decentralized production closely linked to local markets.

Though its growth potential is immense, what is required is supportive infrastructure of credit, training and research institutions. Most of the steps taken to tackle such needs as credit, raw material and marketing have had a centralized structure that has been unable to reach out to the inherently decentralized nature of the industry. The development of support systems that would match the characteristics of the industry is urgently needed today. It is well within our national capability to provide these at no great cost, yet the state has not been forthcoming, and continues to see the sector in welfare terms.

Our practical experience in the field shows that the following are needed in order to ensure the viability of the handloom sector:

(a) extension of credit facility to primary producers
(b) raw material access on reasonable terms
(c) development of innovative market mechanisms
(d) technical and other kinds of research that will support the demands of the industry

1. *Raw materials:* Today, a major difficulty of handloom weavers across the country is the non-availability of adequate quantities of good quality yarn at reasonable prices. The government took certain measures to deal with this problem: (a) the setting up of co-operative spinning mills to ensure supplies to the handloom sector (but the experience in Andhra Pradesh shows that several of these have closed down over the past 3 to 4 years). (b) the obligation on mills to pack 50% of

their total marketable yarn as hank yarn (but this is rarely adhered to). Since the production and supply of yarn vests with the mill sector, the fortunes of the handloom sector get tied to this. The supply of yarn contracts or its price goes up whenever mills require it, forcing handloom weavers to turn to private traders for yarn.

- Non-availability of yarn of the required count and at reasonable prices are continuing problems in the handloom sector. The yarn availability scenario is also affected by the proliferation of the powerloom sector. Though powerlooms use cone yarn, they seek to avoid high yarn duty imposed on it by buying up hank yarn and converting it to cones (the cost of re-reeling being minimal). There is thus a considerable diversion of hank yarn meant for the handloom sector to other players, creating conditions of shortage, high rates, etc. Estimates of this linkage range from 15 to 25%.
- There are other problems as well. Governmental intervention regarding yarn supply is confined to the co-operative sector. For the rest working outside the co-operative fold, yarn access remains difficult. Since it passes through various hands, and dealers at each level add their own commissions, the price is considerably higher than mill rates. Most of this cost burden is transferred onto the weaver, especially since weavers are unable to bargain with yarn merchants or master weavers.
- Weavers in different regions require different counts of yarn. This is not always available, leading to a mismatch in demand and supply. Third, the supply of yarn has fluctuated with the fortunes of the cotton crop as well as with policies pertaining to the export of yarn.

To capitalize on the strengths of the handloom industry, it is necessary to build ancillary support systems specifically suited to its dispersed nature. At present yarn is produced in spinning mills located in distant towns and cities. The pre-spinning process is also technologically intensive which affects the inherent strengths of the cotton fiber. Since the end users of yarn, that is, the handloom weavers in this case, are dispersed across different regions and villages, developing smaller units of yarn production to cater to their needs will be feasible. Small-scale, decentralized yarn production located near cotton fields and weaving clusters will provide crucial linkages between these sectors through which direct flows can be established between cotton cultivation and textile production. This direct relation would also eliminate many of the costly and unnecessary stages of the current pre-spinning process such as baling and reduce the need for carding, as well as generate rural employment.

In addition, continued attention needs to be paid to the right kind of yarn availability (for example, the counts woven and required in a particular region), price regulation and policies regarding the export of yarn, since all of these directly affect the viability of handloom weaving as an industry. While setting up of smaller retail yarn outlets would be beneficial, linkages between credit provision and yarn availability also need to be worked out.

2. *Credit needs:* Credit, or rather the lack of it, is the single largest block in the growth of the handloom industry.

- Despite all the claims of subsidies to the handloom sector, the amount of *institutional credit* that is made available to weavers is abysmally low. While banks have an inbuilt bias against small producers, the credit facilities available to the co-operatives are far from adequate. Very often, master-weaver controlled co-operatives manage to siphon off a large chunk of the credit available. The credit needs of the majority of weavers outside the co-operative fold also remain unaddressed. The existing situation is one where the local master weaver provides consumption loans and/or advances, which, over time, render the weaver completely indebted to the master weaver.
- Also neglected are the *different kinds of credit needs* of weavers. While adequate and timely credit for input

procurement is the main need, at times, capital may be required for repairs or for domestic and social expenses. There is just no agency that can meet this wide spectrum of credit needs, and invariably weavers end up indebted to the local moneylender or master weaver.

- Credit institutions need to be designed which will provide credit in the way that is needed, large number of small loans, to suit the dispersed nature of the handloom industry and to suit market seasonality. Mechanisms must also be developed to support well-functioning producer groups and to ensure productive use of credit. The growth of self-help groups and thrift groups among weavers must be encouraged with matching grants and other incentives for this purpose.

3. *Marketing*: There is a significant mismatch between cloth production (which is dispersed) and marketing which has yet to be seriously tackled. Trader entrepreneurs who may know the market well, and are able to meet new demands often dominate existing marketing channels. But as traders, they also block the trickledown of benefits, even though the profit margin is quite high. The centralized marketing bodies of weaver co-operatives too have been malfunctioning.

A large part of the problem lies in faulty institutional mechanisms of marketing, rather than in the lack of a demand for handloom cloth. The view that a domestic demand for handlooms has no prospects of growth and that there should be more of export-oriented production is far from the truth. Our organization's experience has shown convincingly that there is a large and growing domestic demand for handlooms. Handloom production is well integrated into local demand and this sector cannot be ignored. The potential for growth of this sector in fact lies in the medium and heavier plainer fabrics, rather than the complex patterned or high-count 'fine' fabrics, which are more suited to a small niche market. This is because such production draws on simple and affordable technology and does not require expensive loom attachments. Also, there is a large-scale demand in the burgeoning middle-class markets in cities and towns that can easily be tapped.

WHAT'S NEEDED?

- Market development and market exploration is what is urgently needed today. Though the export segment does need some attention, what is required today is the expansion, or development of the regional and national markets. The demand for handlooms at the middle and lower levels of the market too has to be addressed, and appropriate marketing mechanisms devised.
- Market information-A pre-requisite for all this will be the generation of suitable information about the handloom market, through comprehensive market surveys, and a free flow of such information, which is currently closely guarded by traders.
- These would constitute first steps towards (a) the elimination of trader domination over the market and (b) the development of alternative marketing channels that would better suit the nature of the decentralized handloom industry in the state.

Handloom weavers are the largest group of artisan producers in the country today. Such artisan production has to be recognized by the State as industries and their concomitant institutional supports–pertaining to credit, marketing and management training–met.

THE POLICY FRAMEWORK

The needs of the sector identified above have usually been raised within the framework of the state's textile policy. Textile policy, from the 1950s onwards, has sought to balance demands from different sectors, i.e., mill, powerloom and handloom. There have been a series of early legislations pertaining to the handloom sector, several of which recognized the employment potential of the industry and sought to protect the sector with legislations–for eg., certain items reserved only for production by handloom industry.

All this began changing by mid 1980s and definitely by 1990s. The present crisis has been made worse by successive textile policies, primarily the liberalization agenda.

- Clearest indication was the New Textile Policy of 1985, part of R. Gandhi's early phase of liberalization, where older ideologies of socialism were giving way to new pressures. A shift from old framework of state controlled economic growth to a liberalized market economy and export oriented growth. Terminology shifted from employment, equality, social justices, to modernization, efficiency, market, productivity and competition. (Effects of these seen in successive budgets too).
- In 1985 NTP, stress was on productivity rather than employment; two major processes initiated were: de-regulation of textile industry (i.e., no barriers to expansion and restructuring of mills and powerlooms) and de-control of yarn trade. As a result, over 5 lakh unauthorized powerlooms were regularized in 1985, figure was said to have gone up to 8 lakhs by 1990. These directly and indirectly impacted the rural handloom industry.
- The Textile Policy of 2000, based on the Satyam Committee report had the objective of making India a global player in textile production and exports. It set the target of increasing textile exports in value terms by around five times in the next decade. To achieve this, it de-reserves garment-making from the small-scale sector and throws it open to private investment. Its facilitative policies include allowing 100% foreign direct investment in the textile sector, encouraging the private sector to set up integrated textile complexes, further liberalizing cotton yarn export, funds for technology upgradation 200 crores, mainly for setting up automatic looms, etc. None of these actually address the main problems of traditional handloom and increasingly even small, powerloom weavers.

What is clear, therefore, is a systematic marginalization of a traditional, largely rural-based industry, especially when we look at how protective legislations have worked on the field. For instance, the Handloom Reservation Act of 1985 reserved 22 items for the exclusive production of handlooms. However, it could not be implemented till 1993 due to the legal dispute posed by the mill and powerloom lobby in the Supreme Court. The Mira Seth Committee recommended the reduction of the number of items reserved from 22 to 11 and recent annual report of ministry of textiles indicates that this has been implemented. Even after the Act came into effect from 1993, the number of violations reported in the annual reports has been shocking low, to the tune of five to fifteen all over the country. The approach paper to Tenth Plan suggests that reservation is uneconomical in the wake of liberalization and hence has to be phased out eventually.

While the emphasis on preparing the handloom industry to meet the challenge of the liberalized economy is a welcome one, the facilitative steps that could ensure its competitiveness have not been taken. Given the effects of WTO and liberalization and the reality of international competition in cloth production, it is imperative to expand patent protection. Just as patents protect individual products, we must press for protection on the basis of cultural heritage. Market pressures and the incessant demand for variety are pushing producers to constantly look out for something new. In India, we have a permanent demand for certain kinds of products such as saris and dhotis, since culture defines dress codes. In order to protect this market demand, it is necessary to patent these categories of items, and reserve for ourselves the exclusive right to produce them. Such rights could vest in the hands of the weaving community as whole, rather than specific individuals.

Rural-based industries have often been marginalized in the economic race. The instance of the handloom industry has been presented above. The role of the state in enacting and implementing the right kind of policies regarding these sectors is important in order to strengthen the base of these rural industries.

10

REFORMS AND ITS IMPACT ON THE SSIs–A FIELD APPRAISAL

Sudheesh Kaippachery

We are well past 12 years since India embarked on the reforms course (1991). It is time we analyse the performance of rural industries in the reform period. This paper analyses the performance of Rural Small Scale Enterprises in an Industrial Development Plot (Andoor) in Kannur District of Kerala with the help of primary data for the period 1991-2002. The liberalized Exim policies and de-reservation formed the key areas under trade liberalization. These policies had impacted the RSSEs. Following import liberalization, cheaper raw materials are reaching the domestic markets. With the de-reservation of SSI products, the RSSEs face open competition from the domestic and foreign markets.

This study is based on the empirical method of analysis. Primary data was collected from the RSSEs, using a structured interview schedule. The survey was conducted in the early months of the year 2003. Based on the information on the enterprises in Andoor IDP obtained from the District Industries Centre, Kannur, a list of enterprises set up in this plot was prepared. These units were set up during the period 1991-2002. It covered 82 units in Andoor IDP, which were stratified into ten product groups for the sake of analysis. The selection of this IDP is significant in the sense that it had attracted a lot of investment in the rural industrial activities in the post reform period. Andoor has the duel character of urban and rural setting.

ECONOMIC SUSTAINABILITY

Economic sustainability is one of the three aspects of industrial sustainability, the other two being social and environmental sustainability. An enterprise is economically sustainable if it can improve or maintain its economic performance (in terms of employment, output, productivity etc.) since inception. Sustainability itself is relative and hence to avoid ambiguity economic sustainability is defined here in terms of important economic variables. The following model of economic sustainability is used for this study:

$$Re = Em + Ot + Pl + Ia + Dm + Ep + Cn + Dn + Si + Ra$$

(Re = Economic sustainability of RSSEs; Employment; Output; Labour productivity; Investment adequacy; Market demand; Earning position; Competition; Diversification; Safety inputs; Raw Material availability)

Using the above model, the economic sustainability of the RSSEs is defined as follows: If 60 per cent of the RSSEs responded positively to the variables, then the Andoor IDP is said to be economically sustainable. Two types of scales are used separately (1) three point scale for measuring employment, output, labour productivity, market demand, earning position, competitiveness, and raw material availability (2) two point scale for measuring adequacy of investment, diversification and safety of inputs. The study is more qualitative than quantitative in analyzing the economic sustainability.

DATABASE

Primary data were collected from, the 82 RSSEs in Andoor IDP which were set up in the last twelve years of the reforms. The enterprises were stratified into ten product groups as under:

Table 1
Census Distribution of Units, IDP, Andoor

Product Group	*No*
Wood (W)	26
Handloom, Powerloom, garments, Textiles, Jute, Rubber *	14
Flour mill	2
Food products	5
Agro-Based	47
Engineering	5
Electronics, electricals.	3
Service, repair	7
Metal, Machinery	9
Chemicals, printing plastic	7
Cement, Bricks & tiles.	4
Non-Agro Based	35
Total units	82

There is only one rubber unit in the IDP, which produces rubberized pillows and the like. So it is also included in this product group. About 57% of the IDP units are agro-based and 43% are non-agro based industries. This stratification includes both traditional and modern enterprises, which enable us to capture the emerging tendencies under the reforms in both types of enterprises. Majority of the units are involved in manufacturing followed by service, processing, repair and job work. The manufacturing involved both consumer goods and intermediary goods as well.

EMPLOYMENT

Employment is an important determinant of economic sustainability. Here employment means the annual average person days in the enterprise. In terms of employment generation, an enterprise is economically sustainable if it is able to increase or maintain the initial level of employment.

It can be seen that in Andoor IDP, almost an equal percentage of the agro and non-agro based units have sustained the employment level since the beginning. Capital inadequacy under the economic reforms has forced some of the units to reduce the number of workers. Labour flexibility is an important feature of the liberalized economy. Higher component of hired labour is a way of maintaining labour flexibility. It should be noted that majority of the workers in the IDP are hired labourers. Rising wage bill in the total cost of production also force the entrepreneurs to limit the number of employees. All these have resulted in declining employment in the 23 per cent of the IDP units.

In overall terms, 77 per cent of the enterprises (both agro and non-agro based) have sustained (it means either increased or maintained) their initial level of employment. So the IDP units have fared better under the reforms and hence they are economically sustainable on this count.

OUTPUT

Output is the result of industrial activity. Here output means the amount of products generated in a year valued in rupee terms. Employment and output are closely related.

Non-agro based enterprises (65 per cent) have done better than the agro-based units (55 per cent) in sustaining their output level. In overall terms, 60 per cent of the IDP units could sustain their initial output level and hence they are economically sustainable on this count.

It should be noted that in case of unsustainable RSSEs, while employment has declined in 23 per cent of the units, output level has declined in 40 per cent of the IDP units. Here again as in the case of employment it was found that financial inadequacy under the reforms has forced the entrepreneurs to contract the volume of production in 40 per cent of the unsustainable RSSEs. Declining business orders and the growth of outstanding business credits are found to be the other major factors forcing the business contraction.

PRODUCTIVITY

Productivity is an important determinant of economic sustainability. Productivity here means the labour productivity, which is obtained by dividing the total value of output in a year by the annual average person days. It is found that almost the same percentage of the agro-based and non-agro based (51 per cent) units have sustained the level of labour productivity since

Table 2
Empirical Data from Field

Product Group	*Increased*	*Remained constant*	*Decreased*	*Size of population*
Agro-Based	11	25	11	47
Non–Agro Based	10	17	8	35
Employment	21	42	19	82
	(25.61)	(51.22)	(23.17)	(100)
Agro-Based	13	13	21	47
Non–Agro Based	12	11	12	35
Output Level	25	24	33	82
	(30.49)	(29.27)	(40.24)	(100)
Agro-Based	14	10	23	47
Non–Agro Based	11	7	17	35
Labor Productivity	25	17	40	82
	(30.49)	(20.73)	(48.78)	(100)
Agro-Based	15	7	25	47
Non–Agro Based	14	3	18	35
Market Demand	29	10	43	82
	(35.36)	(12.20)	(52.44)	(100)
Agro-Based	15	23	9	47
Non -Agro Based	15	18	2	35
Earning position	30	41	11	82
	(36.59)	(50)	(13.41)	(100)
Agro-Based	34	11	2	47
Non–Agro Based	24	11	-	35
Competitiveness	58	22	2	82
	(70.73)	(26.83)	(2.44)	(100)
Agro-Based	42	-	5	47
Non–Agro Based	31	-	4	35
Rawmaterial availability	73	-	9	82
	(89.02)		(10.98)	(100)
Agro-Based		25	22	47
Non–Agro Based		21	14	35
Investment Adequacy		46	36	82
		(56.10)	(43.90)	(100)
Agro-Based		14	33	47
Non–Agro Based		8	27	35
Diversification		22	60	82
		(26.83)	(73.17)	(100)
Agro-Based		21	26	47
Non–Agro Based		19	16	35
Safe Sources of Labour and Capital		40	42	82
		(68.78)	(51.22)	(100)

the beginning even though it is significantly higher in the former group. As noted earlier employment and output have fallen in 23 per cent and 40 per cent of the RSSEs respectively which naturally led to a decline in the labour productivity also. Definitely the reform process has precipitated this trend. The sharp decline in output badly affected the productivity of the RSSEs. In overall terms, only 51 per cent of the RSSEs could increase or maintain their initial productivity level. And hence they are economically unsustainable on this count.

ADEQUACY OF INVESTMENT

Adequacy of investment plays a significant role in sustaining the rural industrial activities. Adequacy of investment means that the RSSEs can generate investment out of the own business for the plant maintenance. After some years of operation, a unit is supposed to end financial dependence and reach self-sufficiency for plant maintenance. If a unit can generate investment out of own business, it is treated as economically sustainable. It can be seen that the non-agro based units (60 per cent) have more investment adequacy than the agro-based units (53 per cent). Rising cost of production of these days in general and narrow profit margin in particular leave very little or nothing for the plant maintenance. These factors are severe in agro-based units under the reforms and that is why they generated comparatively less investment. Only 56 per cent of the RSSEs in Andoor IDP are able to generate investment for the plant maintenance and hence they are economically unsustainable on this court.

MARKET DEMAND

Market demand is found to be the most important variable affecting the economic sustainability of the RSSEs. Here market demand means the amount of output of the RSSEs purchased by the consumers. If a unit can increase or maintain the initial level of its market demand, then it is treated as economically sustainable.

Non-agro based units (49 per cent) have done slightly better than the agro-based units (47 per cent) in increasing or maintaining their initial demand. Increased competition from the local and non-local units is the major reason for this poor demand condition in both agro and non-agro based units. The economic reforms had precipitated the competition in both domestic and foreign markets, which resulted in declining decreased for the rural industrial products. The general decline in the income level of the common people after the reforms also affected the demand for rural industrial products. About 83 per cent of units face problems in marketing, of which competition is the most important problem. Delayed payment by the consumers is another important problem influencing demand. Only 48 per cent of the RSSEs in Andoor plot could increase or maintain their initial market demand and hence they are economically unsustainable.

EARNING POSITION

The viability of a plant depends on its earning position. Earning position means the generation of profit, loss, and no profit/no loss in the enterprise. If a unit can earn profit or just have no profit/loss, it is treated as economically sustainable.

Non-agro based units (94 per cent) have done better than the agro-based units (81 per cent) in earning profit or just making no profit/no loss. Here again the rising cost of production eats away the profit margins of the units. It should be noted that the percentage of the units making no profit/no loss is higher in both agro and non-agro units and at any time they can turn into loss making units. These days, a good percentage of the RSSEs are just maintaining their business under the challenges of liberalization and globalization.

Nearly 87 per cent of the units in Andoor IDP are either making profit or have no profit/loss. Hence these units are economically sustainable.

COMPETITIVENESS

Competitiveness of a unit is a crucial factor in sustaining the industrial activity. Competitiveness is measured here in terms of improvement in the quality of product and its price. If a unit can increase or maintain the initial level of competitiveness, then it can be treated as economically sustainable. Non-agro based units (100 per cent) are more competitive than the agro-based units (96 per cent). The stiff competition, which is the hallmark of the globalised market, has forced the units to improve their competitiveness by improving the quality of their products and price level. It is interesting to note that a good number of RSSEs can influence price of their products. Nearly 98 per cent of the RSSEs in the Andoor plot have either improved or maintained their initial level of competitiveness and hence they are economically sustainable.

DIVERSIFICATION

Diversification is another important factor sustaining the industrial activities. Diversification means that the units are producing new products, which are not substitutes for the existing products in the market (Barthwal 2000). If a unit is able to diversify it's products since the beginning, then it can be treated as sustainable. The agro-based units (30 per cent) have done better than the non-agro based units (23 per cent) in diversifying their product structure. It should be noted that nowadays majority of the RSSEs, are just maintaining their existing product structure rather than diversifying the same. Financial difficulties, as found earlier prevent these units from diversification and expansion. But to withstand in the present situation of reforms, the RSSES should diversify their product structure.

Only 27 per cent of the units in Andoor plot could diversify their product structure since the beginning and hence the RSSEs are economically unsustainable.

SAFETY OF LABOUR AND CAPITAL

Safety of Labour and capital create business confidence in the entrepreneurs. The safety of inputs here means that the entrepreneur can continue his business without any fear about adequacy of capital and labour. If a unit has secured source of inputs, then it can be treated as economically sustainable. Unsafe source of inputs create uncertainty in the rural industrial activities. This prevents the entrepreneurs from taking new orders or expanding their business capital is found to be scarce in comparison with labour. The rural financial markets have not developed adequately under the reforms to support the needy rural enterprises. Even if capital is available in some cases, the terms and conditions are 'hard' not 'soft' for the entrepreneurs to borrow the same.

The percentage of units having safe inputs is higher in the non-agro based group (55 per cent) than in the agro-based units (45 per cent). Capital inadequacy, as found earlier, is higher in the agro-based units. The labourers also prefer non- agro based units rather than agro based units. This is due to relatively higher wage in the non-agro based units. All these led to a higher level of insecurity of inputs in the agro-based units. Labour and capital, being flexible in the reforms period, have become unsafe sources to depended on for the industrial activities.

Only 49 per cent of the RSSEs in units Andoor IDP have safe source of labour and capital and hence they are economically unsustainable.

RAW MATERIAL AVAILABILITY

Adequate availability of raw materials is a must for sustaining the rural industrial activities. If the raw material availability has increased or remained constant since the beginning, then it can be treated as economically sustainable.

Both the agro-based units (89 per cent) and non-agro based units (89 per cent) have done equally well in availing the raw materials for their production. Raw material availability has increased especially after the reforms. A large amount of the raw materials are reaching the local markets from the developed countries. Trade liberalization has been instrumental in facilitating their cheap availability.

Nearly 89 per cent of the RSSEs in Andoor plot have increased the availability of raw materials since the beginning and hence they are economically sustainable on this count.

Using the model of economic sustainability, the following result is obtained:

Re = Em + Ot + Pl + Ia + Dm+ Ep + Cn + Dn + Si + Ra = .77 + .60 + .51 + .56 + .48 + .87 + .98 + .27 + .49 + .89

Total score = 6.42

= 6.42/10

= .642 x 100

= 64.2 %1*

If we take account of the increase in the variables alone, (ignoring the cases where the variables remained constant), only a small percentage off the RSSEs will be sustainable. Since in the index, we have included 'constancy' of variables like output, employment, productivity etc. in measurement of economic sustainability, the RSSEs are found to be marginally sustainable in the short run. But in the long run the RSSEs are likely to become unsustainable even with the slightest disturbances from the market. Before these RSSEs die a natural death, some external help, more than mere reservation, from the government is needed. The RSSEs in Andoor IDP have done well in terms of employment, output, earning position, competitiveness and raw-material availability but fared badly in productivity, investment adequacy, market demand, diversification, and safe inputs. It shows that the crucial variables, which sustain the rural enterprises in the challenged world of liberalization and globalisation have turned against the Andoor enterprises. Most of the product groups in this study are reserved items. Still these units have not fared satisfactorily under the economic reforms. Partly, because the reservation has helped other non-rural small-scale industries and now the RSSEs are forced to compete in the domestic market with the former.

It is observed that the non-agrobased units have performed better than the agro-based units under the economic reforms. The changing market situation favours the non-agro based units. The agro-based units are finding it difficult to cope up with the emerging demand pattern in the markets. On the other hand, the non-agro based units cater to the changing taste of the consumers in liberalized and globalised markets.

CONCLUSIONS AND RECOMMENDATIONS

The RSSEs in Andoor IDP are economically sustainable in the reforms period. The entrepreneurs of these units are struggling hard to sustain their units under the challenges of liberalisation and globalisation. The challenges under the reforms have started affecting the sustainability of these enterprises.

Sound business practices are needed for the sustainable development of the RSSEs. The development of rural financial market is needed. Development of institutions providing soft loans to the RSSEs is a welcome step. Improvement in the quality of the products, tradefares in rural markets, advertisements and displays will improve the marketing of rural industrial products. The electricity charge is very high which needs to be modified through suitable policies. The R&D facilities in the RSSEs should be developed. Reduction in cost of production, improvement in the quality of the products and proper dissemination of market information are necessary. The RSSEs should emerge as strong exporting units so that they can withstand the global competition. It requires diversification, expansion and technological development. These are the issues that should be considered while drawing up an agenda among other initiatives that are needed to keep India's RSSEs moving upwards.

NOTE

1. The values given above correspond to the respective variables. By dividing the score (6.42) by the number of variables 10, we get .642. Multiplying it by 100 we get 64.2%. It means that 64 per cent of the RSSEs are economically sustainable in Andoor IDP.

REFERENCES

Barthwal, R. R. (2000), Industrial Economics: An Introductory Text Book, New Age International Publishers, New Delhi.

Bhalla, G. S. and Peter Hazell (2003), 'Rural Employment and Poverty: Strategies to Eliminate Rural Poverty within a Generation' *Economic and Political Weekly*, Vol. XXXVIII, No. 33, August 16.

Radhakrishna, R. L. (2002), 'Agricultural Growth, Employment and Poverty: A Policy Perspective' *Economic and Political Weekly,* vol XXXV, No. 3, Jan 19.

Ray, Sunil (1994), 'Farm-Non-Farm Interaction in a Labour Surplus Economy', *Economic and Political Weekly,* Vol. XXIX, No. 53, December 31.

11

THE PROMOTION OF RURAL INDUSTRY THE FLIP FOPS OF EXTERNAL IMPETUS

Y. Gangi Reddy

Faced with the dismal prospect of a vibrant growth of rural industry, concerted effort is made to lend an external impetus. The official agencies took a lead in pump priming the growth of rural industry. The NGOs joined the race. Yet the results are far from satisfactory and sub-optimal. The external impetus however integral and fine tuned would turn out to be a poor substitute to the internal dynamic of growth. The latter is found wanting. The structural rigidities of the Indian agriculture go a long way in explaining the elusive internal dynamic. The compulsions of doing away with the structural rigidities are felt with redoubled ferocity with each passing year thanks to the pressures born out by the globalisation process. The day is not far off when the rigidities characteristic of its simple reproduction will make place for the much sought after extended reproduction. Internal dynamic of growth serves as the axis to the extended reproduction. Put in place, the rural industry flourishes at a rapid pace. The significance of external impetus does not get minimised nor is it that it would get marginalised in the reign of extended reproduction. The external impetus would rather ignite the internal dynamic to facilitate a much faster growth of farm output and the rural industries. It is time we take stock of the pros and cons of the external impetus; review the experience and draw useful lessons for the future. The many sided interventions call for a comprehensive appraisal. Here is an attempt.

FARM NON-FARM LINKAGES

Large majority of farming community is not more often than not able to realise the remunerative price to their produce. They are forced to go for distress sale. Lack of sectoral integration between agriculture and industry could be one of the serious issues of economic development. An integrated agro-industry promotion would alone provide a solace to the miserable plight of the farming community.

The industry is found faltering both on account of backward and forward linkages. Want of secure and steady supply of farm produce is compounded by the want of reliable markets in the final output from the industry. We are in for a mismatch between the source and the demand. There are a few such attempts at striking a balance between the source and demand. Sericulture could be one such example, where the promotional schemes are attempted to integrate both the agricultural as well as industrial activities. *Leaf to Cloth* scheme under Chetana Plan of Government of Andhra Pradesh could be one such example. There could be many more such examples in Cotton, Wool, Jute, Coffee, Rubber and Horticulture, where the farm and non-farm activities are integrated to successfully address the issue of survival of rural industry in the market.

ANCILLERISATION

Ancillerisation plays no small role in the market survival of industry. A special package of incentives is offered to the industrial units, which in turn help promote ancillerisation. Ancillerisation is considered as one of the important strategic tools for the market promotion of small and rural industries. National Small Industries Corporation is involved in a big way to establish linkages between ancillary units and major industries with a view to solving the problem of marketing of small units. In large number of industrial estates different units are marked for mutual dependence in market support. Majority of units in Waluz Industrial Estate promoted by MIDC are inter-dependant either for marketing or for supply of inputs. The ancillerisation could single handed stabilise large number of small and micro-enterprises over the years. However, the ancillerisation remained elusive to the rural industries so far. True, a large number of small industrial units sustain on sub contracting. We are yet to put in concerted efforts to romp home the ancillerisation in to the world of rural industries?

INSTITUTIONAL NETWORKING-CONVERGENCE AND SYNERGY

Rural industries sector is by far the largest employment provider next only to agriculture. The significance of the sector is not lost on the policy regime. The promotional agencies played no less a proactive role in articulating a host of programmes and schemes. Institutional backing is provided for. Large numbers of these institutions are working independent of each other. There are institutions, which are similar to others with more or less same goals and objectives. There are also institutions within the same sector or ministry created to achieve the same objectives with a special focus. However, all of them work independently. Any coordination worth the name is a amiss.

There is an urgent need to weave in intra and inter sectoral (departmental) as well as regional linkages for better institutional co-ordination. Institutional networking is a crying need at the backdrop of the WTO pressures. Efforts are afoot in the recent past and the results are encouraging. The concept of networking primarily deals with the connectivity of people or organisations or physical structures. The physical structures remain networked (canal systems) even as the networking of people or people's institutions remains elusive over the years. There is no dearth for instances of networking yielding optimal results. NGOs have set forth purposive networking with optimal returns. SEVA did a pioneering job in the networking of SHGs in Gujarat. The SHGs have created a marketing network of their own for the sale of their products. SEWA thus has set a model for others to learn. South India Producer's Association (SIPA) is yet another successful experiment. SIPA is a federation of select NGOs working in the field of micro-enterprise promotion in four southern states. SIPA could successfully address the marketing problems at home. Not content, SIPA vies for making an entry in to the international market thanks to its affiliation with the international federations of its ilk.

Government of India launched a special scheme called the "District Supply and Marketing Society" (DSMS) to provide market support for various products in the districts. DSMSs are established in almost all the districts in the country. There is much to be desired on account of performance. States like Kerala and Orrissa have shown a better performance. There are individual instances of a few other districts marked for better performance elsewhere, where an individual district collector has taken initiative. DSMS is effective in Kerala to the extent of making the district level purchases and marketing of different rural products with the support of DRDAs. The district level societies in Orissa were networked in to a state level agency to achieve the brand loyalty as well as other policy and programme support for marketing of rural products. National Programme on Self-employment i.e. Swarna Jayanthi Gram Swarozgari Yojana (SGSY) of the ministry of Rural Development (GOI) extends necessary financial backing to any state to strengthen the DSMS so as to make the SGSY more effective. Government of Orissa has drawn heavily on the SGSY support to network the DSMS. The effort at networking a host of SHGs under the umbrella of MAC&TS (Mutually Aided Co-operative & Thrift Societies) at the village and block level in A.P is commendable. The connectivity augments financial resources besides extending marketing support to the products of DWACRA.

Lack of institutional co-ordination is one of the major inhibiting factors for the promotion of rural micro-enterprises. Networking of community based organisations and integrating the same with the promotional agencies is the need of the hour. Vertical and horizontal purposive networking would put in place synergy and work wonders. There is the other facet to the networking i.e. the convergence.

There are number of schemes that are meant for providing financial support to those who are prepared to start a micro-enterprise with credit linked subsidy in all departments of rural industry promotion. There are also several other schemes such as provision of raw materials, skill development training, technology transfer, marketing support etc., However, each scheme is being implemented devoid of any linkages with the rest even when the promotional agency is the same. It does not augur well with the promotion of rural industries. Convergence is the crying need of the hour.

NATURAL RESOURCE MANAGEMENT

The rural industries sector is eco friendly. It does not result in the depletion of the resources unlike in the case of most other product lines of modern industry. The resources are renewable and as such the rural industry holds the brightest of the future. Yet, the industry is threatened with want of secure and steady supply of renewable resource base. The lacunae gives an edge to the resource depleting non bio energy based modern industry. Sustainable natural resource management holds the key for uninterrupted growth of the bio energy based rural industries. Degradation of natural resources is yet another area of major concern demanding timely correction. There are several agencies that supply raw material for select enterprises. However, supply of the same in terms of quantity, quality, cost and timeliness is the serious concern for the viability and sustainability of micro-enterprises. Survival of these industries is threatened from both ends of supply of raw material and increasing competition in the market from the synthetic products. Availability, (a) Accessibility, (b) Affordability, (c) State Policy & Facilitation, (d) Vulnerability, (e) Local Dynamics, (f) Maintenance and (g) Protection are some crucial issues of importance crying for immediate redressal. By far the largest concern is the resource endowment in any strategy at promoting the rural industrial sector. The following measures may go a long way in strengthening the resource endowment.

- Resource friendly harnessing of the naturally available resources.
- Pressing in service group dynamics and collective action of the local people in the regeneration and sustainable management of natural resources.
- Identification of prospective areas of natural resources.
- Integration of natural resources management with the local institutional framework so as to promote Eco-friendly rural micro-enterprises, which have got an edge in the global market.
- Shift from the survival approach to the sustainable development.
- Institutional control and management of natural resources making way for peoples (stakeholders) control management.

TECHNOLOGY TRANSFER

There is a large network of scientific institutions established to speed up the process of development in rural areas. Yet the fruits of technology revolution fail to reach the rural communities over the last five decades. The inputs of Science & Technology can speed up the process of development in the rural areas. There seems to be a wide gap between the technology development and transfer. A variety of schemes are pressed in service to bridge the gap relating the farm and no-farm sectors. Integrated package of services attains importance in the context of technology transfer in rural industries. Link up the technology transfer with market promotion to give a boost to the growth of micro-enterprises.

By and large technology transfer is limited to demonstration or making available technologies to the users devoid of a follow up. In most cases of non-conventional energy technologies, it has become a one time activity and its sustainability has thus become a big question mark. Requisite follow up action could help in sustaining technologies in field conditions. Adopting the laboratory born technologies to field conditions is no less a challenge. Transfer of appropriate technology is another major area of challenge. Need assessment on the back of close interaction with the stakeholders is wanting. Appropriate technology transfer could result in Improved Methods of Production, Quality Up gradation, Increase in Productivity, Increased Capacity Utilisation, Increased Value of Production, Increase in Gross Incomes/Net Profit, Higher Purchase Power and Better Quality of Life.

CLUSTER APPROACH

A recent attempt by MRD (GOI) under SGSY has started showing positive results. SGSY envisages adopting group approach to pool together all the players involved in a similar activity. The cluster approach has been successfully experimented. The cluster approach is attended by manifold advantages. Processing facilities, Packaging units, Quality testing centres, Supply of quality raw materials at a reasonable price become available at a single source cutting in to cost of the product. Support services such as the integrated package of assistance, Extension of timely training, Encouragement of Producer Groups or Co-operative societies, Market surveys, Skill development training to meet the market needs and Establishment of Market centres (Marketing Infrastructure) come in to the easy reach of the stakeholders. The cluster approach helps achieving economic viability of the individual units. We will do well to replicate the same. KVIC and SIDBI initiated measures at moving in the direction.

ORGANISATION OF EXHIBITIONS/MELAS

Exhibition or mela is found to be a useful instrumentality in bridging the gap between the small producer at one end and consumer at the other. It enables the littoral producer in avoiding the middlemen and accesses the consumer. The consumer price tends to be lower owing to the absence of the middlemen. The device has the other advantages as well. The interface between artisan and the consumer helps the former to gauge the consumer preferences. There are many other advantages too. A wide variety of products become available at a single source. It helps foster cultural and national integrity.

CONCLUSION

The top down approach of the promotional agencies leaves much to be desired. It has to metamorphose in to a bottom up approach. It is not enough that the promotional agencies are sufficiently proactive, which of course is not forthcoming in many instances. One needs to live through the entire process of promotion from beginning to the end. Promotional agencies suffer the dearth of promotional agents. Impersonal delivery of services is of little help. *Something is certainly better than nothing*. But the philosophy betrays lack of conviction. Indeed, there appears to be an invisible Chinese wall between the promoters at one side and the stakeholders at the other. Successes were not wanting where the wall does not come in the way. The aforesaid NGOs stand to set a brilliant example for the absence of the wall. The GOAP tried semi NGO promotional agencies with little success. The durability of the agencies remained a perplexing question. The want of conviction on the part of the promotional agencies coupled with the want of not so conducive material situation conspired together in dwarfing down the progression of the rural industries. We look for the material situation turn a new leaf making space for the redoubtable extended reproduction. None too conducive material situation is often found dispiriting the actors in the promotional agencies. Conducive material situation will fetch in the spirited promotional agents.

12

IMPACT OF NEW ECONOMIC POLICIES RURAL INDUSTRIES– THE AGONY OF ANDHRA PRADESH

V. Mohan Reddy

The debate on the ensuing Cancun ministerial meet shows that we are far from liberalizing. The implementation issues, the agricultural subsidies, the lowering of tariffs on manufactures and the so-called Singapore issues are all being hotly debated. Reports are that the implementation issues are sidelined by the developed west. We are also not sure whether the developed west would yield any worthwhile ground to the developing countries on the trade in manufactures till the Singapore issues are resolved to their satisfaction. The EU is said to have struck a deal with the US on lowering the tariffs on the manufactures as a quid pro quo so that the latter abstains from pressing the agricultural issues. The trade off between the Singapore issues and the agricultural issues has at the end emerged as the most contentious issue between the EU and Japan at one side and the block of developing countries at the other. The trade off between the EU and US apparently works to their mutual advantage much to the detriment of the developing countries. The developing countries on their part cannot possibly hope to accomplish the impossible feat of agreeing to the suicidal Singapore issues. The failure to concede to the Singapore issues provides an alibi to the EU and the US to continue to wield the threat of inundation of agricultural markets of the developing countries.

Most part of the developing world indeed finds itself in the pitiable position of defending their agricultural markets in the first place as against the onslaught of the developed west leave alone gaining a share in the latter's markets be it in the domain of agriculture or manufacturing. India figures foremost on the loosing side. The governments of the day of the developing countries are mortally afraid that it would cost them the luxury of power should the developed west is allowed to have a free reign in the local agricultural markets. The powers that be make it no secret and admit it in so many words. The Indian delegation led by its commerce minister, Arun Jaitly is believed to take an admirably hardened stance on the Singapore issues come what may. All the same, the delegation hopes to wrest considerable concessions on all other issues in league with 20 other prominent developing countries. It is perhaps possible to make some small gains covering the implementation issues, the agriculture issues and the trade in manufactures in favor of the developing countries. But the concessions may not bring us any cheers. Instead, the concessions might prove to our own disadvantage should we continue to dwell on our own fool hardy course. The reasons are not far to seek. Look at the following.

The Caims group would make for most part of the gains in the realm of agricultural concessions. Countries such as Bangladesh, China and the like are expected to benefit the most from the concessions on the implementation issues. Perhaps, the concessions on the trade in manufactures go the same way while we continue to take the beating in our internal markets on all fronts. A bit of elaboration is in order. The AP case exemplifies the suicidal course.

The GOI is yet to formulate a comprehensive agricultural policy *vis-à-vis* the overseas markets. Nor does it encourage the provincial governments to focus on the export led growth of agriculture. Agriculture apparently is the subject of the state governments. As such, the provincial governments are well endowed to deal with export led growth of agriculture and the agro industry. Any sensible export led growth strategy at the state level awaits the center conceding the provincial autonomy with an explicit mandate to embark on the export led growth of agriculture. One who fails to look for competing in the markets abroad cannot possibly hope to succeed in defending the internal markets as against the competition from abroad.

The absence of such a clear direction from the center's side resulted in the GOAP misplacing its priorities much to the detriment of agriculture sector and the reform process at large in the last many years. An oft-heard recipe was that the agriculture is/was a dying sector. The agricultural sector was subject to fresh imposts (power tariff hike etc) even as a dismal concern was shown to it on the growth front. The lopsided policy boomeranged telling on the very reform process. It goes without saying that a meaningful export led growth strategy, which holds a bright future for agriculture and the reforms entailing the power, irrigation, fertilizer and procurement would have gone hand in hand. Compounding the grievous lapse on the agricultural growth strategy is the misplaced zeal at an ostensible promotion of across the board, all and sundry of the rural industries irrespective of their merit and export prospects. The effort has come a cropper despite claims to the contrary. It is not difficult to see through the game plan either. The poor majority and the women in particular were to embark on the road to self employment and prosperity on the back of a wide variety of 'rural industry' through the instrumentality of DWACRA. All this in lie of the steep cut made in to the subsidy bill of the cheap rice. The job less growth of the industry under the aegis of globalization is believed to have been yet another factor prompting the GOAP to push through the DWACRA devise. FICCI allowed itself to be roped in to this `massive' effort. Yet, the DWACRA plank fell on the rocks of a pauperized agriculture.

EXPORT LED GROWTH AND THE SELECT GROUP OF RURAL INDUSTRIES

Nevertheless, the need of the hour is to focus on the promotion of export led growth of a select group of small scale and decentralized rural industries such as the leather, the textiles (handlooms and power looms), the garments and the ornaments as the debate on the implementation issues makes it abundantly clear. The leather and leather goods, the textiles, the garments and the ornaments figure as the most prominent items and as such the most contentious industries in any debate on the implementation issues. Yet, the GOAP does not appear to have attached the due importance to this group of the rural industries in its growth strategy. What is more, the textile sector is allowed to die down in favor of garments even as the latter is shown scant regard in terms of official promotion. The suicide deaths of over 300 weaving hands in the last 2 years are symptomatic of the crisis gripping the industry. The LIDCAP (leather industry Development Corporation) had to wage a sustained battle at survival. The GOAP was all set to windup LIDCAP. The LIDCAP was not content with mere survival. It made salutary attempts at thrusting a masterly plan at gigantic promotion of leather industry on an unwilling government over the years. LIDCAP promises to generate employment to 432,000 working hands from the madiga community (dalits) overtime as the leather industry grows to full maturation. The sustained pleas by the goldsmith community for a small help fell on the deaf years of the government. According to its own (official) reckoning the garment sector alone is capable of generating employment to 2.5 million rural women.

To be sure, a meaningful strategy at the export led growth of farm and non-farm industry is sure to catapult the state on to the road of all round prosperity. A strategy of the kind would have firmly put in place an internal dynamic of growth. There is more to the GOAP's inability to prioritise the aforesaid right mix of growth strategy. Unfortunately for us the GOAP derides the native talent. If and when the GOAP realizes the need to zero in on the export led growth of a right mix of farm and non-farm industry at a future date, it would perhaps look for the external agencies (FDI) to do the job for it. It would in all probability wait endlessly for the influx of the FDI. That indeed is the crux of the debate at the ensuing Cancun ministerial meet. The EU, the US and Japan are pushing hard for such a consummation in the name of the Singapore issues. They would like to have an unfettered freedom for their capital investment at the cost of our national pride and freedom. Which way do we go? Do we try keeping intact our national identity and competing in the international market as a sovereign equal putting our act together and pooling our native talent or commit suicide as a nation only to return to the status of a colonial possession? It is high time we ponder on all these issues of paramount important.

13

DEVELOPMENT OF A RURAL INDUSTRY BASED ON THE CULTIVATION AND PROCESSING OF CASSIA SENNA

K. P. Sastry, B. R. Rajeswara Rao,
C. P. Singh and Kamla Singh

INTRODUCTION

Cassia angustifolia (Family: Caesalpiniaceae), popularly known as Indian or Tinnevelly senna is cultivated for leaves and immature pods, which are used as laxative. The strong laxative properties of leaves and pods are due to the presence of dianthone glucosides, sennosides A and B in them [1]. The sennosides act chiefly on the lower bowel and are especially effective in case of habitual constipation. The glycosides are absorbed from the intestinal tract; they increase the peristaltic movements through their local action upon the intestinal wall, and this ultimately results in decreased absorption of water and a bulkier and softer fecal mass. Prolonged use of leaves may lead to colon problem; the leaves can also cause gripping in some cases unless they are combined with carminatives [2-4].

In India, Tinnevelly Senna (*C. angustifolia*) is cultivated in Gujarat, Rajasthan, Andhra Pradesh and Tamilnadu states. The total annual production of senna herbage is estimated to be around 7500 tonnes. The leaves and pods of a few other species of *Cassia* also possess laxative properties similar to those of *C. anguslifolia*, the most important being *Cassia acutifolia* or Alexandrian senna. Alexandrian senna is found growing in the wild in North African countries, including Ethiopia and Sudan.

The international market receives leaves and pods of Alexandrian senna obtained from the North African countries in substantial quantities, accounting for about 25% of the international trade.

IMPORTANCE OF SENNA IN THE CONTEXT OF GLOBALISATION

"Globalisation" describes the ongoing global trend toward the freer flow of trade and investment across borders and the resulting integration of the international economy. Because it expands economic freedom and spurs competition, globalization raises the productivity and living standards of people in countries that open themselves to the global marketplace and in turn, promotes poverty reduction, democratization, and higher labor and environmental standards.

After India became a signatory to WTO agreement, globalisation has become a reality and we are living in a global village. The planning commission has identified Medicinal and Aromatic plants as one of the core sectors that can make India a global leader in 21st century. To realize this dream, the Government of India established a National Medicinal Plants Board in the Department of Indian Systems of Medicine and Homeopathy under the ministry of Health and Family welfare. The NMPB has identified 32 plants for promotion and senna is one of them. Senna is the second largest earner of foreign exchange through exports. Indian senna leaves and pods are valued as good sources of sennosides in the international trade. However, Indian senna has to compete with Alexandrian senna for its cost effectiveness and quality. Since the demand for senna products is increasing and the wild collections of Alexandrian senna are unable to meet this demand. India has excellent opportunity to increase its production, trade and export earnings. It is also imperative that India needs to urgently develop processes and products before any other country can develop and patent them. The current scenario in India is summarized in the following paragraphs in the context of globalisation.

AREA AND PRODUCTION IN TAMILNADU

The senna belt of Tamilnadu consists of three important districts, Tirunelveli, Tuticorin and Virudhnagar. The geographical locations of these districts and cultivation of crops in these districts is mainly rainfed because of very small-irrigated area (Table 1). In all the three districts the area under cultivation is less than 8% of the total available area and the area under irrigated agriculture is less than 2.75%.

Table 1
Total Area, Area Under Cultivation and Area Under Irrigated Agriculture in the Three Southern Districts of Tamilnadu

District	*Total cultivable area (ha)*	*Area under cultivation (ha)*	*Area under irrigated agriculture (%)*
Tirunelveli	6,82,308	45,851	2.7
Tuticorin	4,59,054	10,109	0.9
Virudhnagarar	2,21,887	18,282	0.1

The soils in these three districts are predominantly black cotton soils (61.7%), followed by red loam (32.4%) and red sands (3.3%). Based on the productivity of the soils, only 51.1% can be classified as agro climatically good and 36.0 % are average.

In Tirunelveli district, Tirunelveli, Palayamkottai, Mannargudi and Nanguneri are important taluks in which senna is cultivated. In Virudhnagar district, Virudhnagar, Srivallipunur, Sivakasi, Sattur and Aruppukotai are important taluks and in Tuticorin district, Sathagulem, Natikulem, Kovilpani, Srivaikuntam, Ottapidiram and Tuticorin are the important tatuks where senna is cultivated.

The area under senna cultivation in the three important districts during the period 1994-99 is presented in Table 2. The total area under senna has varied from 4081 ha in 1995-96 to

658 ha in 1997-98 and 3500 ha in 1998-99. The production of leaves varies from 4500 to 6000 tones per year depending on the area.

Table 2
Total Area (ha) Under Senna CultivatIon in Different Districts during the Period 1994-1999

District	*1994-95*	*1995-96*	*1996- 97*	*1997-98*	*1998-99*
Virudhnagar	226	990	576	472	300
Tuticorin	1326	2918	172	108	97
Tirunelveli	293	173	257	78	1309
Total	1845	4081	1005	658	1706

CULTIVATION

Varieties: In Tamilnadu two types are available for cultivation, they are Local and ALFT2. Recently a variety by the name Sona was released by CIMAP. The crop is propagated by seeds and about 15 kg seeds are required per hectare.

Season and sowing: In southern parts of India, senna mostly cultivated as a rainfed crop and in certain pockets it is cultivated under limited irrigation facilities [6,9, 10]. It is cultivated under irrigation facilities in places like Tengulem in Tirunelveti district [5,7,8,11]. Under limited irrigation conditions the land is ploughed twice during February- March. It is divided into beds for facilitating irrigation. The seed is drilled in rows 30-45 cm apart. After germination, the crop is thinned to give a spacing of 30 cm within rows and 30 cm between rows. Under rainfed condition in black soils a first crop of cotton, sorghum or coriander is taken and senna is sown as the second crop at the end of the rainy season from end of September to November.

Interculture and fertilizer: One weeding is done 45 days after sowing of the crop. Under irrigated condition, N: P: K (40:40:40) are applied at the time of sowing.

Pests and Diseases: Leaf spot caused by Alternaria alternata and leaf blight caused by Phyllosticta spp. cause severe damage to the crop through leaf drop. Spraying of Carbandazim (0.03%) or Dithiocarbamate (0.03%) at fortnightly intervals for 3 times is recommended. To control damping off of seedlings seed treatment with Thiram or Captan (2.5 g/kg seed) before sowing is advocated.

Harvesting and drying: The plants start flowering 60 days after sowing and the first flush is removed to encourage vegetative growth. About 90-100 days after sowing, fully-grown bluish coloured leaves and golden yellow coloured immature pods are stripped manually. A second harvest is taken 30-45 days after the first harvest. The leaves and pods are shade dried for 10-15 days before packing.

Yield: Under irrigated conditions, 1.0 to 1.5 tones of leaves and about 300kg of pods can be obtained per hectare. If the crop is raised under rain fed conditions, the yield would be about half of that from the irrigated crop.

PROCESSING OF THE LEAVES AND VALUE ADDITION

The leaves are stripped from the branches and dried in shade for 10-15 days till the moisture content reaches 8-10%. The leaves are collected by the local traders and transported to the wholesale dealers and exporters in Tuticorin.

The leaves are processed both manually and mechanically depending on the quantum of trade. The leaves are winnowed to remove dust and stones and then passed through sieves of different sizes to separate them in to different grades. The leaves are graded depending upon the size. The different grades are given in Table 3.

Table 3
The Different Grades of Senna Leaves

Grade	Length
Prime No 1	> 3.5 cm
Prime No 2	2.5 - 3.5 cm
Prime No 3	1.5 - 2.5 cm
Prime No 4	0.5 - 1.5 cm
Prime No 5	0.5 cm and less

The leaves of Prime 1, 2 and 3 grades are exported and grades 4 and 5 are traded in the internal market. Prime grade no 5 is also known as pharma grade and is used for extraction of sennosides and production of calcium sennosides of different grades with in the country (10%,20% etc.,). The left over stem is traded as senna stem and left over leaf pieces are powdered and sold as senna leaf powder. The exporters employ more than one thousand women every day for processing. This can become a rural industry with the village women processing the cultivated leaf in their villages.

TRADE AND EXPORT

There are about eight important exporters and twenty traders in Tuticorin who are engaged in the trade of senna leaves. It is estimated that about 1000 tons of leaf is traded within the country. Data on export of senna leaves and pods to some important countries from Tuticorin port in Tamilnadu in the last six years are presented in table 4. The average export from Tuticorin port was estimated to be around 6000 tonnes. While bulk of the senna exported from Tuticorin port is of Tamilnadu origin, some material produced in other parts of the country is also exported from this port.

Table 4
Export of Senna Leaves and Pods (Tonnes) from the Tuticorin Port to Some Major Countries during the Period 1997-2002

Country	*1997*	*1998*	*1999*	*2000*	*2001*	*2002*
China	338	254	576	924	474	959
Germany	1812	1682	1730	937	819	1458
Japan	861	666	1136	795	438	386
USA	467	1116	707	939	333	161
Total****	4898	4491	5378	6100	7430	NA

**** The total figures include the export to all countries.
NA... Not available.

The export ranged from 4491 tons during 1998 to 7430tonnes in 2001. Major exports were to Germany followed by Japan, USA, China, Spain and France. Many other countries including Argentina, Belgium, Italy, Poland, Portugal, Sri Lanka and Taiwan also continue to import senna leaf and pods from India. The export earnings are to the tune of Rs 15- 18.5 crore.

14

IMPACT OF NEW ECONOMIC POLICY ON COIR INDUSTRIES OF ORISSA: A CASE STUDY OF PURI DISTRICT

Bijaya Kumar Sahu

INTRODUCTION

The New Economic Policy was introduced in July 1991. The basic objective of the policy is to create conducive economic environment for promoting sustainable economic growth in the country. The structural reforms comprise measures such as industrial deregulation, liberalization policies relating to direct foreign investment, reforms of public sector enterprises, financial sector reforms. It is thus, the New Economic Policy is the policy of liberalization, privatization and globalization. Liberalization of industrial and trade policy is another key aspect of New Economic policy. In the eve of new economic policy, it was hoped that with the liberalization, market facilities would become accessible to the rural industries as well as to the traditional artisans. The liberalization policy of India has put much restrain on the process of internal liberalization and the rural industries, are the worst affected. It is true that, the rural industries have been denied a 'level playing field'. Government's policy of liberalization of Indian economy is less sympathetic to such industries. Besides, rural industries always prefer to manufacture reserved items and establish their own identity. But due to non-availability of fund, they failed to adopt modern methods of production and technical know how etc.

COIR INDUSTRIES IN INDIA

Coir industries in India mostly depend upon two types of coir fibres these are; (i) White coir fibre and (ii) Brown coir fibre. The annual production of coir fibre in our country is estimated at about 370 thousand MTs as per 2001-2002 estimation. Out of which 122 thousand MTs (33.0%) is white fibre and the remaining 248 thousand MTs (67.0%) is brown fibre.

The white fibre is generally used for manufacturing of coir yarn, rope, doormat, matting and carpets for internal and external marketing, whereas the brown fibre is used specially for making rubberized coir products, coir brushes, hardboards, geo-textiles and craft items in addition to yarn, rope, mat, matting and carpet production.

The coir industry in India is undergoing rapid modernization that has accelerated the production of coir yarn in primary sector. The extra fiber produced is at present utilized for the production of value added products like poly coir and geo-textile, which has immense export potential.

COIR INDUSTRIES IN ORISSA

The state of Orissa with coastline of about 480 Kms. is having abundant production of coconuts. The availability of husk, Orissa has huge potential for development of coir industry and for generating large-scale employment for the coir artisans in the rural areas of coastal districts of the state.. The coir industry in Orissa is providing employment opportunity to about 9300 people in the said year. The installed capacity of total coir units in the state is 7500 M.T. coir fibre. The total production of fibre in the state is only 1837.5 MTs. It is thus, the total capacity utilization is only 24.5 per cent. Out of the total fibre production 1914 Mt, i.e., 98.7 per cent are brown fibre. It indicates that more brown fibre is produced in Orissa conditions or by the coir industries of the state. The brown fibre production in Orissa was 4480MTs in 1998-99 followed by 2000 MTs in 1999-2000.

In order to know the impact of New Economic policy on coir industries in Orissa since 1991, it is decided to undertake a micro study on the topic titled "Impact of New Economic policy on coir industries of Orissa :- A case study of Puri district". The study has undertaken with the following objectives.

OBJECTIVES

(i) To assess the impact on Employment generation.

(ii) To assess impact on marketing of coir products.

(iii) To suggest policy measures.

METHODOLOGY

The Puri district is the highest producer of coconut (311 lakh nuts i.e., about 19% of the total coconut production of the state Orissa i.e., 1639 lakh nuts in 2000-2001) is selected purposively for the study. The total number of units of coir industry in the district is 265 which is near about the 60 per cent of the total coir industries of the state. Out of which 10 coir industries has selected at random for the purpose of the study. This is about 3.8 per cent of the total coir industries of the Puri district. The units include the coir Industrial cooperative societies, small-scale industries and artisan units. Out of 10 coir industries selected for the study 5 (50%) are SSI units and the remaining 5 (50%) are co-operative and artisan units.

APPROACH

In order to assess the impact of New Economic policy on coir industries of Orissa on Employment and Marketing, a scientifically structured schedule was prepared and canvassed for the purpose of the study. Awareness about the New Economic Policy and its impact on coir industries has also asked to the respondents/workers of the coir industries.

REFERENCE PERIOD

The reference period of the (field) study is 1995 to 2002.

TOOLS OF ANALYSIS

The percentages, ratios are used for the analysis of the data collected for the study purpose.

FINDINGS

The major findings of the study can be seen as follows:

It is observed from the employment generation Table 1, that, the employment opportunities in the coir industries of Orissa has increased from 238 persons in 1995-96 to 249 persons in 2002-2003. The increase of employment opportunity in this sector has registered an increase of only about 4.6 per cent over the period under observation. This change in employment is evident in SSI units and small artisan units. The co-operative sector performed poorly over the period. It is due to closer of one co-operative unit after super cyclone and the static situation of the other one. The employment opportunity for female workers has been remained more or less equal i.e., around 75 per cent of the total workers. The employment opportunity for the male workers has increased marginally by about 10 per cent over the period between 1995-96 and 2002-2003. Where as the increase in employment incase of female workers was only 5.6 per cent over the period under observation. It is to conclude that, the employment opportunity in the coir industries of Orissa has increased marginally. The modernization of SSI units by installation of improved and modern machines is one of the factors of low employment generation in the sector. The declined in co-operative sectors due to the damage of super cyclone of 1999 and non-availability of adequate and timely revival package from the Government and financial institutions are other causes of low employment generation in coir industries of Orissa. The artisan based coir units are small in size and their investment capacity is also poor, failed to generate more employment opportunities in this sector. The employment opportunity in co-operative sectors and small artisan units is maximum to the weaker sections of rural population has declined considerably due to the introduction of New Economic policy.

Table 1
Distribution of Employment Generation (in number)

	1995–1996			*2002–2003*		
Name of the Coir industry	*Male*	*Female*	*Total*	*Male*	*Female*	*Total*
National Coir	15	20	35	18	28	46
Kalinga Ropes	5	15	20	-	-	-
Coir India	7	20	27	10	30	40
Sitaram Coir	10	25	35	12	35	47
Vijay Coir	8	20	28	10	30	40
Teishpur CMA, ICS	4	30	34	-	-	-
Bata Mangala Coir ICS	5	20	25	5	20	25
Veer Arhun Coir Industry	1	6	7	2	10	12
Utkal Coir Industry	3	12	15	5	15	20
Jayagopal Coir Industry	2	10	12	4	15	19
Total	60	178	238	66	183	249
	25.2%	74.8 %	100%	26.5%	73.5%	100%

Source: Compiled from the field study.

Table 2
Percentage Change in Marketing of Coir Products between 1995–96 and 2002–2003

(in%)

Source of Market	*1995-96*	*2002-03*
Own show rooms	25	20
Local (retailers)	20	15
Inside the state (Outside the district)	30	30
Outside the state	25	35
International	0	0

Source: Data compiled from the field study.

It is observed for the Table 2 that, the marketing of coir products in international market is not opened up till 2002-2003. The marketing of such products in the local areas as well as in the own showroom has declined over the period between 1995-96 and 2002-2003. The sale of coir products in outside the district has also remained unchanged over the period of observation whereas; the market opportunity in outside the state has increased from 25 per cent of the total marketable production in 1995-96 to 35 per cent in 2002-2003. Due to privatization, the new markets upon up in the states like, Jharkhand, Chhatisgarh, Assam, West Bengal and North Eastern Sates etc. The International market for coir products in Orissa has not achieved considerably due to the traditional items.

PERCEPTIONS ABOUT NEW ECONOMIC POLICY

- The increased/improved awareness will enhance the learning and education level. While asking the awareness level of the entrepreneurs about the New Economic Policy 4 respondents' i.e, 40% of the total entrepreneurs have answered that they are having knowledge about the new economic policy, whereas the remaining 6 respondents (60%) denied about the said policy and its consequences.
- Only 2 units reported that they have received some benefit out of the introduction of new economic policy in India, whereas, the remaining 8 units could not find any substantial change in their activities.
- The perception of the entrepreneurs about the future of coir industries in Orissa in relation to the New Economic policy is also not encouraging. About 3 (30%) respondents expressed that the coir industries in the state will develop due to the New Economic policy, whereas, the remaining 7 (70%) respondents viewed negatively. The uncertain and declining economic scenario of the state forced them to tell so.

PROBLEMS ENCOUNTERED

- Competition in the coir industries has increased considerably due to the entry of new producer either in local areas or from outside the state, more particularly from Andhra Pradesh, Tamilnadu etc.
- Due to more competition the selling price has not increasing as per the increase of cost of production such as : price of raw materials, labour costs and other dues. This causes low or marginal profit from the enterprise.

- The non-availability of institutional finance and subsidies are the other problems that have been encountered by the coir industries in Orissa more particularly by the Co-operative and small artisan units.
- Inadequate Marketing and other extension services from the government are another problem that has been faced by the coir industries in Orissa.
- The more paraphernalia process, official delays and harassments are the other problems encountered by the coir industries.
- Inadequate awareness, education training and technical support is also causing problem for the small artisan, cooperative coir industries of Orissa.
- Government's defective coir policy is another problem that has been faced by the entrepreneurs in this sector.

FACTORS RESPONSIBLE FOR DEVELOPMENT OF COIR INDUSTRIES

Positive Factors

(For SSI Units)

- Adopt modern known how and Machinery.
- Produced according to the market demand.
- Improved knowledge base.
- Obtained Easy financial assistance from financial institutions.
- Created required infrastructure facilities for development.

Negative Factors

(For Co-operative & Artisan Units)

- Poverty
- Inadequate Education
- Lack of financial support from financial institutions.

- Inadequate Technical supports from Govt.
- Underdeveloped infrastructure facilities.
- Adoption of Traditional methods of production due to lack of fund & technical knowledge.
- Productions of tradition products.

SUGGESTED POLICY MEASURES

The effective implementation of following policy measure may helpful to revive coir industries in Orissa.

(i) Supply of adequate fund for modernization.

(ii) Regular training for up-gradation of technology.

(iii) Uninterrupted supply of raw materials and improvement in infrastructure facilities.

(iv) Adequate supply of institutional credit at reasonable rate of interest.

(v) Prompt and timely financial technical and extension support to the units.

(vi) Procedural delays should be minimized and official harassment to be stopped.

(vii) Regular supply of information, education and communication materials to the entrepreneurs.

(viii) Creation of appropriate market environment for the sale of coir products.

(ix) Implementation of appropriate coir policy in a effective manner.

REFERENCES

Annual Report 1999-2000, Coir House, M. G. Road, Ernakulam, Kochi.

Annual Report 2001-2002, Coir Board, Ministry of Agro and Rural Industries, Govt. of India.

Report on Handicrafts and Cottage Industries of Orissa–2003.

Status Report of Orissa Co-operative Coir Corporation Ltd., Bhubaneswar, Orissa.

Govt. of Orissa, Orissa Review, April' 1997 & September' 1999 issues.

15

W.T.O. AND ITS IMPLICATIONS ON RURAL AND S.S.I.

M. V. Rama Prasad

INTRODUCTION

In the post-independence era, the Government had to synchronize and harmonize the twin considerations of rapid industrialisations and the parameters of a welfare state. The Plan objective of economic growth with social justice was kept in view in the overall strategy of industrial development. All segments of the industry–large, medium and small–were assigned a mutually complimentary role with a view to facilitate an integrated and harmonious growth of industrial sector as a whole. In the context of the major problems of poverty and unemployment faced by the Indian Economy, the development of rural and Small Scale Industries Sector (SSI) was considered essential because of its being labour intensive having implications for equity, capability to contribute to decentralisation, to promote entrepreneurship, optimum use of local resources and talents, etc. Since Independence, a series of six Industrial Policy Resolutions aimed at promoting industrial growth and determining a pattern of state intervention and assistance have been announced by the Central Government. While spelling out the framework of the basic and strategic industries, the Industrial Policy Resolution,

1948 realized Cottage and Small Scale industries to be particularly suited for better utilization of local resources and achievement of "local self-sufficiency" in respect of certain types of industrial goods. The policy of supporting the cottage, village and small industries took shape in 1956.The 1956 Resolution underlined the role that the SSI sector could play in providing employment opportunities, mobilizing local skill sand capital resources and in the process integrating with large industrial sector. The Industrial Policy Statement, 1977, stressed upon wider dispersal of cottage and small industries in the rural areas and small towns. While the Industrial Policy Statement of 1980 was important from the point view of ancillarisations and creation of nucleus plants for the growth of the sector, that of 1990 emphasized the steps for enhancing the contribution of the SSI sector in overall exports, employment generation and dispersal of industries in rural areas.

The Industrial Policy measures announced in 1991 laid special thrust on promotion and strengthening of small, tiny and rural industries. A new scheme of Integrated Infrastructure Development for SSIs with the participation of State Governments and Financial Institutions was initiated and a pro-active role for NGO sector was mooted.

In order to protect their interest and facilitate their rapid development, the Government in pursuance of its policies has initiated a number of support measures from time to time which include policy of reservation, revision of investment ceilings, modernization, technology up gradation, marketing assistance, etc. The emerging economic scenario in the change liberalized and competitive economic environment has necessitated structural and fundamentals changes in the policy framework put into place for the development of the vital sector of the economy. Accordingly, there has been a shift in focus from 'protection' to 'promotion'. In the post-reform period, a number of steps including partial de-reservation, change in investment limits, facilitating foreign participation establishment of growth centers, export promotion, marketing assistance and incentives for quality improvement, etc, have been taken by the government for strengthening of this sector.

The rural and SSI sector has proved is mettle even in the changed liberalized economic environment of the country. The steps required for up of the economy have affected. The need of the hour undoubtedly is to provide sustenance through suitable measures to strengthen it for converting the challenges into opportunities for scaling new heights. In order to enable the government to place more focused attention on the problems of the SSI sector, a new Ministry of Small Scale Industries and Agro and Rural Industries has been created on 14th October 1999, under the Independent Charge of a Minister of State. To give a direction and perspective to the development strategy, the Minister in-charge of Small Scale Industries and Agro & Rural Industries announced an "Agenda for the Millennium" which places special emphasis upon facilities evolution of a new policy, framework, and improved supply of credit, better infrastructural and impetus for modernisation and technology upgradation in small scale industries. The Agenda takes cognizance of the special role to be played by Information Technology, sunrise industries, hi-tech industries, export potent industries, and at the same time stipulated all possible steps to meet the requirements of the tiny and micro-enterprises which constitute over 9 per cent of total small scale industrial units in the country. Though this sector has shown substantial progress, its major problems like inadequate credit flow from banks and financial institutions (FIs), inadequate infrastructure facilities, low quality standards of products, use of obsolete technology, plant, machinery and equipment, inefficient management techniques, etc are still inhibiting the sector. Besides, this sector has to face challenges of competition from the opening up of economy to globalization, need for increasing exports and meet WTO commitments.

POLICY LEGAL FRAMEWORK, RESERVATION & OTHER ISSUES OF RURAL SMALL SCALE ENTERPRISE IN THE TWENTY FIRST CENTURY

The rural and Small Scale Enterprise (SSE) sector has emerged as an engine of growth in most of the developed and newly industrialized countries. India's vision of emerging as an economic power in the 21st century can be realised through the promotion and development of the Small and Medium Enterprises (SMEs). In fact, the SME is the sector of the Millennium. The role that small-scale enterprise sector has to play in the next ten years must be viewed in the dynamic context of a changing world. It must address to the requirements of the time and the changes which are taking place both within and outside the country. Liberalization and globalization are the order of the day. Market forces will determine the system and manner of production. The allocation or resources within the sector must be governed by the criteria of efficiency, productivity and competitiveness. The rural and SSEs will have to move from a regime of a protective environment to a competitive environment. The role of Government is to be that of a facilitator.

The emergence of World Trade Organization (WTO) is a significant event in the realm of world trade. The WTO prescribes the rules of the game based on non-discrimination. These are:

(i) Most Favored Nation Treatment (Any trade concession offered to one member must be offered to all their members).

(ii) National Treatment (Imported goods should not be discriminated, against in favor of the domestic goods–same treatment must be accorded).

(iii) Free Trading System (with barriers coming down through negotiations).

(iv) Predictable Trading System (trade barriers would not be raised arbitrarily).

India is a member of WTO. Thus the policy of the SSE sector in India will have to be WTO complaint. The policies must be in tune with the provisions of the WTO on all issues including the basic issues like actionable and non-actionable subsidies, patents, tariff and non-tariff barriers, sanitary etc. Subsidies support and incentives to the rural and SME sector do not come under the category of 'actionable' subsidies as long as they are horizontal in their application. The Government should take up adequate measures to increase awareness on WTO provisions among the rural SSI entrepreneurs and take appropriate measures to protect Indian SSI sector through bound rates, information and data to prove dumping and help in introduction of anti-dumping measures, create a legal cell to take care of legal problems faced by the rural and SSI units on account of WTO conditions. The DC (SSI) should create a separate Division on WTO, supported by adequate experts in various disciplines. The concept of market is changing very fast. The term 'domestic market' is gradually vanishing. For that matter the term 'international market' also may become irrelevant soon. There will only be one market and hence the products of the rural and SSI sector must be competitive within the country as well as outside. The products are to be sold increasingly with 'brand names' hence the future of SSE development must focus on promoting brands for rural and SSI products. Rapid scientific and technological advancement is taking place in the developed world. The developing countries experience problems relating to technology, raw material and capital. Besides, these countries are under severe pressure to brace up for global competition and to upgrade their skills, competence and technology. More focused attention needs to be placed on these three areas. Information technology should be utilized to the fullest at all levels. SSE should take advantage of e-commerce, e-marketing, etc and internet facilities by making their presence felt through websites. While formulating policies and programmes for the development of small scale enterprises, the following points must be remembered: (a) at a time when employment is stagnant in the agricultural sector and large industry sector is passing through near 'zero employment growth', it is only in the small enterprises, besides the service sector, where employment has been growing. In a labour surplus economy like India, the need for policies and programmes for employment generation is of prime importance, and (b) The SSE sector suffers from certain handicaps and as such needs special support. The rural and SME sectors get special attention and support in the entire world over. The supportive measure to be made available to the three sectors will have to be decided by the government from time to time. The endeavour will be to provide maximum support and protection to tiny units, somewhat lesser support to the SSI units and will lesser facilities and support to the Medium Enterprises. Medium Enterprises would not be supported through reservation, fiscal concessions or credit from banks and Financial Institutions (FIs) under priority lending sector etc., which is normally made available to tiny and SSI units. However, medium enterprises could be helped for technology up gradation and modernization through a separate fund.

The term 'small scale industry' should be replaced by 'small enterprises', which will consist of the following segments.

(i) Tiny Industrial Units;

(ii) Small Scale Industrial Units; and

(iii) Service and Business Enterprises.

REGULATORY LAW FOR SSIs

The vision for the 21st century cannot be realized with a plethora of laws, rules and regulations governing the SSE sector and there is need for a Single Unified Act governing the promotion and development of Small Scale Enterprises in the country. There should be a separate Small Enterprises Development Act for SSEs as the Industrial Development and Regulation (IDR) Act which regulates SSI units covers the industries as a whole.

The rural and SSE units should be free from laws and procedures, which cause under harassment. Inspection should be generally replaced by self-certification. Procedures should be transparent and hassle free. There is need for similar simplifications in other fields as well. Inspections could be prescribed under three conditions: (i) on receipt of complaint; (ii) selection of unit for sample check (10% of total units); and (iii) for audit purposes.

For new units, single window clearances should be arranged irrespective of whether they relate to clearances from Central Authorities or State Authorities or Local Authorities.

RESERVATION

The reservation of products for exclusive manufacture in the SSI sector should continue for the present because the reserved items of the SSI sector are making significant contribution to employment, output and exports.

De-reservation of some selected export thrust items could also be considered since the country is losing valuable foreign exchange by production of low value added items by using traditional or low-grade technology. Production of reserved items could be allowed to be taken up by non-SSI units, subject to minimum export obligation of 30 per cent to be achieved in the first three years.

In the context of quantitative restrictions getting removed by April 2001, which may affect the manufactures of SSI reserved products, the endeavor of the governments should be to make the sector WTO complaint and more competitive during the transition period by way of sensitization to WTO provisions, keeping import duty at bound rates, maintenance of duty differential on raw materials and finished goods, providing interest support for technology up-gradation and easy access of credit to them.

In order to make SSI products competitive in both the internal ad international markets, it is necessary to adopt State of Art technology. Hence the investment ceiling of those items which are important from the angle of exports and also play an important role in employment generation, could be suitably enhanced, e.g. Leather products, ready-made garments, hosiery tools, packaging material, auto components, pharmaceuticals, food processing, etc.

INFRASTRUCTURE DEVELOPMENT

The existing financial provisions for infrastructure development are grossly inadequate. Most of the industrial estates have degenerated into industrial slums due to improper upkeep. New industrial estates also need to be set up in potential areas but they must be equipped with the required infrastructure. While some infrastructures like roads, water supply, banks, telecommunications, etc could be arranged, other facilities like power could be coordinated with the State Electricity Boards. To overcome this constraint, as Infrastructure Development Fund for rural and SSEs with a suitable corpus of around Rs. 2,000 crore needs to be created.

The Integrated Infrastructure Development (IID) scheme should cover all areas of the country with 50 per cent reservation for backward and rural areas. The Industrial Estates need to be managed by levying charges to the user industries so that these could become self-sustainable in the long run. Maintenance of these industrial estates should be done by the associations of user industries and paying charges for utilities, services, facilities made, etc. These industrial estates should be self-sufficient in maintenance.

An Incubation Infrastructure Development Fund of the order of Rs. 1000 crore should be created at setting up adequate of incubation centers in the tenth Five Year Plan to help the skilled young entrepreneurs to start their own ventures with all the required facilities including computers, video conferencing and e-commerce facilities, etc., being available at one place. These centers are aimed to providing an 'address' to the entrepreneurs for a period of three years. These centers would cater to sunrise industries like electronics, information technology, bio-technology pharmaceuticals or any activity which is coming up for which commercial viability is a yet to be established.

SICKNESS IN SSI SECTOR

Sickness in the rural and SSI sector is a serious problem. It is essential to understand the factors which contribute to sickness. To check the further increase in sickness, it is essential that the rural and SSI sector is strengthened by way of providing adequate and timely credit, improved infrastructure market support and support for technology up gradation. Government is aware to these problems. To take care of these problems, the Credit Guarantee Scheme has been formulated. The scheme of Support for Technology Up gradation has been finalised by the Ministry. The RBI has been requested to work out a package for rehabilitating the potentially viable but currently sick units.

TECHNOLOGY UP GRADATION

Technology is the driving force of any economy. The quest for better utilization of human labour an efficient use of natural is endless. Science and Technological capabilities ultimately translate into economic strength. We know that technological obsolescence is a major handicap for the healthy growth of small-scale units more so in the merging competitive economic environment. In order to be effective, the SSI units should not only apply the latest technology but also make continuous efforts to develop and improve technology while integrating with other newly evolved technologies. The government provides support through its countrywide institutions like Tool Rooms, Process-cum-Product Development Centers, and Regional Testing Centers. SSI units should try to obtain ISO-9000 quality certification. The Office of the Development Commissioner (SSI) has been assisting the SSIs by reimbursing up to Rs. 75,000 on acquisition of ISO 9000 certificate.

Information is going to be the key factor in future. The irrevocable economic forces of globalisation would bring in their wake a ceaseless onslaught on traditional production and marketing strategies. The approaches and techniques that have served the SSI till now, are likely to be pushed aside by technology and increasingly by access to information. Therefore, it is not enough to use technology alone, rather the SSIs will have to use information creatively, not only to design technologies and processes that will deliver world class goods and services but also to keep a step ahead in the game. Those who are able to harness the information power will succeed.

FISCAL INCENTIVES

Fiscal incentives have been designed to reduce the manufacturing cost of rural and SSIs, particularly in tiny units. These in a way compensate to some extent, the disadvantages of not being able to manufacture at economics of scale. Manufacturers with a turnover of up to Rs. 53 crore are exempted from paying excise duty up to a turnover of Rs 50 lakh and for turnover between Rs. 50–100 lakh, the duty is levied at 5% advalorem. SSIs manufacturing goods under the brand name of other manufacturers in rural areas are being given the benefit of excise duty exemption.

MARKETING

One of the crucial areas for success of any manufacturing enterprise is its ability to market the products successfully. Marketing is essentially an entrepreneurial function. Many major changes have taken place in marketing strategy in the recent past. The prime mover of this change is the emergence of an information society based on development, exploitation and Communication of Ideas, knowledge and information. The consumer today demands value for money. The rural and SSIs should explore adopting consortium approach towards developing common brands for their products. The NSIC has been asked to help them in this regard. Paying proper attention to marketing should be one of the major tasks before this sector. Rural and SSIs in future should think of taking the services of professional to market their products. Rural and SSIs should use ore of information technology to spread their market share.

EXPORTS

Exports from rural and SSIs have over a period of time acquired great significance in India's foreign trade. This sector today contributes more than one-third of the total exports from the country. Our export promotion strategy includes simplification of export procedures and providing incentives to maximize exporting capabilities. Products of SSI exports are displayed in International exhibitions at government's cost. With a view to acquainting SSI exporters of the latest packaging standards, techniques, etc. training programmes on packaging for exports are organised in various parts of the country. Marketing Development Assistance (MDA) scheme operated by the Ministry of Commerce & Industry provides financial assistance in the form of grant to the export houses, small scale exporters, etc, for undertaking various export promotion activities such as sponsoring of sales-cum-study teams, participation in trade fairs, exhibitions abroad, publication and publicity, etc.

INFRASTRUCTURE SUPPORT

Generally state governments provide infrastructural facilities to the SSIs. The efforts of the State Governments are being supplemented through a Plan Scheme called 'Integrated Infrastructure development (IID) which is being operated since 1994 for creation of infrastructural facilities to set up small-scale units in rural and backward areas of the country. 46 projects have so far been sanctioned in various states of the country. In order to give further boost to rural industrialization to benefit the rural artisans and the unemployed youths and to reduce rural urban disparities, a National Programme for Rural Industrialisation (NPRI) has been initiated with a mission to set up 100 rural clusters every year for the next five years.

FACING THE CHALLENGE OF WTO AGREEMENT

The World Trade Agreements and negotiations have a direct impact on all economic activities including the development and promotion of the small-scale sector. WTO Agreements are likely to affect the SSI sector in the following ways:

(i) Removal of QRS will allow free and cheap imports and will result in stiff competition to the SSIs.

(ii) In view of the Agreement of TRIPS, it would be difficult for the SSI sector to continue with the reverse engineering and manufacture many items without paying royalty to the patent holders.

(iii) In terms of sanitary and Phyto-sanitary measures, SSIs will have to adopt international standards with regard to quality, health and hygiene.

The rural and Small Scale Industry (SSI) sector has emerged over four decades as a highly vibrate and dynamic sector of the Indian economy. Today, this sector account for about 95 per cent of the industrial units and is contributing more than 40 per cent of value addition in the manufacturing sector and about 35 per cent of exports (both direct and indirect). More than 31 lakh units are spread all over the country producing over 7500 items.

Rural and Small scale units, not only play a crucial role in providing large scale employment opportunities at lower capital cost than large scale industries, but also help in industrialization of rural and backward areas, thereby reducing regional imbalance, assuring more equitable distribution of national income and wealth. SSI units are also supplementary and complimentary to large and medium scale units as ancillary units.

IMPACT ON RURAL AND SMALL SCALE SECTOR

The emerging regime of liberalization of international trade and deregulation and privatization of internal economy, in the light of WTO, has rendered the small-scale industry (SSI) sector highly vulnerable. The umbrella of WTO is likely to create some far-reaching implications for the rural and SSI sector in India, specifically with regard to their competitive ability and integration with the global markets. Most of the problems arise due to the unorganized nature of this sector, lack of data and information, use of low technology sometimes obsolete technology and poor infrastructure in the country. WTO will affect all types of SSI units whether producing for the domestic market or for the international market.

The rural and SSI sector which produces over 7500 items will have to be aware of the patents of products including even of the technological patents, trademarks, industrial designs, etc. 95% of SSI units are in the nature of tiny micro enterprises and are weak. Many of them are one man shows. Their capital bases are poor and do not have access to the economics of scale. Their bargaining power is low and do not have access to information and modern management practices. They constitute most vulnerable segment of the SSI sector. Hence, they will need to be guided and supported since they are also employment generators for the economy. Balance 5% of SSI units is in the category of modern SSIs and has already established global links. Indian small enterprises have certain inherent strengths which helped them raise their share in total exports to 35% even in the face of tough global competition. The sector possesses the advantage of immovableness and flexibility. Their inventories are low and have weathered many adverse situations successfully and boldly. Indian SSIs have also advantage of local raw material and besides cheap labour which could be harnessed to the advantage. At the same time, it is essential to note their vulnerability in the context of emerging global environment.

GENERAL IMPLICATION OF WTO

1. The impact of WTO and its agreements are on every economic activity be it agriculture, trading, service or manufacturing.
2. World markets are opening up due to lowering of tariffs and dismantling of other restrictions in developed and developing countries. Enlightened entrepreneurs have greater opportunities to benefit from their comparative advantages.
3. Domestic markets will be increasingly threatened because of lowering of tariffs leading to freer entry of foreign goods and because of foreign companies establishing manufacturing bases locally.
4. Developing countries will have greater opportunities in sectors like textiles, agriculture etc. the developed countries will benefit by opening of service sector and tightening of intellectual property rights.
5. Export markets will become tougher because of competition among developing countries having similar comparative advantages.
6. Products from developing countries will face tougher quality standards in developed markets.
7. The international trade is increasingly becoming knowledge based. The entrepreneurial ability will come into force in the new environment.

IMPACT OF WTO AGREEMENT ON INDIAN SMALL SCALE INDUSTRIES

1. Impact will be on entire gamut of trade in goods. Competition to intensify as more imported products finds

easy access. Around 755 of the products reserved for Small Industries already in OGL, rest to be allowed in due course. Removal of Quantitative Restrictions (QRs) set to further accelerate import of all products.

2. Ignorance among SMEs on WTO is low and will be affected by sudden spurts in imports.
3. Only those businesses whether producing for domestic or foreign markets, which have international vision will survive and grow.
4. Indian exporters of electrical machinery, consumer articles, pharmaceuticals, detergents, automobiles, household electric/electronic gadgets, insecticides, chemicals, fertilizers, toys etc., will benefit as imports of these products are subject to mandatory products standards. However as agreement also covers PPM (Process and Production Methods), it could be used for discriminating against Indian exports for agri/food/pharma products.
5. Companies exporting fresh/processed fruit/vegetables, juices, meat, dairy products etc., should understand the mandatory standards as they have serious implications for their businesses in agri/processed foods and dairy products.
6. Regarding subsidies, the agreement prohibits export subsidies but allows permissible subsidies. Developing countries have to phase them out by 2003 and should freeze their level and coverage during transitional period.
7. On 1st Jan 2000, developed countries reduced tariffs by 40%, developing countries by 30% in five equal installments, which has resulted in massive increase in competition for domestic manufacturers.
8. Important development for textiles/garments exports from India. Quotas will be phased out. Real benefit to accrue from 2002 onwards.

REMEDIAL MEASURES

- More Industrial/Technology parks with all facilities for small industries will be established.

- Quality will be uppermost concern in customer -oriented economy. Acquiring ISO 9000 and other standards will be crucial.
- Rapid Technological obsolesce exerts tremendous pressure on SSI to upgrade/modify/process technologies.
- Small units will be environments friendly and necessary certifications will have to be obtained.
- Access to global markets, tie-up with foreign partners for import of technology and buy-backs.
- Preferential treatment in allotment of infrastructure facilities, setting ups of mini-industrial units and cluster industries.
- Thrust on agro-industries, food-processing industries export promotion industries and high technology industries.
- Greater weightage to tiny units will required to continue.
- Co-operative arrangements between units manufacturing the same products will consolidate the negotiating power in the market will not be far.
- Making available integrated (Composite) term loan for higher amounts on preferential terms.
- Collateral guarantee from institutions will boost the establishment of tiny and small scale units.
- Credit rating institutions will play a prominent role in acting as intermediaries and arranging of loans etc.

PROSPECTS AND OUTLOOK

- The process of liberalization, while providing tremendous opportunities, has thrown up new challenges for the Indian rural and small scale industries sector.
- For SSIs, the globalization of economic activities has two interfaces. Form some, the process opens new opportunities to expand and grow, for others, a much larger group the process is a threat from abroad.
- In view of the importance of SSI sector and to provide a further impetus to its contribution in the overall economy,

a new Ministry for Small Scale Industries and Agro Rural Industries has been created.

- With regard to the definition of Small Scale Industry, a school of thought has propagated the introduction of a new concept of Small and Medium Enterprises in Indian context. This would be in line with the concept of SMEs prevalent the world over.
- In view of emerging WTO regime and a high level reservation redundancy, there may be a need to reconsider orienting of the existing Government policies so as to achieve a phased dereservation of reserved items.

CONCLUSION

- To enable the rural and SSI entrepreneurs in facing the emerging challenges, there is a need for creating awareness about the implications of WTO and educating entrepreneurs suitably.
- It may be desirable to conduct product -wise market research on the implications of WTO and other related aspects. The outcome of such studies could be made available to Industry Associations/Entrepreneurs for wider market understanding and use by the members and SSIs at large.
- Due to the unique characteristics of resilience and flexibility, the SSI sector has generally performed better than the manufacturing and the overall industry sector.
- Exports from the SSI sectors also have generally shown better growth as compared to overall exports of the country.

REFERENCES

Aswathappa K., Business Environment.

Francis Cherunilam, Business Environment, Himalaya Publishing House.

D. Panduranag Rao, WTO & Competitiveness, Excel Books.

Laghu Udyog.

16

FUTURE OF RURAL MICRO-ENTERPRISES AND DECLINING COMMONS

V. Annamalai and Y. Gangi Reddy

INTRODUCING THE RATIONALE

Contrary to popular belief, CPRs hold the nerve centres of the agriculture and rural economy at large. The two fold contribution of CPRs to the rural economy is very often glossed over by academics and policy makers. It makes a direct contribution to the income of the rural households. No less significant is its contribution to the irrigation sources of the agriculture. As much as 50% of the rural income is traceable to the CPR source (Sarvekshana, 2000). Fuel wood, fodder, green manure, grasses, bamboo, small timber and palm leaves, wild fruits and leafy vegetables are both marketed and used for household consumption. Fuel wood and fodder in between them sustain a good chunk of forest based population according to NSS Survey 2000 as much 58 per cent and 25 per cent. The income from these two sources is often found rivalling the income from the agricultural source.

CPRs serve as the sprawling green pastures for hordes of goat and sheep besides the milk and draught animals. Part of the cultivable CPR land is brought under plough by the land hungry poor. CPRs serve as the vast bastion of rainwater catchments to feed in to the groundwater as well as the surface water sources of irrigation. Besides, CPRs are a major source of primary product supply for a wide variety of cottage industries/household enterprises. Rural micro-enterprises owe a great deal to the CPRs for their sustenance. These include bamboo, wood, reeds, grass, roots, fruits, nuts, gums, resins, honey, wax, herbs, honey and weeds. These resources have been available earlier in plenty. They have been cheap source of raw materials for these enterprises. In the past the lower cost of these resources, have sustained activities. There is much more to it from the living memories.

The older generation fondly cherishes the memories of the rural population satisfying all and sundry of its needs from the CPRs with the only exception of staple food and clothing. The older generation was brought up in the belief that forest is the mother for it takes care of every other need of rural residents. Forest served as a constant source of supply of primary produce, which went in to the acquisition of fixed assets (house building, agricultural implements etc) at one end to durable consumer goods (mats, baskets, musical instruments) at the other besides meeting the day to day consumption needs (fuel wood, fodder and water). A host of micro enterprise mediated the primary produce taking the shape of the final product. The micro enterprise thrived at its best as late as in the 50's and 60's of the just concluded century. Fewer people were found in the agricultural operations (40%) and the majority (60%) had its stakes in the industry and service sectors.

A sympathetic observer might in desperation hold that we are well past the good old days and little is the hope for any return to the great glory of the past. We do not believe in putting the clock back either. All the same, the recent developments suggest that the international community is decisively moving towards replacing the fossil fuel based synthetic industrial economy with renewable energy (bio-energy inclusive) based bio degradable product oriented industrial economy. The former holds a potential threat for the very survival of the globe. The latter promises a new lease of life to the globe and therefore the bright future to it. The future in short belongs to the bio energy latter.

The present study purports at making a strong case for the regeneration of the vegetative cover of the CPRs. The case study highlights the fact that the degradation of the CPRs wiped out the micro enterprises from the rural map. The study brings out that the micro enterprises of yesteryears are breathing their last. Consequently immisarisation and the distress out migration are on the rise as is seen through the plight of the rope makers. The degradation of CPR wealth went hand in hand with the disappearance of the bulk of micro enterprises in to thin air resulting in the wholesale pauperisation of the artisan and service castes over the last three decades and more. The loss of CPR wealth led to the loss of rural micro enterprises and loss of productive jobs. The loss of CPR wealth had its pernicious impact on the water resource and by implication on the crop output. The loss of jobs led at one side to distress out migration and redoubled pressure on the water scarce agricultural land at the other. The study stops short of getting in to unfolding the whole gamut of the vicious cycle, which may await a future date. For the present, the study confined itself to outlining the road map of marginalisation of the micro enterprises from the rural setting.

THE CASE OF KARURA

Micro-enterprises in rural India produced user goods based on locally available resources and basically meant for local consumption. The barter system mediated the exchange of the user goods. The basic premises and conditions which made this micro-enterprises generating employment and income in rural non-farm sector is undergoing tremendous changes. The sweeping changes in the pattern of resource use in the recent past engulfing the countryside swept out the micro-enterprises en-masse resulting in mass unemployment and pauperisation.

Micro-enterprises such as rope making in rural areas depends mainly on the primary products supplied by CPRs like community forest in rural areas of Punjab. The families who depend on them use simple technology to make ropes, which are useful in bundling wheat and paddy. This is true in case of around 40 families in the Gram Panchayat Karura in the Rupanagar district of Punjab.

Agriculture constitutes the single largest source of employment and livelihood and provides employment to 44.74% of total workers in the Rupanagar district (1991Census). The district is quite important in forestry and ranks second in area in the State. An extent of 47,800 hectares (1991 figures) was shown under forest; out of which 6,400 hectares were government held and the rest privately held (41,400 hectares). The 1979-80 figures make a bit of variation. Total extent under forest was put at 44,192 hectares and within it the government held at 6,700 hectares and the privately held at 37,472 hectares. Protected forest is the other name for the government held forests and the same bordering the rail lines, roads, canals and embankments is maintained by the forest department. The records of 1982-83 show an area of 5,546.22 hectares under the 'protected forest' and 1,154.66 hectares under unclassified forests. The forests in the district are spread across the Shivalik foothills. The types of grasses available as primary produce are locally known as Palwan, Sariala, Jheuri, Khavi, Kant and Bhabbar. Bhabbar is valued the most among all and it is used for making pulp for paper besides ropes. The official figures put it that an income of Rs. 413, 827 was raised in 1982-83 in the forest produce from the government held forests alone. There is both demand for ropes in the rural economy and supply of Bhabbar for rope making aplenty in the vicinity. The demand and supply together gave rise to a cottage industry in rope making. Roughly 40 dalit households took to the rope making to eke out a living.

The jurisdiction of Karura Gram Panchayat extends to an area of 481 hectares. 185 households showing a total population of 1013 (1991 figures) are resident of Karura. The pattern of land distribution under Karura Gram Panchayat is as follows: Irrigated by source: 15.00 ha (3%); Rain fed: 178.00 ha (37%); Culturable waste: 38.00 ha (8%) and Area not available for Cultivation: 250.00 ha (52%). The land under Karura (Nurpurbedi block) is mostly dry and hilly. Karura is located down the foothills of Shivalik Range. Dalits make a preponderant presence with 80 families and 500 population.

SOURCES OF DIFFERENT RAW MATERIALS

Karura is marked for the predominant presence of the CPRs (60% of GA). Common lands, community forest, *bhanjar* lands and forest-all put together make up to the CPRs at Karura. The forest area in turn appears sub divided in to (a) the government held (250 hectares) and (b) community/the Gram Panchayat held. The people are kept out of access to the government held forest. Yet, the poor forces its way in to the government held forest and collects fuel and fodder. The people owning lands keep away from the government held forest. The community forest was wrested back by the panchayats from the hands of the FD under the Punjab Common Lands act, 1961. This is contested even now by locals citing to the community (*shamilat)* character of the land.

The *Shamilat* lands were the creation of local people. Each according to their will and capacity contributed to the common pool. These were meant for grazing of cattle, collection of fodder and fuel for the whole village. The shift of control from community to the gram panchayat has its own problems. Firstly the community lost control over common lands thereby neglecting the interests of the community. It is possible for the panchayats to convert these lands into source of income for gram panchayat rather than serving the community for supply of fodder and fuel to the poor. Secondly, under Panchayat rules in Punjab the income derived from common lands are vested in the hands of the government. Unlike Harayana, panchayats in Punjab cannot plow back their income to develop the village. Thirdly, community ownership is lost resulting in people taking not much interest in the maintenance of CPRs. In many cases in Punjab they get illegally occupied leading to litigations and depravation of income to gram panchayats. People have a limited access, which at times is interrupted by a total denial of access. In case of a need, the individual households have to approach Gram Panchayat and obtain a permit. The permits materialize following a resolution in the Gram Panchayat meeting. In case of auctioning out of the forest in favor of contractors, the individual households are kept out of access. Access to the government held forest appears to be far easier. The government held forest and the panchayat held forest share a common management model. The model is inspired by threat perceptions and the communities are seen holding a threat to the regeneration of the forest. The model seeks to regenerate the forest by keeping the community away at arms length. The laws are made stringent to the effect that the trespassers shall be punished. It is a far cry from the community management of the forest where in a need based forest growth is planned and executed followed by devising an appropriate sharing mechanism. The collective will of the people goes in to the planned growth and sharing of the fruits. The top down command and control model built on the trespasser threat perceptions worked at the cost of the interests of both commons and the communities.

DECLINING COMMONS AND MICRO-ENTERPRISES

Gram Panchayat makes money from the sale of Bhabbar grass. Around 40 families took to rope making. The rope is in peak demand on occasions of wheat and paddy harvesting. The collection right of Bhabbar is acceded by the panchayat following group auction by the rope makers. Actual collection of Bhabbar is open to any one willing to cut and carry the Bhabbar to a select place. The labor is rewarded at the rate of Rs. 2 per KG. On an average, an individual is found collecting 40 kg of Bhabbar per day. The collection agents increasingly find it difficult to pool together 40 kg per day. The thin presence of Bhabbar comes in the way. Perhaps, the collection practices are not Bhabbar friendly. The agents in their anxiety to collect an extra bit harm the Bhabbar growth risking their own interests at the end. The collection agents are prompted by their immediate individual interests to make the most out of collection. It harms the long term interests of all the stakeholders involved in the rope making enterprise. It reminds us the overriding need of embarking on the community management of the commons.

SYNTHETIC ROPES THREATEN TO OUST BHABBAR ROPE

The Bhabbar rope is constrained by insecure supply of primary produce and consequently cost escalation. Given these big constraints, the rope making micro-enterprises cannot possibly supply ropes at a competitive price in the market. Meanwhile the nylon rope threatens to make big inroads in to the rope market. The nylon ropes have an edge over the Bhabbar rope in terms of durability. Therefore the farmer's preference for the nylon ropes. There is steady erosion in the demand for Bhabbar rope resulting in the huge stockpiling of finished Bhabbar ropes. The Bhabbar rope makers are yet to ensure durability to the home made rope if only to be able to withstand the onslaught from the nylon rope. The possibilities are slim as the availability of the primary produce is none to encouraging and the institutional support is conspicuous by its absence.

ABSENCE OF INSTITUTIONAL SUPPORT

The rope making dalits are an unorganized lot. They are not even aware of the existence of a wide ranging official and quasi official support structures covering finance at one end to the R&D at the other. The support structures are found wanting to reach the needy either.

SITUATION ELSEWHERE

The situation in other parts of the country is no better characterized by declining supply of raw materials from commons, challenging of market in terms of more cheaper and durable products like plastics, nylons etc and absence of institutional and policy support for micro-enterprises. Take the case of villages from Khammam district of Andhra Pradesh where most of the population of these villages depended on special reeds from nearby forest for making baskets. In the recent years, they also face similar problems like in Punjab and elsewhere like declining raw materials supply like reeds from nearby area, changing preference of market and lack of institutional support for these activities. Decline in agricultural activities due to drought and deficient rainfall adds to their woes.

HOW NOT TO ALLOW THE MICRO-ENTERPRISES TO DIE DOWN?

The rope makers are haunted by uncertain future. Insecure supply of Bhabbar grass from the commons, obsolete technology and changing market preferences conspire together to marginalize the Bhabbar rope making. The rope makers are on the verge of folding up the activity in favor of out migration. How not to allow the micro enterprises to die down? Is it that the enterprises have no other go except to meet a natural death?

Introduce a meaningful community forest management and rope in both the government held and panchayat held forest under its embrace. The single measure would give a powerful impetus to the rope making industry to come alive with redoubled zeal. Besides, it will fuse life back in to a wide variety of the so called dead and moribund rural micro enterprises. Combine the native talent with the advanced skills and technologies on top of it. The rural micro enterprises will soon start out witting the synthetic products. Emulate SEWA (Gujarat) and ensure a manifold growth of the rural micro enterprises.

REFERENCES

Survekshana (2000), Survey on Common Property.

V. Annamalai (2001), The Role of Panchayats in the Management of Common Property Resources for the Benefit of Rural Poor: A Case Study in the States of Karnataka and Haryana, Hyderabad: NIRD.

V. Annamalai (2001), Panchayati Raj and Natural Resource Management: A Study of two Village Panchayats in Tamil Nadu, Hyderabad: NIRD.

V. Annamalai (2004) , Common Property Resources and Livelihood Patterns: A Study in Punjab and Sikkim on the Use and Accessibility by Different Sections of Rural Society, Research Report, NIRD, Hyderabad.

V. Annamalai and Y. Gangi Reddy, "Declining Commons, Obsolete Technology and Shrinking Market in Punjab" paper presented in NIRD Foundation day Seminar held in 2001, Hyderabad

NIRD-World Bank Evaluation Report–Deepam (Gas Stove) Scheme in Andhra Pradesh, 2002.

17

RURAL INDUSTRIALIZATION: PROBLEMS AND STRATEGIES FOR PROMOTION IN THE POST-LIBERALIZED ERA

N. V. Madhuri

INTRODUCTION

The past experience of the developed economies has shown that industrialization has a major role to play in the economic development of the Less Developed Countries (LDCs) of which India is one. Net value of output per person, scope for internal and external economies of scale, marginal propensity to save and invest etc. is greater in industries than in agriculture. So, it makes industrialization both a means of higher productivity and a cause of higher income. It is, therefore, rightly called the engine of growth; especially in situations of unfavorable trends in world trade for primary commodities. Therefore, there is no second opinion on the importance of industrialization but the question is industrialization of what pattern?

This question arises because the diversion of unemployed and underemployed rural labour to non-agricultural occupations is the basic need of the developing economies for their sustainable development and balanced development. Historically industrial development has proceeded in three stages which can be explained in a simple way by the relative importance of consumer goods and capital goods output.

Halffman explains the three stages. In stage I, the consumer goods industries are of overwhelming importance; their net output being on the average five times as large (5:1) as that of capital goods industries and the ratio is 2.5:1 and 1:1 in the second and third stages. This transition through the stages has seen many variations in different countries. But the transition in less developed economies is largely guided by the relative scarcity of capital. The problem is not how to economise the use of capital but how to increase its supply. Since the labour is plentiful and unemployment is large causing poverty, and capital is scarce, the development of labour intensive consumer goods marks the beginning. It is in this context that the small scale industries, which are highly labour intensive, assumes importance and rural industries are of this type. They are important for their employment effect.

RURAL INDUSTRIES

Rural Industrialization means the spread of industries to the countryside. Rural industries embrace all industries which are run by rural people in or near their homes as a spare time or whole time occupation, as a traditional profession. Its objectives are to utilize local resources both human and material; and to meet the needs of the local masses. Necessarily the industries are decentralized, locally based, labour intensive and agro-based because India still remains predominantly a country of villages and agrarians. Rural Industries are usually classified into two categories:

(i) Agricultural sector or agro based industries. These industries include industries processing agricultural produce and by-products.

(ii) Non-agricultural sector

- Professional service sector
- Cottage industries
- Small scale industries.

Professional Service Sector

There is a certain class of people like barbers, cobblers, blacksmiths and carpenters etc., in the rural area which can become a great source of strength to the economy. This sector can easily provide gainful employment to a sizable section of the rural unemployed labour.

Cottage Industries

Cottage industries are generally associated with agriculture or whole time occupation in rural and semi-urban areas. Cottage industries or village industries refer to those industries which flourish in the rural and semi-urban areas, such as bee-keeping, pottery, soap industry, ghani oil, bamboo and cane work, manufacturing of gum, agarbathis etc. These industries now provide full and part-time employment to about 43 lakh persons in India.

Small Scale Industries

Small scale industries are usually classified into two categories:

(a) Traditional small scale industries include Khadi and Handloom, village industries, handicraft, coir, sericulture, etc.

(b) Modem small scale industries produce a wide range of goods, particularly ancillaries to large scale industries electronic control system etc.

The traditional small industries are highly labour intensive and are based on locally available resources, especially farm products. In contrast, modern small industries make use of highly sophisticated machinery, equipment and skilled labour and professionals. They are mostly located in the urban ridge.

PROBLFMS OF RURAL INDUSTRIALISATION

Rural industries play a vital role in the development of Indian economy. But these industries are facing a number of problems in the post liberalisation era which are discussed below:

Size of Rural Industrial Units

The size of rural industrial units is generally very small, both in terms of the number of workers employed and the volume of output. One of the reasons for their small size is their household character. Even though rural population is high, when compared to urban population, the size of rural industrial units is very small. Employment in rural industries is generally limited by the number of workers in the owner-household, and the major motivation in operating the units is to earn livelihood for the family rather than for purposes of accumulation and expansion.

Finance

Finance facilitates growth and its absence is a constraint for the growth of any sector. Mainly in rural industries like pottery, carpentry, wire machine etc., the availability of finance had favourably influenced their recent growth. On the other hand, majority of units like leather, hand loom, food-products, blacksmithy, oil mills, beedi making etc., suffer due to lack of finance. Banks are the most frequent source of finance. However, various financial agencies including commercial banks have not been adequately effective in meeting the credit needs of the weaker sections in rural areas. The traditional view in the lending policy, influence of vested interests, the rampant corruption are responsible for this situation.

The serious problem of rural industries is in respect of credit both of long-term and short-term purposes. It is evident from the fact that the supply of credit has not been commensurate with their needs associated with fixed and working capital. The credit has lagged much behind the volume of activity that the small units generate in the fields of storage, transport, distribution etc. Further, very often the credit has not been timely. Its delayed availability is a major problem for the rural industrialists. The credit situation is particularly hard for the very small or tiny industrial units. As a result, quite a significant proportion of these units is dependent upon high cost credit of private money lenders which our rural industrialists could not bear.

Marketing

The problem of marketing is likely to be a serious handicap for those independent small units which produce a wide variety of articles. The experience has been that marketing of such products suffers due to faulty organisation, poor product standardisation, quality variations, lack of market information etc. Further, marketing difficulties are accentuated from the hard facts that most of the goods produced will have to be sold in the urban areas where large investment on advertisements is required in an intensively competitive market in the post liberalised era. A small manufacturer can, perhaps, make as good toothpaste as a multi-nationals but his product is unlikely to sell against the flair of publicity of the multinationals who are great experts in manipulating the publicity media. Marketing of the products, therefore, is going to be the most difficult part of the efforts for industrialization of the rural areas.

Technology

Artisans in the rural industries still adhere to the traditional and outmoded techniques of production. They have no knowledge whatsoever about the latest technology. Moreover, the methods of production which the small and tiny enterprises use are old and inefficient. The result is low productivity, poor quality of products and high costs. The producers for want of information know very little about modern technologies which have revolutionized production in small units in advanced countries. There is little research and development in this field in our country. Whatever new is available in the field is not easily transferred to them, for want of a satisfactory technology delivery mechanism, such as arrangements for demonstration in respect of their use, cost etc. There is almost no agency to provide venture capital to cover risks associated with the introduction of new technologies.

Communication

Information technology is the key element of modern business world. The communication has joined in the list of basic needs of human society. The post liberalised era saw the advanced technology in many frontiers. The insulation of world wide telephone network, the invention of Radio and

Television, unprecedented growth of computer industry, launching of satellite communication have shrunk the world boundary.

To-days fiercely competitive business world is greatly dependent on communication system. Modern communication is an indispensable aid in meeting basic needs and is an essential element to facilitate development activities such as agriculture, construction, sanitation, water sourcing and likes. Communication systems turn local news to global news and local events to international events.

Communication in to-day's world plays an indispensable role in promoting accessibility, accountability, connectivity, democracy, and decentralization—all qualities essential to effective social, economic and political development. It binds people's ideas and initiatives. It has become a primary tool for nation-building as essential as the basic needs like water, shelter, agriculture, health etc.

The basic function of advertisement and sales promotion is obviously the communication of salient features of products and service to the potential users and developing the urge to buy products and services apart from retaining the loyalty of the existing users. Publicity of new methods of cultivation, use of modern production techniques and inputs are very important for the development of rural industries. In the absence of communication facilities in the village artisans do our get the realistic scenario of market prices, the taste, the preference, domestic demand, export potentials etc. Competing with the multi-nationals who have access to communication technology is another major problem.

Social Sector

Socio-economic development of rural areas is of crucial significance in the framework of integrated growth and social justice. The most pressing problem in India to-day is that of improving the economic and social condition of the vast number of people in rural areas who live below the poverty line. They include landless labourers, small farmers, artisans and other weaker sections of the society. These sections have been subjected to economic discrimination, exploitation and oppression of all types.

On the basis of National Sample Survey (NSS, 38th Round), the World Bank report calculated the incidence of poverty among different categories of rural households. It was revealed that persons in wage dependent families (including those working in non-agricultural jobs) comprise 46 per cent of the poor in rural areas.

Various factors account for this high incidence of poverty among rural labour households. Firstly, there is a considerable degree of unemployment and underemployment among rural labourers. It has been established that incidence of unemployment is the highest among casual labourers. Another major cause of rural poverty is the low asset base of the poor. The next major cause of poverty is low educational attainments of the poor.

Social environmental improvements will attract our attention to rural housing and sanitation. This is the most crucial sector which differentiates a rural-area from the urban complexes. Most educated people do not like to live in the villages because the standard of sanitation, water supply and rural housing is not adequate to their needs. The poor quality of environments existing in the rural situation does not attract people to the villages as has been the trend in the developed countries of the world. On the contrary, with the advent of education the process of migration starts from villages to the towns for the rural elites. This brain drain to the cities is perhaps responsible for the backwardness of our rural economy. If the slogan 'back to villages' has to succeed we must provide provision for better social environment in our programmes of rural regeneration.

Infrastructure

Economic development of a country depends to a great extent on infrastructure. *Ex:-* Transport, communication, power, health service, raw material, banking, etc. But most of the Indian villages are lacking in these facilities because of various problems. These infrastructure problems hamper the growth of rural industrialization.

Foreign Investment

Most countries are making use of foreign capital to accelerate the pace of economic growth. The utilisation of foreign investment depends on the absorptive capacity of recipient country. But various factors such as lack of infra structural facilities, lack of technical know-how, inadequacy of administrative machinery etc in the rural areas of our country affect this absorptive capacity, due to which foreign Investment tends to flow to high profit areas rather than to priority areas.

Apart from the above mentioned problems, rural industries also have to face the problem of:

(i) *Non Availability of Raw Material:* Not only the supply of essential raw materials is scarce but they are available at high prices and their quality is not up to the standard. This increases the cost of production and puts them in an ad verse position.

(ii) *Power Shortage:* Rural industries always suffer from power failure. Due to this, there is no continuity in the production.

(iii) *Lack of Guidance:* Rural industrialists suffer from improper guidance. They should be motivated and encouraged by proper training. Because of lack of training and guidance, their money is improperly invested.

(iv) *Lack of Transport Facilities:* Even though Government takes adequate steps for the improvement of transportation, proper transportation facilities to rural area is lacking.

(v) *Tax:* Rural industries also face the problem of the payment of local and other taxes.

STRATEGIES FOR PROMOTION OF RURAL INDUSTRIALISATION

(i) *Planning:* Planning for rural industrialisation should be made at the grass root level. This could be integrated into the national plan to avoid lopsided development. A team of social workers, local officials and experts should make a detailed assessment of the natural resources, per-capita income and capital, wage-rates, land holdings, level of literacy and the attitude as well as aptitude of the rural people by holding discussions with the cross-section of the rural population in the concerned place. Involvement of the local population in the planning and execution of such projects is essential if there should be a sustainable development of these projects.

(ii) *Infrastructure Development:* Infrastructural facilities like roads, power, transport and communication must be created prior to the implementation of the rural industrialisation programme. Village must be linked by roads from all sides and rural electrification should be given utmost importance.

(iii) *Skill Development:* There is a misunderstanding prevailing that out rural artisans are not good entrepreneurs. But such a notion is absolutely baseless. They have lots of creative ideas and are highly innovative.

They have the requisite skills to handle any new technology introduced, with re-orientation of skills. However, proper training must be provided to upgrade their skills, diversify their production process and make their products more acceptable.

(iv) *Finance:* The success of any rural industrialisation programme very much revolves round the availability of financial assistance at a reasonable cost. Inadequate availability of finance has been the major obstacle to the growth of small enterprises. The existing co-operative structure has to be strengthened and reorganized into viable units. Rural artisans also being impoverished have a different set of priorities. Whatever external assistance is given to them they will spend according to their own priorities. Household consumption followed by redemption from old debts are the major priorities. Working capital to carry on the existing activity takes the third priority.

The banks therefore need to have permanent arrangement to take care of monitoring and recovery aspects of their credit. If there is a separate agency to monitor and recover the credit, the size of bad debts would come down drastically.

(v) *Marketing:* The next problem before the rural industries producing a variety of commodities is to sell their products at fair prices. Neither the producers have the knowledge of the potential consumers nor do the consumers have the idea of the goods so produced. The marketing efforts of the existing village industries lack proper organisation, product standardisation, due publicity and accessibility to market. It is natural the product of rural industries would find a place in the urban market if intensive publicity is given to the product. A small manufacturer can make an article of good quality but cannot compete with a large scale enterprise which produces an article of inferior quality but has the capacity to capture the market by publicity.

A large part of the products of village industries must find market in the surrounding areas. It should be ensured that articles produced by village industries should not be produced by large scale enterprises and their ancillaries to avoid competition.

(vi) *Communication and Management:* The industrial development of any nation is achieved not only through its major industries but also through the small scale industries which are situated both in rural and urban places. There are certain exclusive vocational advantages and disadvantages for these industries. There are two dominant issues pertaining to rural industries are, How to promote-rural industries? How to manage them? Management is not only a science but also remains as an art, due to the fast developing technological innovations. Among the science and technological developments the role of communication on managing industries is to be thoroughly and repeatedly reviewed.

Getting things done is largely dependent on communication. The importance of communication is generally felt in its absence. Similarly the effectiveness of communication is directly related to technology. The emergence of IT industry and its innovation play very important role in the success of communication. Communication in turn helps in so many dimensions to solve managerial problems in industries.

Due to technological changes, rural industries face a number of day-to-day managerial problems. The impact of technological changes is more powerful and pervasive than it has been considered and will continue to increase. The managers of rural industries do worry about coping up with this fast development. As a catalyser, the government should do its best to overcome these barriers in industrial development. "When water jet looms were invented in Japan, the government supported it with an edict which scrapped 90,000 obsolete looms in five years" (Rao, 1994).

Indian government introduced a number of schemes for rural people in order to make them entrepreneurs. However, a large gap is felt in providing them with infrastructural facilities, particularly, communication network. The minimum facilities pertaining to communication are to be reviewed very frequently. All arrangements to improve such facilities are to be made by the governments and local bodies.

Sustainable Management

There are abundant resources in rural India. They can be used for rural industrialisation. Land, water, climate, flora, fauna and human resource are the basic resources for industrial development. Utilization of these resources needs sustainable management. It is imperative to develop strategies for conservation and improvement of these resources for better results in the process of rural industrialisation.

The concept of sustainable management implies that the needs of the present can be met without compromising the ability of the resources to meet the needs of the future. Achieving this target needs cooperation from the government, policy implementors and public in general. Science and technology personnel must work in partnership with rural entrepreneurs to create a new industrial environment where communication facilities are provided to strengthen the management. Apart from providing facilities, enough training should be given to the personnel of rural industries to solve the emerging problems. Problem solving needs a scientific approach. Understanding the nature, process, style elements of problem solving would enable the entrepreneurs to work for sustainable management of industries.

Credit to Weaker Sections

With a view to augmenting credit to rural sector, commercial banks were advised by the RBI to provide at least 10 per cent of their net bank credit or 25 per cent of their priority-sector advances to weaker sections including rural industries. As at the end of December 1997 the amount of outstanding advances to weaker sections accounted for 8.7 per cent of their net bank credit and 20.3 per cent of the aggregate priority sector advances.

Technology

It is important not only to generate rapid development in rural areas, but to reduce the economic and technological gap between rural and urban areas, and seek to achieve a greater degree of integration between the two. The development of low technology and low productivity industries in the rural areas together with the growth of modern high technology industries in the urban areas would inevitably result in accentuating the technological and economic dualism between the two sectors. Therefore, the industries located in rural areas should generate not only linkages; to the extent possible, in the villages, but also become a link in rural-urban integration. Besides, reducing the income gap between the two sectors, it is also desirable that rural industries should use technologies which are in line with the technological pattern of the emerging industrial structure in the country as a whole. The upgradation of the technologies of "dynamic" rural industries and the introduction of relatively modern-technology industries in rural areas alone are likely to make rural industries an integral part of the industrialisation process in the country.

The choice of technology has to meet the criterion of 'appropriateness' not only in terms of the use of locally available materials and manpower, but also in terms of generating reasonably high levels of incomes for the workers as well as meeting the changing patterns of demand. The use of technologies which require a heavy labour input but yield a very low productivity per unit of labour is unlikely to serve the basic objectives of rural industrialisation. The technology used in rural industries varies in terms of the use of machinery, equipment, non-human energy, and therefore, of capital intensity; but, by and large, the activities in which mechanical devices and capital equipment are used yield a reasonable income only to those who are engaged in them. At the same time, the use of such devices and equipment does not turn these industries 'capital intensive' nor does it reduce the employment potential. It only makes employment more, effective in terms of income generation.

Environmental Improvements

A well planned and executed programme of rural housing can act as a vehicle of modernisation of rural life. It is capable of changing the attitudes towards education, health, and employment and of even changing physical structures of villages; bringing about a whole series of community improvements, for example, in drainage, sewerage, water supply, sanitation habits etc. The immediate consequence is social awareness of higher standards of living and an urbanised outlook.

Capacity Building

While framing the policies for rural industrial improvement, the Government must set up separate cells to study the location, resources, availability of labour, nature of work etc. According to this, suitable programmes which suit the particular locality may be framed and implemented by the Government. The skills of industrialists and the rural industrial workers must be upgraded through suitable programmes. Unnecessary expenditure by the construction of huge buildings should be reduced and funds may be utilised for the construction of community halls, training-cum production centres, children homes, old age homes, widow homes etc.

CONCLUSION

Rural Industries in India are now facing more threats for their survival. They have begun to feel hardship in doing their business on two accounts. As the Indian Economy has been practicing open market economy from the year 1991, India's market is integrated with world market which resulted in severe competition from Multi-National Corporation (MNCs) for local industries including SSIs.

On the other hand, small scale industries are subject to many hardships due to the policies of World Trade Organisation (WTO) on its member countries. As India is a signatory of WTO, it has to adapt to free imports of many consumer goods which in turn affects the rural industries as these goods are exclusively reserved for production by SSI Units. So far, small units do not have any financial and managerial resources to play in the Global Market.

Rural Industrialization has been a widely spread phenomenon. The relative merits of less capital intensity and more labour absorption capacity, among others, have endeared the sector to the policy-makers as an instrument to achieve a variety of economic objectives such as employment generation, production of mass consumption goods, balanced regional development, equitable distribution of income etc., since India's independence. Rural industries also suffer from variety of weaknesses. Some of the policy recommendations to tackle the problems of the rural industries are mentioned below:

POLICY RECOMMENDATIONS

1. The Government should start raw-materials bank in order to solve the problems of shortage of raw material in small scale sector.

The public sector banks should identify correct beneficiary and help them to start small industries.

Micro Credit for Women to be Increased more

Special attention must be paid on account of the global changes to enable domestic rural industry to enhance competitiveness on a continuous basis.

The government support machinery has to be revitalised.

Effective Research and Development networks to be developed and the small industry association have to be involved intensively.

Adequate infrastructure facilities have to be created in rural areas for setting up small industrial units.

The government will have to give special fiscal concessions to SSI units to setup in rural areas.

Information of state-of-the-art technology should be disseminated.

Creation of awareness on using international quality assurance standards.

Improving conditions of roads, ports and airports to strengthen the transport system.

Simplification of export procedures.

In tune with the overall Philosophy of New Economic Policy the Government sponsored Khadi and Village Industries must be slowly privatized and the existing industries to be modernized.

Thus, by adopting the above strategy, the process of rural industrialisation may be stimulated which will result in poverty alleviation by generating jobs and income for the most vulnerable communities as well as providing an essential element in the value added chain of manufacturing activities.

REFERENCES

Chaudhri, M. R. (1992), *Indian Industries, Development and Location,* Oxford University Press, New Delhi.

Haffman, W. G. (1958), *The Growth of Industrial Economics,* Oxford University Press, New Delhi.

Knaut, R., Mukhopadhyay, T., Szczypula, J., Kiesler, S. and Scherlis, W. (1998), *Communication and Information: Alternative Uses of the Internet in Households,* in proceedings of the CHI 98 (pp. 368-83), New York, ACM.

Planning Commission (1991), GOI, *Eighth Five Year Plan,* Vol. II.

Rao, A. S. (1994), *Management of Technology Change,* Delhi, Global Business Press.

Soundarapandian, M. (2000), *Industrial Resurgence in Rural India,* Delhi, Kanishka Publishers.

Thomas, K.W. and Schmidt, N.H. (1976), A Survey of Managerial Interests with Respect to Conflict, *Academy of Management Journal,* June, p. 317.

The Economic Survey (1977), Government of India, New Delhi.

Uppal, J. S. (1975), *India's Economic Operations,* Tata McGraw-Hill Publishing Co. Ltd., New Delhi.

18

RURAL INDUSTRIES AND NEW ECONOMIC POLICIES–HRD INTERVENTIONS FOR SUSTAINABLE RURAL INDUSTRIALISTATION

P. SivaRam

INTRODUCTION

Since time immemorial, Rural Industries had significantly been contributing to the development of rural economy by providing full employment to the people. These Industries were not only providing full employment to the landless laborers and rural artisans but also generating part-time employment and additional income to the small and marginal farmers for meeting their household needs fully and also make sufficient investment in agriculture and also contributing an important segment to the Indian economy. The Rural Industries are classified into eight sectors, which are as follows– (1) Khadi; (2) Handlooms; (3) Sericulture; (4) Handicrafts; (5) Coir; (6) Village Industries; (7) Small-scale industries and (8) Power-looms (Sury. MM-2003). In view of the emergence of New Economic Policy in the country, the Government of India and the State Governments have taken several important steps to accelerate economic and social development among these people, who have adopted rural industries as primary occupation for their livelihood. In addition to this, the Government of India has recently created a separate Ministry for Agro and Rural Industries for promotion and development of village and cottage industries, micro enterprises as well as tiny units in both urban and rural areas of the country.

The unorganized traditional industries are artisan-based, located mostly in rural and semi-urban areas. These industries are being used by the local knowledge, skills and resources for producing the products, which are being sold their products locally or near by areas. They are as follow - Handlooms, Khadi, Sericulture, Coir, Bidi-making, Embroidery, Knitting, Woodcarving and Other handicrafts. The field evidences (Sivaram P. 1990) revealed that the traditional artisans are giving up their occupations such as weaving, pottery etc because of the occupations is non-remunerative and unable to compete with machine made products. Consequently, they are migrating to urban and semi-urban areas in search of livelihoods. These field evidences have also revealed that the artisans are lacking macro and micro HRD services such as up gradation of knowledge and skills in their respective traditional occupations and lack of drinking water and sanitation, health and education facilities in their villages.

Modern small industries including 'tiny' units and power looms use power-driven machines and possess some technological sophistication. The market for these industries is relatively wider and quite often includes export market. Generally, these industries are located close to the urban and semi-urban areas including large industrial centers. Their products include hosiery goods, ready-made garments, motor-parts, electronics, sports goods, and engineering goods. Small-scale industries are defined that they were invested in plant and machinery up to Rs.3 crore. For tiny units, the investment limit is Rs. 25 lakh. The rural industries are-Employment Opportunities, Low capital investments and Regional based development. They are important source of employment and development in the rural areas and could provide large-scale employment and self-employment opportunities to the rural populace in the country. This rural industry sector output contributes almost 40 per cent of the gross Industrial value-added and 45 per cent of the total exports directly as well as indirectly from this industry in the country. In addition, this industry is the second largest employer for the human resources after agriculture in the country.

RURAL INDUSTRIALIZATION–OVERVIEW

The rural industrialization is an important strategy for employment generation and poverty reduction in the rural areas of the country. However, several Government sponsored programs have not resulted to the expected levels of people as well as Government due to a multifacet-shortcomings such as improper direction of subsidies, over emphasis on targets, unscientific methods in selecting and compensating the programme implementing agencies. The organized sector has not been able to generate additional employment opportunities. In the recent past, employment elasticity to output growth of all sectors has been falling drastically. The agriculture sector is over burdened with unproductive employment in other words that even if a good percentage of workers is with drawn, output may not suffer (Sudhakar Rao. B... 2003). The mega industries are significantly providing jobs to the urban people, as they are located in the vicinity of urban areas. But the liberalization and globalization have brought heavy competition to these industries. These competition can be tackled by improving their quality products in the international and national markets of urban and rural areas of the country. The modern small industry is mainly concentrating in and semi-urban centers. Because of this, the migration of both skilled and unskilled workers of rural areas is increasing to the semi-urban areas for utilizing the remunerative employment opportunities in modern small industries. However, the only hope is to generate employment opportunities in the sustainable non-farm sector in the rural areas, as there is no dearth for resources amenable for value addition. Considering the above, rural industrialization can provide an answer to the growing problems of poverty, unemployment and migration. Under certain programmes, the stakeholders are considered only as beneficiaries rather than as entrepreneurs. The approach is concentrated on providing subsidy to the beneficiaries and not as partners in a development project. In this process, they are identified and rated low, as there is no motivating environment. As a result, genuine self-employment that moves them towards a competitive world was not created. Self-employment as a method to help people to help themselves was also not there what is required is participation, involvement, employment and empowerment. Therefore, a new method needs to be introduced that provides as integrated package of services in project, technology, marketing and development.

Rural Industrialization has a mixed record of strengthens and weaknesses. Considering its contributions to the economy and the need to generate self-employment opportunities to the rural areas, several programmes have been conceived and implemented by Governmental and non-governmental organizations. In the rural development progamames, the relevance of micro-enterprises have always been related to poverty and employment issues. Also, the generation of service sector to service the rural areas has been a part of rural industrialization process. The targets for this approach are semi-skilled and skilled artisans, unemployment youth and women and families who have been left out in the growth process. The hope is see that value addition takes place to rural resources and rural entrepreneurs would contribute to employment generation and to stop further migration to urban centers. However, in these programmes, Methodologies for market integration have mot been attempted. In this context, SIDBI's Rural Industries programme takes a special place, due to its unique methodology for providing integrated services, with higher levels of investment, technology back-up and market integration.

SMALL INDUSTRIES DEVELOPMENT BANK OF INDIA (SIDBI) INITIATIVES IN PROMOTING RURAL INDUSTRIALIZATION

The SIDBI is the premier bank with the national responsibility of promoting small and micro enterprises in the country with a view to addressing problems as rural unemployment and urban migration under utilization of rural resources and skills. Apart from loaning from Banks, State Finance Corporations (SFCs) and other selected financial institutions, SIDBI has launched a rural industries programme (RIP) to extend critical services to the potential entrepreneurs in information, motivation, and training, appropriate technology support and market linkages for the growth of viable and sustainable rural enterprises. The RIP is being implemented through 23 agencies spread across 44 districts by March 2000. The RIP is in progress in the following States-Andhra Pradesh, Assam, Bihar, Karnataka, Madhaya Pradesh, Orissa, Rajasthan, Skkim, Tamilnadu, Himachal Pradesh, Tripura, Uttar Pradesh, West Begal. In total, 6022 enterprises have been promoted by the end of financial year 2000 by the SIDIBI.

The Table 1 showed the distribution of RIP units across the states. The table clearly showed that the highest number of units was existing in Andhra Pradesh (2329), while Orissa occupies the second place amongst the states (1779). The causes may be that the liberalized policies of State Governments (Andhra Pradesh and Orissa) towards RIP observation. However, some states still have to utlise the benefits of RIP. The details of number of units promoted under RIP are presented in Table 1.

Table 1
Distribution of RIP Units-Statewise

State	*As on 31.03.1999*	*1999-2000*	*Cumulative as on 31.3.2000*
Andhra Pradesh	2329	196	2525
Assam	59	28	87
Bihar	498	150	648
Himachal Pradesh	358	21	378
Karnataka	182	6	188
Madhaya Pradesh	37	54	91
Orissa	1779	36	1815
Rajasthan	84	62	146
Tamilnadu	0	4	4
Tripura	1	0	1
Uttar Pradesh	84	36	120
West Bengal	8	10	18
Total	5,419	603	6,022

Source: Rural Industries Programme–An evaluation (2003) by B. Sudhakar Rao, NIRD, pp. 12.

RURAL INDUSTRIALIZATION AND NEW ECONOMIC POLICIES

The decade of 1990s has witnessed sea change of economic policies in the context of Liberalization, Privatization and Globalization. These economic policies have tremendous impact on primary, secondary and tertiary sectors of production. The rural areas with enormous surplus labour in agricultural sector, rural industries have been employment provider for many unemployed hands. However, the rural industries have been facing with number of problems such as lack of capital, obsolete technology, lack of marketing facilities etc. In this context, there are distinct views on the impact of the new economic regime on rural industries. While many social scientists argued that it would intensify the existing crisis and spell doom for many indigenous small rural industries. In the country. But some other social scientists argued that it would provide a boost with new opportunities and markets to expand the rural industries. The Field Studies of Center for Rural Industries and Employment (CRIE) of NIRD revealed that the rural industries were unable to compete with giant multinationals because of poor infrastructure, lack of marketing facilities, facilities, lack of modernized technology, lack of capacity building, lack of proper training, exploitation by middle men and lack of basic minimum services like drinking water and sanitation, housing, roads etc.

Current Challenges of Rural Industries in the Context of New Economic Policies

It is recorded that after independence there has been a considerable increase in the number of small-scale units and the range and total value of their production. However, there undo concentration of small-scale units in urban conglomerates and near the industrial complexes. There is no appreciable penetration small-scale sector has tended to limit the spread of entrepreneurial base in the country to desired extent. In the matter of credit availability also, the smaller among the small-scale units have not benefited adequately and continue to depend on the moneylenders for borrowing funds at exorbitant interest rates. Similarly, excise concessions in certain cases have resulted in unintended splitting up of the capacities into uneconomic units, inhibiting their smooth transfer to the medium sector.

'Income effect' and entry of products of industrial giants in the rural markets pose a great threat to the sustainability of rural industries unless they are equipped with modern technology and adopt an aggressive marketing strategy. With the growth of farm income due to higher agricultural productivity, rural demand pattern will continue to change in favour of high value products. Publicity campaign and market research and intelligence network of big industries and multinationals are likely to dominate rural markets, which constitute more that two-thirds of the aggregate demand. But, on the other side, New Economic Order appears to be a good source of motivation for the traditional and other rural industries to go in for modernization/technology up gradation to improve their competitive efficiency through micro HRD interventions. Presently, the challenges faced by the rural industries are presented below.

- Majority of the rural industries depend on locally available raw material. They have to purchase raw material in small quantities, as they do not have purchasing capacity and often-on credit. Therefore, they cannot compete with large-scale industries in the procurement of raw material. In many cases the raw material is an imported one. Often, rural industries have to pay a higher price for inputs and suffer uncertainty in their procurement.
- Quality assurance and standardization of products conforming to national and international standards to compete on quality fronts in both national and international markets.
- The technology that is being used in many rural industries such a weaving and woodcarving is obsolete. This is leading to high production cost and output of inferior quality goods.

- Rural industries face marketing difficulties because their products are not properly advertised through various media of communications. Therefore, they face competitive disadvantage *vis-à-vis* large scale-units. And, it is necessary to provide information about the products of these industries and to bring producers and consumers into close contact to eliminate the middlemen. Moreover, Government should help rural industries in exporting their products to foreign countries in view of globalization.
- Lack of financial resources is another hurdle in the development of rural industries. The capital base of the small entrepreneur is usually weak and often has to procure credit at high rate of interest. A system of integrated credit should be evolved to meet the long term and short-term credit requirements of the rural industries at reasonable rate of interest.
- Majority of rural industries in back ward areas are still deprived of infrastructure facilities such as power, transport, and communication services. These have hampered their proper and efficient working thereby retarding their development.
- The development of the rural industries has been hampered due to the shortage trained and experienced managerial and supervisory personnel. Provision of technical services is needed to stimulate productive efficiency and new product lines.
- The rural entrepreneurs are facing a cost effective management of the project and utilizing the promotional services. Potential clients are geographically widely distributed. Their needs are often diverse. Maintaining a continuous with such entrepreneurs is a formidable challenge. At present, the data and information systems at all levels are poorly maintained.

All these constraints have resulted in a high cost structure placing this sector at a disadvantage *vis-à-vis* the large industries. In view of the importance of small-scale industries,

Government continues to lay emphasis on their growth and various measure have been taken to enable them to stand competition with large and medium scale industries. Small industries are helped by the Government in the following manner–Reservation of items for exclusive production by small-scale industries; exercise duty concessions; Priority in the disbursement of loans by the financial institution.

HRD INTERVENTIONS FOR SUSTAINABLE RURAL INDUSTRIALIZATION IN THE CONTEXT OF NEW ECONOMIC POLICIES

These interventions involve a planned approach to learning aimed at changes in knowledge, skills, understandings, attitudes and values, and in the behaviour of a learner or group of learners involved in the rural industries. It is often associated with a technical goal to provide a trained work force, to promote the knowledge and skills required by rural industrialization in a society to acquire greater prosperity; in short, to provide or build productive capabilities. However, for some educators and development planners HRD is an end in itself, and its goal should be realising human potential and developing individual self-reliance.

The HRD interventions are classified into two categories, namely, Micro and Macro, which are presented below.

Micro-HRD Interventions

Individual is as a resource. HRD is a distinct one from Human Relations in as much as the latter was at best a human welfare strategy: (1) HRD treats an individual as a "resource" and (2) endeavours to make the individual "develop" his propensities in order that (3) individual as a developed or developing resource, contributes to organizational effectiveness. A resource is never an end by itself. Making some one qualified or competent is not an end by itself. The individual has to act as an agent for the development of the organization and has to register his own individual contribution towards meeting organizational needs and demands. HRD, in this context, is basically an intervention strategy to meet specific requirements of Rural Industries in view of specific situations and as the milieu and the sub-systems keep changing, organizational frame and strategy too has to adapt correspondingly and all this, in turn, requires the primary stakeholders to modify behaviour and styles through a mix of training and conditioned exposures.

Capacity Building of Institutions, Families and Individual

Capacity-building efforts should highlight on institutional strengthening, including the design of new organizational structures to improve capabilities among the institutions for sustainable development and enacting institutions in both the public and private sectors. These institutions include KVICs, SIDBI and training institutions as well as extension agencies, research institutions, NGOs and community organizations among others. A multiplier effect can be achieved if strong linkages among KVIC, SIDBI, NGOs, research organizations, public and private extension services etc are fostered. This approach recognizes that there are multiple sources of technology development and dissemination and that integrated institutional network capacity building is required.

Institutional analysis is a pre-requisite for Rural Industries' institutional capacity building. It involves assessing how the talents and energies of staff at KVICs, SIDBIs, NGOs etc can be enlisted and upgraded on a regular basis to improve these institutions' operations. In many institutions, there is a lack of an effective human resource management system (HRMS). An institutional analysis should assess the existing HRMS and design improvements. Among other areas, there should be attention to results-oriented performance appraisal; mechanisms for improving communication to and from staff; identification of knowledge/skill gaps and staff training needs; teams skills development and the reinforcement of teamwork; and transparent staff selection and promotion processes. These institutions should impart training programmes to the people of rural industries in the areas of promotion of entrepreneurs, skill development, awareness creation, marketing, motivation etc.

MACRO-HRD INTERVENTIONS

The UN-ESCAPE envisaged that two-thirds of the world's 1.3 billion poor live in the Asian and Pacific region. Over 75 per cent of these people are living in the rural areas. Their progress is hampered by poor access to HRD opportunities and consequent low levels of education, skill development, health, remuneration and participation in rural development including rural industries. This entraps them in a cycle of deprivation that is marked by social and economic disempowerment. HRD has been effective strategy for developing the rural industries in the country. This situation is closely associated with the quality of human resources. The time is changing. Therefore, HRD is defined that investing in people and enabling them to access socio-economic benefits, rights and entitlements constitute the core of the philosophy and practice of HRD. The rural industries programmes' endeavors are to increase socio, economic conditions of the people in turn improving the quality of life. But what was missing was well laid out strategy to enable the people to help themselves. The field studies revealed that the development interventions especially state-sponsored programmes viewed that the beneficiaries thus signifying 'a provider stance' and a 'dependency syndrome'. The creation of a ministry for HRD by the Government of India bears testimony to this awareness and concern at the national level. Efforts are afoot at various quarters in the country today to devise and implement methods of developing human resources.

Development Plans for Macro-HRD Services

The macro-HRD services mainly discusses on education, health care, drinking water and sanitation services etc. To ensure these areas, there is a need of public action if human development has to gather momentum. Together, these facilities comprise a social infrastructure that is a critical as physical infrastructure for a widely shared and inclusive development. Literacy is the first step towards empowerment. The economic returns, both private and social investing on education are high as it is revealed by the reviews of World Bank (1995) are 39 per cent,

19 per cent and 20 per cent for primary, secondary and higher education, respectively. This was before existence of the Internet. At present, the returns would be much higher. Therefore, the people who have involved in rural industries have to be made literate for understanding the existing market facilities for their goods through out the world by using internet facilities as these facilities are reached to even rural areas. In addition, the literacy can bring and adopt modern methods in their rural industries. Of course, the country has significantly progressed in life expectancy and mortality but there is a long way to go. While life expectancy at birth of 62.4 years in 1997 is nearly double that in 1951. Our infant mortality rate of 71 per 1000 live births should be compared with kerala's 12. This reflection indicates the poor state of Public Health, inadequate medical attention during pregnancy and at birth and poor-natal care. To reduce infant and child mortality , there is a need nearly cent per cent immunization, supply of portable drinking water and provision of sanitation facilities to prevent infections and professional attention during child birth. The government in collaboration with people's contributions may provide these facilities. And the operation and maintenance of these infrastructures should be handed over to the people for a greater success.

SUMMARY AND CONCLUSIONS

Development of rural industrialization on a sustainable basis is a strong need for facilitating the speedy socio-economic transformation of rural India with the transparency of perceptible change in the quality of life of the rural communities in the country. These Industries have tremendous potential for employment generation for landless labour, educated job seekers and additional income for small and marginal farmers, besides export market. In the context of globalization, liberalization and privatization, the Rural Industries will have to strengthen its competitiveness by focusing special attention on technology up gradation, modernization, productivity improvement, cost efficiency through achieving economies of scale and professional management for creating full employment in the rural areas so as to reduce pace of chronic problems such as poverty and rural migration. Moreover, due to shift in the rural industrial culture towards capital intensive technology, change in organizational pattern, rising wage bill, increasing awareness of dignity of labour, etc., greater pressure is likely to be occurred on the removal of under-employment and disguised unemployment from agriculture sector, thus resulting in creation of a large army of un-employment, which may be a cause of great concern in the future. Bringing a few industrial units to the rural areas will not solve the chronic problems of rural poverty and unemployment. In such a situation, if the functioning of rural economy is confined to the doctrines of free market, this will not help in mitigating the rural problems in the short run. Industry sector is likely to become more prone to the adopting of capital-intensive technology requiring less labour input. Rural problems will rather get aggravated, adding to the social cost of the big cities due to rural migration. Therefore, The State's interventions are essentially required to evolve a comprehensive perspective plan for development of infrastructure to make the rural areas more attractive for setting up industries.

Besides the development strategy of rural industrialization, Government should also focus more on HRD interventions/ components with regard to professional management and training for updating the skills and knowledge of rural artisans and workers, research and development, common facilities, quality control, marketing support, financial assistance, transfer of technology, encouragement to cooperatives and associations of micro rural industrial units, etc. In the same manner, Capacity Building has to be given top priority on the aspects of awareness building, education and training, attitudinal change, confidence building, participation in decision-making and action to the rural people. Because of these, the individuals and families are empowered to expand their abilities to participate in the sustainable rural industrialization process. Besides, the development of partnerships between Government, NGOs, community and institutional building is need to be addressed properly for the community based HRD. Also, there is a need to plan and delivery of macro-HRD services such as Drinking water, Health, Education, Skill development and informed participation of people in conceptualizing as well as designing and implementing HRD in rural industries programmes for a sustainable rural industrialization. Some more recommendations are as follows:

- Formulation of a National Policy on rural industrialization for addressing or tackling of uneven development (not to concentrate on only few regions) of rural industrialization.
- Strengthening of existing infrastructure both physical and social including electricity, road, transport, communication, potable water, education, health, etc., for motivating entrepreneurs to set up industries in the potential rural areas.
- Development of Rural Growth Centres in potential rural areas for promotion of large and medium industries.
- A special package of incentives for setting up of industries based on rural resources and skills.
- Encouragement to rural women entrepreneurs through Krishi Vigyan Kendras (KVK) having necessary infrastructure could be involved in providing necessary techno-economic support and training to rural women entrepreneurs/artisans.
- Establishment of linkages between agriculture and agro-industry by encouraging joint venture, assisted sector with growers' participation as members of the industry and cooperatives of the growers.
- The overall database should be improved to include, for example, more reliable estimates on annual production. Furthermore, state efforts in collecting data must be improved, as it is primarily the state's responsibility to collect data on such issues as employment.

- An institutional base should be established for providing raw materials, training and marketing assistance.
- An improvement should be made in housing and work space for artisans, especially those whose production process is space intensive, such as carpet weavers, handloom silk weavers etc. In addition, Protection from factory competition should be provided for a wide range of products that are experiencing severe problems from loss of competitive edge for example, had-woven carpets, hand-printed textiles, brass and bell-metal utensils, silk, hand-embroidered products, and hand-made pottery are all facing severe competition from factory-made substitutes.
- Improvements in tools and the overall production process should include designs on a large enough scale to cover a substantial portion of the work force.
- The Nationalized Banks, which were earlier assigned some social obligations are now being restructured to function on commercial lines of privatization. RI sector particularly traditional industries are likely to suffer most for want of institutional credit support. This would force rural artisans to move out of their traditional occupation/craft works and join vicious circle of miseries in the cities. Therefore, setting up of a National Rural Industrial Development Bank is necessary to cater to the investment requirements of this sector. NABARD (National Bank of Agriculture and Rural Development) may only look after financial need of the agriculture sector.
- Encouragement to the setting up of rural service centers for repairs, maintenance of agricultural implements and machinery, auto parts, transport services, repairs of TV/radios and other electrical and electronic items.

REFERENCES

Arul M. J. (1989), *'HRD: Not Everyone's Cup of Tea'* Institute of Rural Management, Anand. (Downloaded on 22.8.03) (Paper presented at the *Seminar on 'Emerging Trends in Human Resource Development for Poverty Alleviation'*, held at NIRD, Hyderabad, on January 18-20, 1989).

Durgaprasad P. and Srinivasan S. (2002), *'HRD for Sustainable Rural Livelihoods: Perspectives and Field Realities'* (This paper is presented in the National Seminar on 'Impact of Liberalization and Globalization on Rural livelihoods' held at NIRD, Hyderabad, on May 18, 2002).

Gangi Reddy Y. (1996), 'Empoloyment Pattern in Rural Industries – A Case of Drought Prone District', *Manpower Journal,* Vol. XXXII Number 2, July-September.

Purushotam P. (1990), *'Entrepreneurship Development and Rural Youth', Khadi Gramodhyog,* Vol. 36, No. 8, May.

Purushotam P. (1997), 'Micro-Enterprise Development in the Regions of High Poverty: Lessons from An Action Research Project', *Journal of Rural Development,* Vol. 16 (2).

Raj Kapila and Uma Kapila (Edited By) (2002), *A Decade of Economic Reforms in India–The Past, The Present, The Future*....Published by Academic foundation, Ghaziabad.

Sudhakar Rao B., Purushotham P., Gangi Reddy Y., Ramachandraiah G., Krishna Murthy V., Murugesan R. (2003), *'Rural Industries Programme-An Evaluation'*, Discovery Publishing House, New Delhi.

Sury M. M. (2003), *'India: A Decade of Economic Reforms 1991-2001'* Published by New Century Publications, New Delhi.

Van Crowder L. (2003), *'Human Resource and Institutional Capacity Building through Agricultural Education'*, Extension, Education and Communication Service (SDRE); FAO Research, Extension and Training Division (Downloaded on 22.8.2003).

19

RURAL DEVELOPMENT PROGRAMMES AND POVERTY IN INDIA: A STUDY WITH RESPECT TO GANDHIJI'S THOUGHT

Shankar Chatterjee

Mahatma Gandhiji was deeply worried about poverty of the masses. As is evident from his autobiography that, "The grinding poverty and starvation with which our country is afflicted is such that it drives more and more men every year into the ranks of the beggars, whose desperate struggle for bread renders them insensible to all feelings of decency and self-respect." According to him self-employment should be the basis of production. Economic system should aim at the welfare of all the citizens but not the majority. Gandhian economic system is based on certain assumptions. Some of these are mentioned below (Bharathi 1999).

(i) Every person has right to live. Every individual in the society has a right to the basic economic needs like food, shelter and clothing.

(ii) Man's body requires bread. So man should earn his bread by manual labour. Intellectual labour should work for the benefit of the society.

(iii) When a man works for the sake of the wage, he cannot bring out the best in him. When he is motivated by love, he makes the best use of his inner strength and abilities. So it is the love for others which is to be developed and encouraged.

(iv) The Indian economic system should be built on the principle of Swadeshi. Swadeshi is not based on narrow and regional considerations. If everyone make use of locally produced goods, all the goods produces in the world will be locally consumed. Swadeshi in economic field has some objectives. It tends to revive and encourage the home industries. It provides employment to millions of unemployed and starving people. Every village is expected to be self-supporting and self-contained exchanging such necessaries with other villages. Swadeshi aims at decentralized economic system.

(v) The means of production should be easily owned and operated by ordinary people. Self employment should be the basis of production. Mass production should be by the masses. When the people are self-employed, the wealth of the nation would be in the hands of the masses.

Gandhi by establishing his Ashram at Sabarmati (Ahmedabad) wanted to do some development works. One of the reasons of establishing Ashram in Ahmedabad was that "Ahmedabad was an ancient centre of handloom weaving; it was likely to be the most favourable field for the revival of the cottage industry of hand spinning'. (Gandhi 1927). Main activities in the beginning were: worship, sanitary service, sacrificial spinning, agriculture, dairy, national education, khadi, technical school, etc. Gandhiji not only restricted him to the Ashrams but launched satyagraha, initiated constructive programmes, convened prayer meetings, adhered to eleven vows: truth, non-violence, chastity, non-possession, non-stealing, bread labour, non-palatable, fearlessness, equal treatment and respect to all religions, swadeshi, and untouchability-for the transformation of self and society simultaneously. His practice during his stays in South Africa and later in India proved rewarding in cadre building for the liberation struggle for a nation and reconstruction of the society.

Gandhiji was not in favour of large scale production. As large scale production divides society into exploiter and exploited. In his own words, "By nationalising the means of production you can only minimize the exploitation within the four walls of the country but you cannot prevent the exploitation of the weaker backward nations by the powerful advanced nations". So he pleaded small scale production, which would reduce poverty also. The central concept of Gandhian theory is man not the material wealth. Gandhiji believed that in a country like India, where a poor man earned about an anna everyday, it was a crime to keep hoards of money lying idle by means of ornaments and decorative pieces. His wife processed no ornaments (Bandyopadhyaya, 1964).

Poverty is a major concern till today although it has come down in many states of the country in relative terms but numerically poverty figure is still very high, particularly in rural areas. For example, in 1973-74 numbers of poor in rural India were 2612.90 lakh which declined marginally to 2209.24 lakh (based on URP) and 1702.99 lakh (based on MRP). The explanation on MRP & URP may be seen later on. Although after independence, Government of India took several measures to eradicate poverty, from the country, but these were all in ad hoc in nature up to 1970s. The poverty alleviation measures were taken up systematically from late 1970s/ early 1980s when the country introduced two types of programmes– Self-employment and wage- employment, which are discussed below.

MAJOR SELF AND WAGE EMPLOYMENT PROGRAMMES

The major self employment programmes which were introduced in the early 1980s were:

(i) Integrated Rural Development Programme(IRDP)

(ii) Training of Rural Youth for Self-employment (TRYSEM)

(iii) Development of Women and Children in Rural Areas (DWCRA)

(iv) Supply of Improved Tool-kits for Rural Artisans (SITRA)

(v) Million Wells Scheme (MWS)

(vi) Ganga Kalyan Yojana(GKY)

All the above programmes were merged together on 1st April 1999 and a new self-employment programme has been introduced under the banner of Swarnajayanthi Gram Swarozgar Yojana (SGSY), popularly known as SGSY. Swarnjayanti Gram Swarozgar Yojana is financed on 75: 25 cost sharing basis between the Centre and the States. The Focus is on group-approach (minimum 10 members). Persons are assisted mainly after forming Self-help Groups (SHGs). *Some important features of SGSY are –*

(i) SHGs are given projects for income generation activities.

(ii) Initially SHGs have to save regularly and saving fund is used among the members as internal lending.

(iii) Performance of SHGs is assessed by government officials and bankers after six months.

(iv) A paltry sum of Rs 25000 is given after First grading as Revolving Fund (RF) and Cash Credit Limit (CCL).

(v) With RF & CCL when activities are carried out properly then after Second grading, bank loan is given.

In fact SGSY is programme meant for economic development for the rural poor through rural enterprises. Many poor persons in the country have taken up different type of activities including rural industries under SGSY. Important activities are handloom, toy making, different type of rope making, bulb making, carpet making, detergent making etc. As a result of SGSY, many poor persons have become viable entrepreneurs. In other way what Gandhiji thought about rural industrialization was being achieved through SGSY. Regarding achievement of SGSY, data show that since inception of the programme (April 1999) to September 2007, 26.68 lakh SHGs have been formed. Of these 5.09 lakh SHGs have taken up economic activities that mean these SHGs have been extended bank loan supported by back-end subsidy.

A CASE OF SELF-HELP GROUP BENEFITED UNDER SGSY

Gayatri SHG of Kakrahi Village (Robertsganj block), Sonbhadra district of Uttar Pradesh was formed in 2003 with 12 women members belonging to OBC and OC category. They started their savings with an amount of Rs. 30 per member per month. In 2004, the SHG was Graded-I, accordingly CCL and RF were given. Second grading took place in October 2006. A sum of Rs. 2.40 lakh (50:50 loan and back-end subsidy) was given to the SHG for vegetables cultivation as every one is having little bit of agricultural land. So they used the amount for purchasing of HYV seeds, better fertilizers, etc. By cultivating crops in two times in year, each member earned in between Rs. 25000 and Rs. 35000 per year. The area is not having irrigation facility; otherwise their income would have increased. The members informed that an amount of Rs. 45, 000 was repaid to the bank till the day of the visit (October, 2007). Thus by forming SHGs and by taking the advantage of SGSY many rural poor persons have been benefited in the country.

SGSY is major self-employment Programme for eradication of poverty presently going on in rural India. On the other hand NREGS is major wage employment Programme in this regard.

WAGE-EMPLOYMENT PROGRAMMES

Major wage employment programmes launched in recent years, inter alia, included–

(i) National Rural Employment Programme (NREP)

(ii) Rural Landless Employment Guarantee Programme (RLEGP)

(iii) Jawahar Rozgar Yojana (JRY)

(iv) Employment Assurance Scheme (EAS)

(v) Jawahar Gram Smridhi Yojana (JGSY)

All the above wage employment programmes are merged together and at present, single wage employment programme is continuing in rural India which is known as NREGS-National Rural Employment Guarantee Scheme.

The NREGS has been passed as an Act in the Parliament in September 2005. It is known as NREGA (National Rural Employment Guarantee Act). Employment has to be provided to every rural household whose adult members volunteer to do unskilled manual work. Cost component is shared between Centre and State on basis of 75: 25. Some salient features of the Programme component are:

(i) Such household is to be provided work for 100 days in a financial year.

(ii) Central Government will bear entire cost of wages of unskilled manual workers.

(iii) Central Government will bear 75% of the cost of material and wages of skilled and semi-skilled workers.

Benefit derived from NREGS is presented here:

The author studied some NREGA beneficiaries in last part of 2007 at Anwarpur village, Prantij taluka of Sabarkantha district of Gujarat. A few of them are Hiraben (58 years), Romilaben (40 years), Monguben (55 years), Maniben (50 years), Dibaben (58 years) and others. They all belong to poor families and scheduled caste community. Before implementation of NREGS, they and their family members were working as daily laborer where earning and working days were uncertain. But after launching of NREGS, they informed to this author that each family was earning in between Rs. 6500 and Rs. 7000 per annum. This is their additional earning. Thus NREGS has been helping to poor house holds to earn additional and assured income for some months.

INDIRA AWAS YOJANA (IAY): HOUSING PROGRAMME

As a housing scheme, Indira Awas Yojana (IAY) has been launched for the poor people of the country. IAY was launched in 1985-86 as sub-scheme of RLEGP from 1989 it was sub-scheme of JRY. However from 1st January 1996, IAY has been launched as an independent housing programme. Some salient features of the Programme component are:

(i) Fund is shared between Centre and State on basis of 75: 25.

(ii) In the plain areas a sum of Rs. 25000 is given for construction of house against Rs. 27500 in hilly/difficult areas.

(iii) It is the responsibility of the beneficiary to construct the house. The beneficiary is expected to construct the house at least 20 square meters plinth area along with a sanitary latrine and smokeless Chula.

(iv) No specific design has been stipulated for an IAY house.

(v) Since inception of the programme about 167 lakh houses have been constructed with an expenditure of Rs. 32793.84 crore up to 25 October 2007.

With the launching of all the above programmes from time to time, poverty in percentage term has declined substantially in rural India (Table 1). Declining figure is found in almost all the states of the country.

Table 1
Percentage of Population below Poverty Line in Rural India

		2004-2005	
States/U.T.	*1973-74*	*Based on URP**	*Based on MRP***
Andhra Pradesh	48.41	11.20	7.50
Arunachal Pradesh	52.67	22.30	17.00
Assam	52.67	22.30	17.00
Bihar	62.99	42.10	32.90
Chattisgarh	—	40.80	31.20
Goa	46.85	5.40	1.90
Gujarat	46.35	19.10	13.90
Haryana	34.23	13.60	9.20
Himachal Pradesh	27.42	10.70	7.20
Jammu & Kashmir	45.51	4.60	2.70
Jharkhand	—	46.30	40.20
Karnataka	55.14	20.80	12.00
Kerala	59.19	13.20	9.60
Madhya Pradesh	62.66	36.90	29.80

Contd...

States/U.T.	1973-74	2004-2005 Based on URP*	2004-2005 Based on MRP**
Maharashtra	57.71	29.60	22.20
Manipur	52.67	22.30	17.00
Meghalaya	52.67	22.30	17.00
Mizoram	52.67	22.30	17.00
Nagaland	52.67	22.30	17.00
Orissa	67.28	46.80	39.80
Punjab	28.21	9.10	5.90
Rajasthan	44.76	18.70	14.30
Sikkim	52.67	22.30	17.00
Tamil Nadu	57.43	22.80	16.90
Tripura	52.67	22.30	17.00
Uttar Pradesh	56.53	33.40	25.30
Uttarkhand	—	40.80	31.70
West Bengal	73.16	28.60	24.20
A & N Islands	57.43	22.90	16.90
Daman & Diu	-	5.40	1.90
D & N Haveli	46.85	39.80	36.80
Lakshadweep	59.19	13.30	9.60
Pondicherry	57.43	22.90	16.90
All India	56.44	28.30	21.80

*URP = Uniform Recall Period consumption in which the consumer expenditure data for all items are collected from 30-day recall period.

**MRP = Mixed Recall Period consumption in which the consumer expenditure data for five non-food items namely clothing, footwear, durable goods, education & institutional medical expenses are collected from 365-day recall period and consumption data from 365-day recall period & the consumption data for the remaining items are collected from 30 day recall period.

Source: Planning Commission, India.

CONCLUSION

With the launching of self-employment, wage employment and housing programmes in rural India not only employments have been generating but poverty in relative term has substantially come down. The days are not very far where all the rural persons will have food, shelter and cloth (*roti, kapra aur mokan*). Thus Gandhiji's dream will be fulfilled.

REFERENCES

Gandhi, M. K. (1993), *An Autobiography*, Navajivan Publishing House, Ahmedabad.

Gandhi, M. K. (1927), *An Autobiography*, Navjivan Trust, Ahmedabad.

Bharathi K. S. (1999), *The Economic Thought of Gandhi*, DATTSONS Publisher, Nagpur.

Bandyopadhyaya, Anu (1964), (Foreword by Jawaharlal Nehru), *Bahuroopee Gandhi*, Popular Prakashan, Bombay.

20

A UNIQUE BANK RUN BY RURAL WOMEN SELF-HELP GROUPS (SHGs) OF ANDHRA PRADESH

Shankar Chatterjee and N. V. Madhuri

Aadarsha Welfare Society (AWS), a based voluntary organization located in Mahabubnagar district of Andhra Pradesh organized 3250 women in 37 villages of Addakal Mandal, (in Andhra Pradesh Mandal is smaller than development block) in 416 self help groups (SHGs) in 1995. During that time, district administration also launched 'Maa Laxmi' campaign in October, 1995 throughout the district in which entire administration, public representatives, youth and voluntary organizations were involved. As a result of this, another 3000 women were also organized under self help groups at Addakal Mandal taking the total number to 210 SHGs. In October, 1996 all these groups formed a network under the banner of 'Aadarsha Mandal Mahila Samaikya', which is synonymous to Federation.

Aadarsha Welfare Society (AWS), a based voluntary organization located in Mahabubnagar district of Andhra Pradesh organized 3250 women in 37 villages of Addakal Mandal, (in Andhra Pradesh Mandal is smaller than development block) in 416 self help groups (SHGs) in 1995. During that time, district administration also launched

'Maa Laxmi' campaign in October, 1995 throughout the district in which entire administration, public representatives, youth and voluntary organizations were involved. As a result of this, another 3000 women were also organized under self help groups at Addakal Mandal taking the total number to 210 SHGs. In October, 1996 all these groups formed a network under the banner of 'Aadarsha Mandal Mahila Samaikya', which is synonymous to Federation.

This is a unique case as in many parts of the country even at village level SHGs have not taken a deep root but in Andhra Pradesh due to initiative taken by NGOs, Government departments and others, at the village level SHGs have not only formed but also taken a deep root as a sequel Federations have been formed. Next to village is Mandal where Federation has been formed as Mandal Samakhya. At the district level also, there is Federation which is known as Zilla Samakhya In most of the villages and in all the Mandals and districts of Andhra Pradesh Federations have been formed. Till 2008, a little more than 7 lakh SHGs have been formed in Andhra Pradesh. These SHGs have been federated in to 34236 village organizations (VO) and then to 1088 Mandal Samakhya (Mandal Federation) and 22 Zilla Samakhya (District Federation).

For the benefit of readers the structures of these Federations are presented in the following charts. However the meaning of Federation is given below.

MEANING OF FEDERATION

The meaning of Federation is "an association of autonomous bodies uniting for common perceived benefits" (FWWB, 1998).

"A Cluster Level Federation is a network of several SHGs and a structure or body evolved by SHGs themselves consisting of representatives from all members SHGs, with a motive of supporting member-SHGs to attain the goals of economic and social empowerment of women and their capacity building" (TNCDW, 1999).

NEED FOR FEDERATIONS

The literature suggests that SHG federations have been promoted over the past 15 years in India. The Academics (Ajay Nair, Malcom Harper), NGOs (MYRADA, and their net-works (Sa-dhan), and the development professionals (CS Reddy, Shasirajagopalan) (for all these source APMAS, 2007) have pointed out the rationale behind the promotion of Federations:

(i) to strengthen existing SHGs

(ii) to promote new SHGs of the poor

(iii) to access various services to the member SHGs

(iv) to provide a sense of solidarity among members of different SHGs in an area

(v) for sustainability of SHGS

(vi) to facilitate linkages and

(vii) to empower women.

Besides the above, federations play an important part in SHG capacity building and conflict resolution-both internally and externally.

Structure of Village Organisation

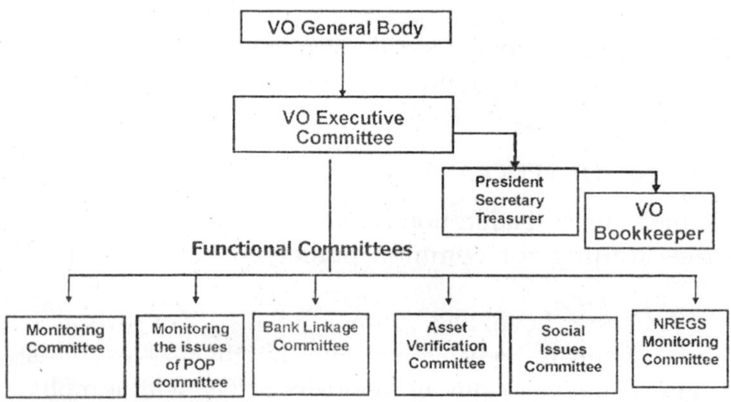

Legal Frame work:

Village Organisations - registered as Primary Cooperatives under APMACs Act-1995

Structure of Mandal Samakhya

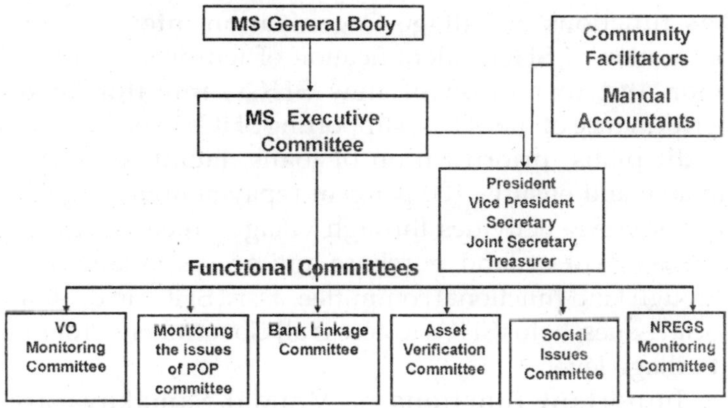

Legal frame work

MSs are registered as federation of VOs under APMACs Act - 1995

Structure of Zilla Samakhya

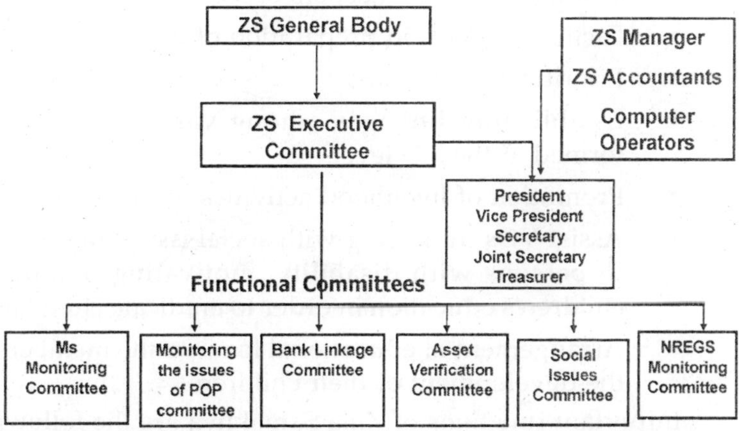

Legal frame work

ZSs will be registered as confederation of MSs under APMACs Act - 1995

IMPORTANT FUNCTIONS OF VILLAGE ORGANIZATION, MANDAL SAMAKHYA & ZILLA SAMAKHYA

The functions of Village Organization inter alia, include promotion of SHGs, identification of left over poorest of the poor and formation of new SHGs, monitoring of the performance of the SHGs, supporting SHGs in preparing micro credit plans, prioritization of loans, facilitates SHG bank linkage and ensures 100 per cent repayment, management of food security activities through village procurement centers, management of land purchase and access to land activities through land functional committee, assist SHGs in dealing with social issues, helps SHGs to access all Government Programmes at village level.

Important functions of Mandal Samakhya are the following:

- Promotion of VOs
- Formation of VOs
- Capacity building of SHGs through community resource persons and organizing trainings
- Training the book-keepers of VO
- Facilitating VOs in preparation of micro credit plans
- Prioritization of loans
- Establishing linkages among various committees formed at the VO level.
- Promotion of livelihood activities of the poor
- Assist VOs in dealing with social issues like support to persons with disability, motivating parents for children's education in order to eradicate child labour
- Arrangement of educational loans to the members for the development of their children

Important functions of Zilla Samakhya are the following:

- Promotion of mainstream Mandal Samakhyas and exclusive Mandal Samakhyas for vulnerable communities viz., Persons with disability, tribal, Chenchu, fishermen and others

- Formulation of policies that promotes self-management and financial sustainability of CBOs.
- Capacity building of SHGs, VOs and Mandal Samakhyas through Community Resource Persons strategy.
- Monitoring of the performance of Mandal Samakhyas
- Training the mandal level Community Based Organization staff & leaders.
- Conducting Audit of Mandal Samakhya books of accounts.
- Promotes livelihood activities of the poor.
- Assisting Mandal Samakhyas in dealing with social security issues such as insurance etc.

ABOUT THE STUDY

To get an idea about the functioning of the "Aadarsha Mandal Mahila Samaikya" as well as Mahila Bank a study was carried by the authors in September 2008. The Samaikya is involved in many activities but one unique activity is managing of a bank managed by the women members. The study was carried out in Mahabubnagar district of Andhra Pradesh. Mahabubnagar is one among 12 droughts prone districts of Andhra Pradesh situated in the Southern part of Telangana area and in the Western part of Andhra Pradesh. Basing on the geological status it is receiving 3rd lowest rainfall in the entire country after Jaisalmar (Rajasthan) & Anantapur (Andhra Pradesh). Major livelihood in this district is agriculture and the returns from agriculture are very low due to low and erratic rainfall. According to 2001 census and BPL survey the percentage of people below the poverty line is 60 per cent.

The district has a population of 35.09 lakh (as per 2001 census) of which 17.81 lakh are the male and 17.28 lakh are female. Among the total district population 24.18 lakh stay in rural areas and the rest in urban areas. Mahabubnagar is the largest district with 64 mandals covering 13 Assembly constituencies. The number of villages in the district is 1533 with 2496 habitations and comprising with 7.52 lakh families. Literacy levels in the district with a percentage of 38.6 are lowest among all the districts of the state.

There is a high incidence of distress migration among the rural Poorest of the poor and Poor as the district is having meager resources for providing livelihoods through out the year. Further the district is having more arid and rain fed areas, which gives only one crop a year with rain support. The irrigation facilities and water resources are very less which made the district as the poorest one among other districts.

GENERAL PROFILE OF MAHABUBNAGAR DISTRICT

1.	Area of the District	:	18,432 Sq KMs
2.	Forest Area in the District	:	6.59 Lakh Acres
3.	Population (a) Men	:	17.82 Lakhs (50.77%)
	(b) Women	:	17.28 Lakhs (49.33%)
	Total Population	:	35.10 Lakh
4.	Literates (a) Men	:	8.75 Lakh (64.48%)
	(b) Women	:	4.82 Lakh (35.52%)
	Total Literates	:	13.57 Lakh
5.	No. of Gram Panchayats	:	1346
6.	No. of Habitations	:	2496
7.	Cultivated Area	:	22.53 Lakh Acres
8.	Cropped Area in Kharif	:	20.44 Lakh Acres (2002-03)
	in Rabi	:	4.20 Lakh Acres (2001-02)

STRUCTURE OF SAMAIKYA

Samaikya is having a General Body (RGB), Executive committee (EC) and Board of Directors as explained below:

- RGB (832 members)-One leader from each of the SHGs forms RGB and this body meets once in six months to take major decisions including selection of EC members and Board of directors.
- EC (42 members)-Six members from each of the clusters (the groups have an intermediary tier of

cluster which is 4 to 6 adjacent villages major to share information and there are 7 clusters in the Mandal) form in to Executive committee. The EC meets once in a month to work on the activities of Samaikya.

- Board of Directors(14) - Two members from each of the cluster(from among the 6 EC members) form in to Board of Directors which meets once in a month to look in to day to day activities of Samaikya and also to implement the decisions taken in EC meetings.

REGISTRATION OF THE SAMAIKYA

The Samaikya has been registered under the Mutually Aided Co-operative societies Act, 1995 in September 1998.

After forming Mandal network in October, 1996 the SHGs realized the importance of having a network at village/ habitation level. From 1997 Village Organizations (VOs) which is network of SHGs at village/habitation level also have come up. Two leaders from each of the SHGs constitute the Executive Committee of the VO. Apart from economic activities; VOs have been working in education, health and village development etc.

The major activities of VO inter alia, include

- To mobilize financial resources and on lend to member groups
- To facilitate SHGs to solve their problems
- To take up and work on the issues that individually a SHG can not do
- To help Panchayat Raj Institutions to work more effectively
- To participate in village development activities.

FUNCTIONING OF AADARSHA MAHILA SAHAKARA SAMAIKYA LTD

'Aadarsha Mahila Sahakara Samaikya Ltd.' (Samaikya) is the Mandal network of all the 416 SHGs of Addakal Mandal.

Though functioning from October 1996, it improved on its structure and systems and got registered under the Andhra Pradesh Mutually Aided Cooperative Societies Act, 1995 in September 1998.

The important activities of Samaikya are:

- Lending to SHGs (informal women bank)
- Train SHGs in group management
- Organize exposure trips
- Facilitate training on Income Generation Activities
- Train SHGs of other parts of the District and State
- Support members in social issues like health, education etc.,

The Samaikya is having following assets:

1. Market building and super bazaar
2. Training hall
3. Informal Bank and Office
4. Dormitory
5. Highway restaurant
6. Milk chilling unit

For establishing the above units a sum of Rs. 40 lakh has been spent from different programmes like MPLAD (Rs. 10 Lakh), District Rural Development agency (DRDA) Rs 15 lakh and Andhra Pradesh Livelihood project & Drought Prone area Programmer Rs. 15 lakh.

WOMEN BANK MANAGED BY SAMAIKYA: AADARSHA MAHILA SAHAKARA SAMAIKYA LTD

Initially Samaikya was involved in lending among the members for 2-3 years and thus gained knowledge about financial transactions. It started banking operations from January 1999 with its own fund of around Rs14 lakh, where all the SHGs contributed at the rate of Rs 300 as share capital to the Bank.

As Samaikya gained the required confidence it started approaching different financial institutions for bulk lending.

Now the bank is a popular bank in the area. The SHG members happy to inform that at any time they can take loan from the bank. They do not have to face any sort of problem to get the loan. Even bank has been extending loan to individual member also. Moreover it is heartening to note that the SHG members always felt it was their bank. Repayment is almost 100 per cent. Apart from the members of the SHGs the Bank also gives credit to other persons from the locality. The Management and staff members of the bank are women. Every after three years based on profit of the bank dividend is distributed among the SHGs. Out of total profit, 40 per cent is distributed and rest 60% is ploughed back to the bank for its business. In the year 2005, bank earned an amount of Rs. 10 lakh as net profit and in 2008 the amount of profit came down marginally to Rs. 8 lakh.

The Samaikya apart from managing bank has also been managing a restaurant and milk chilling plant. The restaurant is located near the national highway. Due to its location advantage and hygienic condition, restaurant has been giving good return. Samaikya is also managing milk chilling unit with a capacity of 2000 liters, where hundreds of dairy -farmers are being benefited.

CONCLUSION

With the formation of SHGs *vis-à-vis* launching of SGSY, poor persons in general and women in particular are not only socially empowered but proved entrepreneurs. Functioning of SHGs, village and Mandal (Samaikya) Federations is really praiseworthy. Not only it is acting as "Demonstration Effect" to nearby villagers but many a times other SHGs of different districts of Andhra Pradesh *vis-à-vis* from other states visit and study women bank, restaurant and milk chilling plant as 'exposure visit'.

(Authors are grateful to Sri K. P. Rao, State Marketing Adviser, Society for Elimination of Rural Poverty, Andhra Pradesh and staff members of the Bank for their cooperation during the course of field study).

REFERENCES

APMAS (2007), Hyderabad "SHG Federations in India-A Status Report".

FWWB (1998), "India's Emerging Federations of Women's Savings and Credit Groups", Friends of Women's World Banking, Ahmedabad, India.

Tamil Nadu Corporation for Development of Women Ltd. (TNCDW, 1999), "A Guide to SHG Federation".

INDEX

G

H

J & K